Choose Abundance

Powerful Fundraising for Nonprofits

A Culture of Philanthropy

Choose Abundance

Powerful Fundraising for Nonprofits

A Culture of Philanthropy

Laurie Herrick

Rainmaker Media

Choose Abundance: Powerful Fundraising for Nonprofits—A Culture of Philanthropy
By Laurie Herrick

Cover Design by Ginny Glass

ISBN-13: 978-1-7369424-6-8
Also:
Hardcover: 978-1-7369424-9-9
Ebook: 978-1-7369424-3-7

Published by Rainmaker Media
www.rainmkr.com

Publisher's Note
The publisher does not have any control over and does not assume any responsibility for author or third-party websites or their content.

Contents

Praise for *Choose Abundance*

Take a stand. We need the work you do to make things better, and this clear and generous book will help you see how walking away from scarcity can change things for the people you serve.

Seth Godin, Author, *This Is Marketing*

Laurie Herrick is the kind of professional I turn to when I require expert advice on all matters of fundraising and advancement—from strategic planning and special campaigns to annual fundraising and major gift portfolio management. Laurie's training has helped drive organizational growth and contributed to my ability to achieve greater levels of success personally and professionally.

Having worked with Laurie for more than six years, I have regularly enrolled in her training programs and sought personal mentorship. I've come to rely on her guidance as a gold standard in fundraising. She's made a profound impact, holding me accountable to setting—and then achieving—goals. She has helped me reframe strategic planning to include abundance and generative language, as well as industry best practices to ultimately engage constituents in meaningful and relevant ways. In turn, I've seen fundraising grow exponentially and a new Culture of Philanthropy take seed.

Melanie Gerard, Director of Advancement, UMass Hillel

As Laurie Herrick reminds us, fundraising is more than a list of prospects, tactics, techniques and a good program. To do it well requires a full-body reorientation of our nonprofit organizations and the adoption of a Culture of Philanthropy. In this valuable, grounded and practical book, Herrick holds our hand and walks us through the process of organizational transformation toward abundance.

Chuck Collins, Institute for Policy Studies, Author, *Born on Third Base*

If you find yourself deliberating whether buying this book is in your organizational budget, let Laurie Herrick enroll you in the idea that your scarcity mindset is holding you and your organization back. Using memorable stories, curated resources and an easy-to-understand framework, Herrick is with you, step by step, as your organization makes the shift from scarcity thinking to abundance—in thinking, relationships and resources.

Donna Haghighat, CEO, The Women's Fund of Western Massachusetts

The only way to achieve long-term fundraising success in an organization's culture is to intentionally choose abundance. It's the intentionality that makes the difference. It has to be chosen. This book shows you how to accomplish that.

Mark Shapiro, CEO of The Harry & Rose Samson Family Jewish Community Center

Just as your mission is the heart of your organization, fundraising is the lifeblood, and strong fundraising demands fostering a Culture of Philanthropy. Such a culture transcends best practices. It permeates and transforms organizations. Laurie Herrick's *Choose Abundance* shows you how to get there.

It was through our work with Herrick that we came to understand and commit to growing a Culture of Philanthropy that helped us increase leadership giving by 12 percent, year over year.

Herrick's book is focused and well-organized. It shows you how to align and leverage your teams. How to avoid pitfalls. And, most importantly, how to implement and find fundraising success. If you are serious about changing your Culture of Philanthropy, start here.

John D. Bidwell, Executive Director, United Way of Hampshire County

GIFT [the Culture of Philanthropy course] is where I learned to listen—to really hear—what motivates my team members, staff, and donors (i.e., investors) to be involved and to contribute. This learning continues to bring deeper meaning and intention to our planning, breaking down silos, and strengthening relationships. We focus on abundance, and the structure needed to support the attitude and behavior changes necessary for a Culture of Philanthropy to thrive.

Marsha Rothpan, Development & Engagement Director, Shalom Institute

When Laurie Herrick first introduced her framework of Scarcity & Abundance in my fundraising graduate class in 2008, it sparked a conversation around the charity mentality many nonprofit organizations and staff find themselves caught in. The larger conversation that followed led to positive discussion on the methods of breaking out of that mentality and bringing along an organizational culture to raise more money. This book is a solid companion to students of philanthropy who are reading textbooks in their classes because it is written from a practitioner's experience. This is a solid guide to think through how breaking out of a scarcity mindset in your organization can inform your total development plan to change the Culture of Philanthropy to better meet your mission. Greater abundance means many more Mission Moments for your community.

A. Rima Dael, WSHU Public Radio, General Manager, and Bay Path University, faculty, Nonprofit Management & Philanthropy

A difficult undertaking and a product that I think will be useful to many. A real contribution to the field. Brava!

Anne Teschner, Executive Director, The Care Center

Reading *Choose Abundance* is having a deep conversation with a fundraising master. Isn't that what you'd want for the organization you care about most? Go ahead—read the book, have the conversation, share it with others and see the difference it will make.

Sam Daley-Harris, Founder, RESULTS, Microcredit Summit and Civic Courage

I wish that I'd had this book when I entered the field. I think every Executive Director and Board President should get a copy.

Daisy Pereira-Tosado, Director of Philanthropy, Community Foundation of Western Massachusetts

Laurie Herrick is right on target! What stops many nonprofit leaders from fundraising success is a mindset of scarcity and a lack of confidence. They forget that people with wealth are looking for great places to put their philanthropic dollars. In *Choose Abundance,*

Herrick provides important lessons on how to become an organization that attracts donors' dollars to reach shared goals.

Harold Grinspoon, Founder, Harold Grinspoon Foundation

Choose Abundance combines the practical with meaningful to produce a useful implementation guide for building a solid Culture of Philanthropy in your organization. I recommend it for anyone committed to this transformational aspiration.

Jennifer McCrea, Author, *The Generosity Network*

Fundraising with a weak culture is like driving with the emergency brake on. In this book, Laurie Herrick deftly helps culture pioneers unstick the brake—exploring the why, how and what behind creating an extraordinary culture of abundance that transforms ok organizations into amazing and impactful ones.

Alia McKee, Sea Change Strategies

The Culture of Philanthropy course has been one of the most powerful learning experiences for me as an individual and for our cohort at Mandel JCC. While the course's primary purpose is to strengthen the individual and organization's focus on philanthropy, it has provided so much more. Cohort style learning provided insight into what can be gained by business planning with individuals from varied perspectives of the organizational structure. We coalesced around prioritizing and strengthening the culture of the organization and empowering other professionals and volunteers to find their "inner philanthropist," in order to drive the agency and all its parts forward towards greater success in building a culture of philanthropy.

Gilon Rubanenko, Senior Vice President,
Programs and Engagement
Mandel Jewish Community Center of Cleveland

This is one of those books, one of those approaches to work and life, that can change everything.

As quietly and unassuming as Laurie Herrick goes about telling her stories and offering practical steps for people committed to making a difference in the world, she is a powerhouse in the best sense. If you have any spark in you of contributing to the world around you, and especially if you are part of an organization with a pro-social mission, take the time to not only read this book, but put it into practice. It will deepen your connection to what most matters and will extend both your belief in and your ability to help create a world that actually works for everyone.

I've been a teacher, and a student, of both personal growth and organizational development for three decades, and Laurie is one of those precious few teacher/practitioners who have radically expanded my understanding of how to bring more good into the world.

Zemo Trevathan, President, The Aligned Team,
East Coast, USA

To my students, peers, clients and family:

Thank you for your insights, wisdom and perseverance that have contributed to this work of building a Culture of Philanthropy. I appreciate your partnership in making a world that works for everyone.

To my mother, who first taught me to use my words to intentionally alter my attitude, and my attitude to alter my results—starting with my earliest chore-mantra, *I love to do what I have to do!*

Acknowledgments

Much as building a Culture of Philanthropy requires the engagement of your surrounding community, *Choose Abundance* is truly a collection of lessons that I learned from my many teachers and supporters. Lynne Twist kick-started that learning while I was in my very first development job. She introduced me to the Myth of Scarcity in her book *The Soul of Money,* and it fit perfectly with my desire to have my work make an impact in the organization where I was employed, and throughout my career.

My supervisor, who introduced me to Lynne and who embodied her lessons, was Lynn McMullen, and she was especially influential, giving me a chance to enter the blessed field of fund development. Lynn also introduced me to Terry Axelrod, whose Benevon Model took abundance thinking and created a wonderful structure for fundraising that was also highly influential to me.

There were a few people over the years who truly cheered on my work in building a Culture of Philanthropy. Here are a few key players.

Back in the early 2000s, Kathleen Dowd, a friend and Rainmaker colleague, heard what I was attempting to articulate and helped me put it into words. She was the first to notice that we were on to something. We teamed up with Rachel Kuhn, and launched Quantum Jump, a series of webinars for development professionals. The curriculum we created has been at the foundation of our Culture of Philanthropy work. Kathleen has been a true partner in making *Choose Abundance* happen, as well as a thought partner and cheerleader for this work.

My Rainmaker Consulting partners, including my colleagues Beth Spong, David Sharken and Eric Phelps, have taken up the mantle and continued to develop the body of work with countless individual clients. We have learned from each other and from our clients as we have discovered the nuances of what makes a Culture of Philanthropy work, what makes it stick and what gets in the way within varied organizations.

In 2004, I began my consulting work with the Harold Grinspoon Foundation. This opportunity allowed me to not only coach and consult their grantees—overnight and day camps for Jewish children throughout North America—but also to be empowered to create and lead professional development courses on building a Culture of Philanthropy. It was a true blessing, as it allowed me to pilot and run a program—first, GIFT for development professionals, and then GIFT Leadership Institute (GLI) for teams of professionals and board members, both of which were project-based, peer-learning courses to establish a culture change that embraced philanthropy. I am grateful to Harold Grinspoon and his wife, Diane Troderman, for giving me the opportunity to do this work. And to Winnie Sandler Grinspoon for embracing a Culture of Philanthropy.

Students in GIFT and GLI have taught me countless lessons, many of which you will read about in this book. Outstanding is the team of people associated with the Harry & Rose Samson Family JCC's Camp Interlaken and Rainbow Day Camp. Harriet Rothman, Ruth Wallace and Elyse Cohn embodied the lessons from GIFT and brought them back to their camps and ultimately the entire JCC. It got the attention of their CEO, Mark Shapiro, who embraced their ideas and started to expand them throughout his agency. I went to Mark for input on how to expand GIFT to include full teams. It is my belief that the creation of GLI was a game changer for the field of development. I'm indebted to Mark for his ideas, grounded in his experience as CEO, his co-leadership of GLI and for being a champion for this program in the field.

During my tenure at the foundation (which continues today), I've had many champions who have embraced this work and supported my further development of it. All the members of the camp consulting team (called JCamp 180) have been very supportive. In particular, Dan Kirsch was someone who looked me in the eye and told me I should jump into this Culture of Philanthropy pool, headfirst. I deeply appreciate his encouragement and coaching. Also, program directors Sue Kline, Eric Phelps, Mark Gold and Sarah Eisinger have all been highly supportive and influential in the development of the GIFT or GLI curriculums, or both. Each of the

JCamp 180 team members has played an important role in further developing the Culture of Philanthropy model, including Jill Paul who co-led the first GIFT program with me, Julia Riseman, Natasha Dresner, Kevin Martone, Michael Miloff, Janina Kruzel, Tara Acker and Herschel Singer. Tara and Herschel were especially helpful in building the baseline study to evaluate and measure a Culture of Philanthropy.

Another champion who has been there through thick and thin is Anne Weiss, my friend and executive coach. She has encouraged and supported me through the inception of Rainmaker Consulting, as well as coaching our team as we've grown and blossomed. She also made a very important introduction.

In April of 2019, Anne insisted that I meet Donna Haghighat, the Executive Director of the Women's Fund of Western Massachusetts. What started out as the casual introduction of two strangers turned into a life-changing event for me. Donna asked me about my passions, and I shared about my Rainmaker Consulting and Harold Grinspoon Foundation efforts to build a Culture of Philanthropy. She listened intently. When I stopped speaking, she said, "You need to write a book!" I blinked a few times, taking it in. I decided in that moment that I would take it on. Thank you, Donna, for that life-altering conversation and your powerful words.

Zemo Trevathan, culture change consultant from The Aligned Team, was initially brought on as a guest presenter for GLI. Our partnership has grown, and not only has Zemo contributed a number of brilliant concepts cited in *Choose Abundance*, but he has also been very helpful in editing and giving me feedback on the book.

Consultants Mark Rovner and Alia McKee of Sea Change Strategies have also been GLI presenters. Their pivotal work in the field and their white paper, "Inside Out Fundraising," have been very useful in informing the concepts in this book. It's been wonderful to work with this powerful team, and I am thrilled that we will continue this work into the future.

As you will read in this book, many teachers have influenced, inspired and contributed to my body of knowledge. I want to be sure to thank Jennifer McCrea, author of *The Generosity Network*; Terry

Axelrod, author of *The Benevon Model for Sustainable Funding*; Benjamin and Rosamond Zander, authors of *The Art of Possibility*; Robert Gass of the Social Transformation Project and inventor of the *Wheel of Change*; Richard Perry and Jeff Schreifels of the Veritus Group, authors of countless useful blogs and the book *It's Not Just About the Money*; Seth Godin for his many blogs and podcasts about culture and culture change; the Evelyn & Walter Haas Jr. Fund and Compass Point authors Jeanne Bell and Maria Conrnelius for *UnderDeveloped*; Cynthia Gibson, author of *Beyond Fundraising*; and, again, Lynne Twist for *The Soul of Money*.

A number of people helped by reading, reviewing and giving me feedback on *Choose Abundance*, including Natasha Adele Albornoz, Aaron Cantor, Rima Dael, Sam Daley-Harris, Kathleen Dowd, Sarah Eisinger, Joel Hefty, Phil Herrick, Meryl Lowell, Kevin Martone, Kathy "Hootie" Osterhout, Daisy Pereira-Tosado, Eric Phelps, Marsha Rothpan, Mark Shapiro, David Sharken, Cindy Sherman, Anne Teschner and Zemo Trevathan. All of you shared critical insights that helped me make this complex concept accessible to the readers. I thank you for your patience and for your precious time.

This book could not have been possible without the work of two publishing industry experts. Ginny Glass has provided unlimited patience, brilliant editing and the cover design. Publisher K.D. Sullivan of Untreed Reads has taught me all things publishing. I've learned a tremendous amount from the two of you, and I'm eternally grateful. I know who I'm calling if there is a second book in me!

Davin Pasek did a brilliant job with the illustrations in the book as well as designing the downloadable posters and resources on the Book Hub. Thank you, Davin, for your hard work and creative insights.

Lastly, this could not have been accomplished without my Chief Champion and husband, Dan Zukergood, who read, reread, encouraged and gave feedback to me over the last two years. It's not always easy to take feedback from a spouse, but Dan knows how to push hard, expect the best and be kind. Thank you for your steady and stalwart partnership.

Foreword
by Lynne Twist

One of my true joys in life is when someone fully embraces the ideas that I write about in *The Soul of Money* and makes meaningful transformational change with them. Laurie Herrick and I have known each other since the 1980s. When I first met her, Laurie was a new development professional, and I was hired to provide coaching to her and the board of RESULTS, a grassroots citizens' lobby committed to ending hunger. I encouraged Laurie to throw her hat over the fence and take a stand to find a million-dollar funding partner for RESULTS. In fact, Laurie threw that metaphorical hat over the fence and never looked back.

Laurie has taken her experience and expertise in organizational culture change to teach her students, clients and readers how to dismantle the hold that scarcity thinking has on our important social profit organizations. She guides organizational leaders in rebuilding something much more powerful—a Culture of Philanthropy.

Similar to other groundbreaking innovators, Laurie is not creating something new out of nothing, but embracing knowledge from several great leaders and making connections among them to build, test and strengthen a unique model. Her deep experience and understanding of the lessons embedded in my work as well as that of Seth Godin, Simon Sinek, Brené Brown, Terry Axelrod, Jennifer McCrea, Dave Logan, Steve Zaffron, Cynthia Gibson, Maria Cornelius, Jeanne Bell and Benjamin and Rosamond Zander are integral to the Choose Abundance Model.

Laurie's innovation has led her to be the first person to be insightful enough to see the connection among these concepts and their potential, when combined together, to drive meaningful, positive change for mission-driven organizations. While developing and strengthening this model, Laurie draws upon years of experience working with hundreds of organizations and amplifies what she has learned from them: best practices, common challenges and practical solutions.

We can all agree that these are extraordinary times. It is a time when our entire species is so humbled and sobered by the issues confronting us. Our collective society has been waking up to issues that have been building and festering for years. Racial issues that were hidden to people of privilege have become revealed and present in ways that has them now undeniable. We've seen a collapse of our economic systems, the near collapse of our democracy, the breakdown of the media's reliance on the truth and of our reliance on the media to be truthful. We've witnessed the pandemic's impact on our collective health and the collapse of our healthcare systems.

The outcome of excess and waste on our planet has resulted in a climate crisis with fires, floods, super storms and the melting of the polar ice cap. These events are horrendous expressions of mother earth giving us feedback that we hadn't been paying good enough attention to our environment.

Importantly, we've also witnessed the absence of spiritual depth in the way people are living and getting along. This was revealed powerfully in 2020.

These awakenings are an opportunity to have "20:20 vision," if you will, and create the future that we all want. We are on the precipice of a great cultural awakening. A cultural evolution. And we've got work to do. Because of this 20:20 vision, we know what to focus on in ourselves and in the world, and, ultimately, we will look back and say that we saw what was wrong and we made the appropriate change happen. It is a very healthy thing to stop and reflect and recognize when we are on the wrong path, and then adjust and change our trajectory. At this time, in the beginning of this new decade, we have the most precious opportunity to visualize and then fully create where we want to go.

That is where all of you, the readers of this book, come in. I know that you are up to great things. You are leading organizations that are addressing many of the issues that I just mentioned above—the inequities, the social and environmental injustices and the care of our sisters and brothers all over the planet. You are generating possibilities…of art, of beauty, of music, of justice, of health and of laughter and joy.

In fact, it has always been social profit organizations that have seized the moment to transform the world. There are nearly 1.7 million such organizations in the US and Canada. So many of them are struggling to acquire the resources they need to fulfill their missions. And our society needs your organization to thrive, now, more than ever. Your organizations are lifelines to a better world.

You picked up this book because you believe your organization can do better. You realize that you need more money, more partnerships in the community and more teamwork among your board and staff. You are intent on accomplishing your organization's mission. In other words, you desire a vibrant Culture of Philanthropy.

This is where Laurie Herrick's *Choose Abundance: Powerful Fundraising for Nonprofits—A Culture of Philanthropy* can be your map. Just as we need to have 20:20 vision as a society and face the ways that we are not on track with our highest values, our social profit organizations need to do similar reflective work to identify where we are not aligned with our highest values.

To do this, Laurie will guide you to look into the eye of that 20:20 vision and recognize what may be in the way of your desired Culture of Philanthropy. Where have you been stopped by fear of rejection, an old narrative about money or stories that you can't make a difference? Where have you made up that it's a zero-sum game and there must be losers? Notice where you have thoughts, a mindset or a framework that has you believe your organization, you or your life are insufficient.

Laurie wisely points out that you cannot build a Culture of Philanthropy without first digging deep and revealing where fear and scarcity thinking are present. Once we reveal that we have a scarcity mindset, we can begin to dismantle that framework. This helps us become aware of our own blessings, what we already have in our lives that we are grateful for. Laurie refers to this as an *abundance mindset*. When we get in touch with the plentitude of what already surrounds us and we allow that to permeate our perceptions of our organizations, we can start to get in touch with what is possible.

When we begin to see and then articulate what is possible, this enables others to get in touch with their generosity, their own abundance, and their philanthropy, their love of humankind. When you powerfully share your organization's vision of a different world and inspire others to be generous, you are giving them a gift—the opportunity to make a difference. You are also giving your community a gift by helping to realize your organization's mission and vision.

Once you gain this newfound vision, you will find an abundance of generous individuals within your orbit who will want to contribute their ideas, money, skills and wisdom (their abundance) to help manifest a world that works for everyone, with no one excluded.

Change happens when a person recognizes that something is not right and seizes the opportunity to transform it. This book represents your opportunity to lead your organization in achieving unprecedented breakthroughs. Seize it!

Choose Abundance

Powerful Fundraising for Nonprofits

A Culture of Philanthropy

Introduction

It's likely that you picked up this book because you're deeply committed to a cause and an organization that's addressing it. You may be an Executive Director, development professional, program staff person or volunteer board member. Whether or not you get paid for this work, you contribute your time and your energy, and you give your heart and soul to supporting this mission.

Before we go any further, thank you for your work on behalf of our society. We need you, and we need your organization to make our lives better. You may work on behalf of a social justice cause addressing environmental, racial, gender or other issues. Your agency may bring us the beauty of the arts or care for our community's health and well-being. Or you might do some other important work that helps make the world a better place. I'm grateful that you are doing the hard work to make life a little brighter, a little cleaner, healthier and more peaceful and joyful.

My guess is that you found yourself drawn to this book because you see some sort of deficit—a gap between what your not-for-profit is currently achieving and what it can become. Most likely, that gap has to do with the financial resources that come to your organization.

Over the last twenty-plus years, I've been the owner of multiple successful businesses. I've been a grassroots fundraising professional, Development Director, Executive Director, board member, donor, consultant and instructor. I've consulted for food banks, arts organizations, religious organizations, alternative-education programs, entrepreneurial programs, children's camps, healthcare agencies and environmental and social justice organizations. I've worked in the social service sector. I've worked with tiny, medium and large organizations. Through these varied experiences, I've seen firsthand the funding challenges facing not-for-profit organizations across North America.

I have repeatedly heard the frustration of countless leaders who strive for abundant resources for their agencies and seem to be constantly struggling to make ends meet. I've seen common mistakes made repeatedly that keep organizations from being able to realize their full potential and make maximum impact. In fact, I've made some of these same mistakes myself.

In 2014, a seminal report called "Underdeveloped: A National Study of the Challenges Facing Nonprofit Fundraising" (Jeanne Bell and Maria Cornelius), was released by Compass Point, with support of the Evelyn & Walter Haas Jr. Fund. Compass Point interviewed 2,700 Executive Directors and development professionals. Their study validated what many of us already knew—development shops across North America are struggling. Donor-retention rates are abysmal, boards and staff members are disengaged, and the turnover rate of development staff averages approximately eighteen months. The missing link, according to the report, is a *Culture of Philanthropy.*

There are many useful how-to books and resources available that teach the process of fundraising, but none address the complexity and deep impact of creating a Culture of Philanthropy throughout your organization. Across the field, many have been seeking the path to build this elusive culture, but few have done what I'm suggesting here—*create a strong team and intentionally name, build and put into practice your desired culture.*

Building a Culture of Philanthropy in your organization, while often difficult, is entirely possible. It takes tremendous effort and focus. The rewards for this effort are even greater.

Imagine what it would be like if you had the dollars to expand your program and serve more constituents, or if your best staff members were better paid and could remain with your agency and comfortably support their families at the same time. What if you had the resources to go the distance within your programs, adding features that are visionary and exciting—features that would allow you to come closer to fulfilling your mission? What if changing your culture could change the trajectory of your organization's financial future? And what if culture change could help your cause weather hardships that other organizations couldn't?

In the fund-development world, I have trained and taught fundraising skills, and people have met inspiring goals. These achievements were wonderful, but in many cases, they did not leave a lasting impact. Since offering training in transforming the culture and having more permanent change with teams, leaders have found a Culture of Philanthropy to be a game changer.

In early 2020, we began to shut down our economy, society and organizations because of the COVID pandemic. What happened was unprecedented on a number of levels. We had never really suspended so many systems and structures before on such a tremendous scale. Many things came to a screeching halt: schools, businesses, transportation and in-person socializing.

Interestingly, we changed our habits, ways of thinking and behaviors in a very short period to adapt to the new set of circumstances. It was suddenly common and acceptable to work from home, do video meetings and travel less. And despite the challenges, there were unforeseen benefits to this about-face in our routines. Now, what happens when all travel bans are lifted? Will flights from NYC to London for two-hour meetings be a thing of the past?

But it wasn't only the isolation and the change in our ability to travel or interact that influenced my thinking—or that of many others—during the writing of this book. In 2020, in addition to the pandemic, our nation saw the rise of the Black Lives Matter movement and the racial reckoning of our country. Coupled with a period of strong political divisiveness, equality issues have come to the forefront and caused many to examine scarcity and abundance from important new perspectives.

We've seen through this example that radical change—though never easy—can happen. We must not waste this crisis and go back to the way things were. It's time to use this lesson to seize the moment now. We truly have the ability to make change happen. And by that, I mean that you can use the mission of your organization and the urgency of the need to fuel a demand for culture change that leads to the resources you require to fulfill that mission.

There is tremendous opportunity to shift how we think and how we do things. As a fundraising consultant, I coached development professionals and Executive Directors to build Major Donor programs and have one-on-one meaningful calls and meetings with top donors. Many struggled to make donor meetings regularly happen, given the multitude of fundraising tasks on their lists. They seldom did check-in calls with donors just to see how they were doing.

In the beginning of the pandemic, I once again (but this time more adamantly) encouraged people to reach out and check in with their donors to share their authentic care and concern for them. A number of clients took that on. They began connecting more deeply and intimately with donors in a way that they had not been able to prioritize previously. They checked to see how people were.

For those who did this, it paid off. A few months later, when these agencies were hurting badly from months of closure, they asked their funders to help, and the funders stepped up. Those agencies that shied away from calling people early in the pandemic did not get the same warm response when the first communication from the organization was an ask.

As I tell you that story, you can see that it is not just about behaviors and structures, but about the culture that is often hidden to us. If we don't pay attention to the culture, we are missing something very important. This book will help you be more aware of your organization's culture, and then guide you in the steps, exercises and changes in mindset that must occur for sustainable culture change to happen.

When you start to implement a Culture of Philanthropy following the set of instructions and exercises within this book, remember that the information in these pages is not just theory or general information—these practices are tried and true. If you take this on, you will begin to see that there are numerous people who are already connected to your agency who care deeply about your work. They will step up and help you in a multitude of ways if you treat them kindly and stay connected to them.

Instead of feeling a scarcity of funding, you will recognize the potential wealth of human ideas and resources you already have.

Instead of having transactional relationships with donors, you can get to know them. Your cause can build systems to not just track the gifts and the direct-mail pieces, but begin to track people's passions and how they might want to be more involved in your work. Instead of staff members being lone wolves struggling to keep up with their tasks, your agency can take on development as a group effort, with everyone playing a role in making connections and building partnerships.

You'll probably find a number of small ideas in this book that you can quickly take on. In fact, you might think that many of these things are standard fundraising practices. Absolutely, you can pick up several good fundraising tips and tricks from reading this book. Some of them might be extremely helpful to your agency if you start doing them yourself. Building a Culture of Philanthropy is not about a one-time trick, nor is it a job for a Lone Ranger; it's impossible to break through an organization-wide scarcity mindset and change the path of an agency (and the lives of those it serves) all alone.

I will introduce a powerful tool for organization-wide change—the Choose Abundance Model—to build a Culture of Philanthropy. I hope, as you read this book, you'll see that there's no better time to use this systematic approach than now. Each of these ideas would bring powerful momentum to your cause, whether in a time of economic challenges or in everyday life, taken individually. When combined, these practices can be the beginning of a fresh, new Culture of Philanthropy, or the path to enhancing and strengthening an existing Culture of Philanthropy.

Whether your organization is doing quite well in development or is below average, there are few organizations that are extraordinary across *all* fronts. I'll explore the impact of culture as a way to help your organization be the best it can be, raising the funds that will keep it healthy and sustainable and thriving in all situations, regardless of the economy or other outside forces. I'll help you look more deeply at your organization's existing culture, and then I'll help you unpack it, revealing where it supports your efforts and where it undermines them. I'll help you redesign your culture into one that's steeped in abundant resources.

The following concepts will distinguish this book from other resources in the field:

- **A team approach**—My system brings the key leaders of board and staff to the table and requires transformation of the leadership team.
- **Look within**—Building a Culture of Philanthropy mandates both looking outward *and* looking inward. I'll strongly encourage you to look at your own *and* your organization's behaviors, systems and overall mindset.
- **A method that *includes* implementation**—In fact, simply by picking up this book and making the commitment to put your team together and work the program, you've already taken step one to positively changing your agency.
- **Not a one-size-fits-all!**—This approach can be easily customized to your organization so you can create effective change wherever you are, at whatever size you are.

As I've found in working with clients over the last decade, creating a Culture of Philanthropy requires commitment, a willingness to step up to the plate and think outside the box, and every other figure of speech that means to *think differently*. Success requires the shifting of our perspectives—and following those shifts with bold actions.

Together, we will intentionally push against commonly held not-for-profit and culture misconceptions, and I'll teach you what I have learned about building a Culture of Philanthropy. I will provide examples of what this culture looks like in practice. I'll guide you through case studies (which I call Guideposts) from clients and friends who have successfully made organizational culture change. I'll provide you with practical tools designed to strengthen your team's skills.

It's important to understand, going into this book, that there isn't a shortcut to success in building a Culture of Philanthropy. Building a strong foundation takes time. There are steps you can take immediately, but complete organizational culture change typically takes three to five years to accomplish. It will require your perseverance, patience and planning. And once you start to have a Culture of Philanthropy in place, you will still need to maintain the culture to assure that your organization doesn't slip back into its old habits.

My goal with this book is to reach many levels of reader. It's a great practical companion to students of philanthropy who might be reading other textbooks. It can provide immense benefit to a spectrum of organizations, from those that have one-person development departments, to all-volunteer organizations, to large safety-net agencies across our country.

To get the most out of this book, don't just passively read *Choose Abundance*. Reading and doing are two different things. You will see places where we refer to resources we have created to aid you in taking action. All of our *Choose Abundance* resources can also be found on our Book Hub at www.ChooseAbundanceBook.com. We developed them with you, our reader, in mind. I highly recommend you use them.

Treat this book like a workbook. Try out the ideas. Do the exercises, even if they seem simple—or uncomfortable. Because organizational culture is so intangible, it's difficult to discuss in the abstract. The exercises I lay out are intentionally created to make you think differently about how you do things, to consider approaches you might not have considered previously. You can also read more at www.rainmkr.com about how my business, Rainmaker Consulting, works directly with clients to help implement a Culture of Philanthropy.

I hope that regardless of your years and your past accomplishments in the not-for-profit field, you'll be surprised and challenged by this book. Even if you have had fundraising success and already do some of the things I outline in this book, there is always an opportunity for your organization to achieve so much more. I'm optimistic that the following pages will provide you with important insight.

This will require you to look deeply not just at your agency, but also at yourself. As you'll see, the future of your organization is dependent on this awareness. I hope you undertake this journey of transforming your agency into one infused with a mindset of abundance and is distinguished by a Culture of Philanthropy. May this book be a resource to help you build a more effective and powerful collective, one that you could not have imagined possible—one that is *extraordinary*.

Part I

Is Your Fundraising Program Less Than Extraordinary?

Chapter 1
Your Current Reality

The most common way people give up their power
is by thinking they don't have any.

—ALICE WALKER

As you begin this Culture of Philanthropy journey, think about this Chinese proverb: "When is the best time to have planted a tree? Ten years ago. When is the next best time? Now." As we discussed in the Introduction, a Culture of Philanthropy is something that is relevant now. It's a tool that you can use for future planning, but you can also use it this very moment to build a stronger foundation.

Before we go further, let's define the problem we are addressing. You have found yourself involved in an organization that needs to fundamentally change *something* to increase its donations, its engagement of more volunteers or its enhancement of public awareness of your cause in order to achieve the extraordinary.

I make the following assertions about what *extraordinary* means—it's about long-term sustainability and resilience. It's about reaching for your boldest vision. Extraordinary is about building a community of champions around your agency, people who love your cause and will be there for you through thick and thin. These individuals will understand that fulfilling your mission is not easy, yet they are in it with you for the long haul. They'll thrive in a culture that allows leadership to be authentic with them, sharing the challenges and seeking their help with solutions. Together, you will build a solid framework to be deeply effective in the work you do. Your agency will be stronger because there are many of you, with a wide variety of attributes and assets, with a united vision and—most likely—with a spectrum of ideas of how to best fulfill that vision.

An agency with a Culture of Philanthropy has:

- Valuable community partners
- Increased donor loyalty and retention

- Greater board and staff engagement
- Larger gifts
- Abundant resources of all kinds

If your experience is that your organization is not on a trajectory to manifest this vision, you may have already seen that the benchmarks of stagnation are there—low morale, tepid fundraising efforts, inconsistent donor response, lackluster community involvement, and little or no upward movement in the number of individuals you serve or the quality of services you deliver. By recognizing that these are all symptoms of a cultural deficit, you've taken the first step toward recognizing that cultural change is needed.

At this point, you might be starting to think that you don't have a Culture of Philanthropy. Or perhaps you have a number of things that are working well, but there is opportunity to do much better. Regardless, you're ready to get to work building your Culture of Philanthropy.

Many of us are drawn to the tactical. We tend to want to get to work and take action. You'll see in the next section that culture change isn't just about taking action steps. You need to first understand what is pushing up against your desired Culture of Philanthropy. I've seen countless organizational leaders make the mistake of attempting to build some change into their agency without first looking at the mindset, attitudes and feelings of key stakeholders.

I promise that there will be a moment when you can get to work implementing a Culture of Philanthropy. In the meantime, I want to share some concepts that might help you understand the powerful, negative effect that a misaligned culture has had on the not-for-profit industry. I'll share the lessons that I've learned surrounding the problem, and, importantly, what I've discovered about how you can transform it.

Chapter 2
Unexpected Results

Until one is committed, there is hesitancy, the chance to draw back, always ineffectiveness. Concerning all acts of initiative (and creation), there is one elementary truth, the ignorance of which kills countless ideas and splendid plans. That the moment one definitely commits oneself, then providence moves, too. All sorts of things occur to help one that would never otherwise have occurred. Whatever you can do or dream you can, begin it. Boldness has genius, power and magic in it. Begin it now.

—WILLIAM HUTCHISON MURRAY

Slinging dog shampoo and tanning lotion doesn't seem to be the fast track to becoming a development professional, but for me, it was. In my twenties, I'd intended to be an artist, but the path to becoming a lucrative handmade-paper maker appeared to be fraught with disappointment. I was attempting to use this art form as a vehicle for motivating the public on social justice issues. Clearly, that short-lived vision was also shortsighted.

So, I got a job, and it happened to be selling dog shampoo and tanning lotion. The manufacturer that employed me did a great job of teaching me how to become a professional telemarketer to their retail stores. It turned out I was actually good at sales, and I ended up eventually owning a wholesale distribution company, employing twenty-two people and selling millions of dollars of dog shampoo and tanning lotion. I did that for about seven years in my thirties. I loved having my own business and managing people, and I enjoyed sales. I learned a lot during that tenure.

There was a problem, however. I wasn't particularly committed to the products, and I still wasn't moving and inspiring the public on social justice issues—well, that's not completely true, but I wasn't doing that for a living.

I was volunteering for a wonderful organization called RESULTS. RESULTS is a grassroots citizen's lobby that teaches advocacy for people living in poverty. It's a brilliant model where volunteer chapters all over the United States join international chapters to simultaneously reach out to our political leaders and ask them to support legislation that addresses the root causes of poverty. As a volunteer, I was learning a tremendous amount about working with other volunteers, public speaking and about the issues we addressed. Each year, I would go to our international conference and cry. Why was I still selling dog shampoo? I wanted to sell the end of hunger!

Before long, my opportunity presented itself. The Founder/Executive Director decided to move on, and the Development Director moved into his place. I saw my chance and applied to become the Development Director. The new Executive Director kindly responded to my inquiry and told me that I was not a good candidate for the job, as I had no development experience. I was crushed. I wrote a letter explaining in great detail the connection between sales and development, only to get back another No. This back and forth happened multiple times. Months passed, and I continued my pursuit. In the meantime, I sold a ton of dog shampoo.

Finally, it happened. After another one of my attempts to get the job, the Executive Director sent me a letter saying that under no circumstances would I be the Development Director for this agency. She stated that it would not be responsible for her to hire me when I didn't have development experience. That didn't deter me. After months of gentle pestering, I was offered the post as RESULTS's grassroots fundraising director! Not the Development Director job, but it was close enough.

It was my big opportunity. I closed my company and shifted my focus to fundraising. At last, I was selling something I was committed to. I coached groups across the United States in rallying their volunteers to invest their money for the end of hunger. I got to know our Major Donors, and I was thrilled to be there. I was promoted to Development Director. I had my dream job.

Until one day, when the pressure was on.

My boss told me that we were experiencing a shortfall, and that I needed to raise an additional $40K by the end of the year. That was a mere three months away! I had no idea how to do it. Time passed with no great progress, and she asked me who I would fire if I didn't raise it.

I went to my go-to donor, someone who I knew, though he'd made a big gift recently. When I asked him for $10K, he declined; he and his wife had recently given, and they had other commitments at that time. I got off the phone and did what any professional would do. I cried. At that point, no one had told me that there's no crying in development.

I was filled with self-doubt. Maybe I should have stuck with dog shampoo. Maybe I was in the wrong career. I just couldn't take this pressure. Who were they going to fire? Maybe they should just get rid of me.

I called my boss and relayed all of this. And while she had been very direct about our needs, she was equally kind with solutions. She suggested that I call one of her friends, Lynne Twist, a fundraising consultant and author of the book *The Soul of Money*. Perhaps Lynne would do a fundraising training and help us get out of this situation.

Little did I know that the No for $10K would be the most influential No I ever received.

Lynne Twist did come to RESULTS, and she did a training for a group of staff and board members. Lynne said a lot in that training, but here is the conversation I remember:

> At one point, I mentioned that I had heard of an organization that had received a million-dollar gift. I said, "We should have a million-dollar donor!"
>
> Lynne looked at me and said, "It takes a stand. Laurie, are you willing to take a stand to get a million-dollar donor?"
>
> I started backpedaling, thinking, *I can't even get $40K!* How could I possibly find a million-dollar donor?

> Lynne said something critical then that forever changed my life—*if you really want it, take a stand for it. Publicly declare that you are committed to achieving that result. Once you take a stand, you essentially throw your hat over a fence. Once you throw your hat over a fence, what do you have to do? You've got to climb over and get it.* She didn't promise that we'd get our million-dollar donor. But if we didn't take a stand for it, our chances were certainly much lower. Taking a stand for a million-dollar donor is what will give you a fighting chance to get a million-dollar donor.

With some trepidation, I said I would take on the challenge. I declared to my peers that I was committed to getting RESULTS a million-dollar donor. Lynne had also suggested that I find someone who could be an ally, someone who wouldn't tell me that my idea was crazy, someone who saw the same possibility that I did. She called that person my *Committed Listener*.

I immediately thought of a volunteer, my friend Peter, who I believed to be particularly visionary. A small-business owner living in California, Peter was very passionate about our work. We shared that passion, and we also had running in common. Each time we got together, at each of our regional or national conferences a few times a year, we would take a run and think through our strategy and action plan. Who could we approach?

Aside from actual conversations with potential donors, we spent a fair amount of time dreaming of pie-in-the-sky wealthy individuals who didn't even know we existed. We set up a small gathering of some Silicon Valley young entrepreneurs. I traveled to California using some of RESULTS's meager travel budget. It went nowhere. We talked to countless individuals, sharing our big idea. We would start to get some traction, and then nothing significant would happen.

Meanwhile, every time we met, we got more excited about what it would mean for RESULTS to find a million-dollar donor. We'd be able to start more chapters. We'd be able to advocate for more people living in poverty. We could perhaps leverage more funding through the Child Survival Fund, a program of UNICEF that saves millions of children by providing them with proper nutrition, safe drinking water, affordable vaccines and other basic necessities.

One time, as Peter and I were getting together after several months, I could see he was bursting with enthusiasm. He seemed so upbeat, and I started to become hopeful that perhaps he had met someone rich (this was my misguided mindset at the time, I'll admit it). As we started running, I said to him, as I had on nearly every run before this one, "Peter, we need to find our million-dollar donor. Who is our million-dollar donor?"

Peter smiled. He stopped running, and he looked me in the eye and slowly said, "Laurie, I'm your million-dollar donor. My wife and I have figured out a way that we can make an annual gift of $100,000." I could not believe my ears! He and his wife made a pledge to give a million dollars over the span of ten years to RESULTS.

This was a tremendous breakthrough for me and for the organization, and it was a definite turning point in how I thought about internal organizational resources (and not just in the monetary sense). My friend was deeply involved in the cause. While none of us knew that Peter and his wife had that sort of capacity of financial resources, we otherwise knew him well. He had years of history as a dedicated volunteer and Major Donor, and he understood the vision of RESULTS. Unknowingly, I had been engaging this donor in deepening his commitment to the organization. Each time we ran together, he got more in touch with what was possible in the organization, and how he could make a difference.

Through his volunteer work prior to my project, and then enhanced by meeting regularly to discuss what was possible for RESULTS, Peter was brought deeper into the agency as a key insider and stakeholder. He was empowered through our conversations to step into an even greater leadership role, one that he hadn't previously considered to be possible.

Equally powerful was what happened for me. Through this experience, I saw this—taking a stand required me making a major shift in my mindset. I had to move from a place of fear and scarcity (I'll define these in the next chapter) to one of great possibility. This was the beginning of my understanding the critical role that we each play in the success within our agencies, and how each role, when properly calibrated to a Culture of Philanthropy, can power significant success.

It's important to make a couple of points about how aspects of this story about Peter were inconsistent with a Culture of Philanthropy. So often, organizations seek a single donor who can save them. A single-donor focus was part of my thinking, initially, but I've learned better since then, that it truly takes a diversity of funding from many people. One person will not save your organization. Also, I never actually asked Peter to give. Asking is necessary.

I eventually left my role at RESULTS, though I still love the organization and the many lessons I learned from both my boss and Lynne Twist. While I fought hard to become the Development Director of RESULTS, I knew that when the opportunity came along to serve as the Executive Director of a small foundation, I needed to seize it. I saw the potential to share those countless lessons with a wider number of agencies, the grantees of the foundation. And each of these agencies taught me as much as I taught them.

I quickly noticed that there was a pattern. So many organizations had very similar challenges. In fact, I started to see that there was an industry-wide cultural mindset problem—one that was fixable. This clearly became my work, starting with lessons with my boss and Lynne Twist, and continuing through that initial foundation working with grantees. It continues in my current business, Rainmaker Consulting, and through a foundation where I teach courses on building a Culture of Philanthropy.

Making any large cultural adjustment involves changing hearts and minds. Discovering that culture change was the solution to the problems in fundraising—and that I was empowered to help—involved these changes for me as well. I had a meaningful turning point in my career, where I realized my true power to be a catalyst for change (something we all possess).

In this book, we will dig into what can cause personal and organizational breakthroughs for *you*. These will require some authentic and open introspection. They will require you (and your entire organization) to stand in a place of vulnerability in order to change hearts and minds. Think about your organization now. Do you or your staff feel unable to gain momentum toward organizational goals, no matter what you do? If so, this can be a sign that you're due for a culture change. And when your organization culturally stands as one, can you imagine the momentum-gaining power of that?

Together, through the ideas and practices outlined in this book, we can create efficient, aware organizations that aren't just sustainable, but also have an abundance of resources, allowing leaders to be nimble and responsive to the needs of their clients, and ultimately, to aid in fulfilling their missions. Instead of grasping for short-term, Band-Aid solutions, we will achieve lasting impact with our clients by building a Culture of Philanthropy and having the right mindset to drive phenomenal results. As I experienced with my friend Peter, the impact of a changed mindset can be remarkable. If I hadn't shifted from "I can't do this" to "I will take a stand for this happening, and I can make it happen," it never would have happened.

In the next several chapters, I will provide tools to help you make this culture change, tools to help you think differently about how to do your work, run your agency or be a great volunteer. Regardless of your skill level or experience, I intend to shine a light on the things that are hidden from all of our view unless we intentionally expose them.

Part II

Foundational Tools and Resources to Build a Culture of Philanthropy

Chapter 3
What Is This Culture of Philanthropy, Anyway?

They always say time changes things, but you actually have to change them yourself.

—Andy Warhol

The phrase *Culture of Philanthropy* has been held out in the industry as the holy grail of fundraising. And, of course, who wouldn't want a holy grail? It sounds wonderful, right?

I was working with an agency a few years ago that asked me to help them hire a new Development Director. We interviewed several individuals. In the interview questions, we asked one individual, "What do you know about a Culture of Philanthropy, and what could you do to help us build one here?"

The candidate stumbled a bit and said, "Yes, of course, I can build it here. We'll get lots and lots of rich people all clamoring to give to this organization. I'm confident I can make that happen!"

For many hopeful not-for-profit leaders, this is what they envision. Somehow, magically, the right development person comes along with their contact list and gets their rich connections to love your cause and make the biggest gifts of their lives. Not only is that incredibly unlikely, but it's built upon a number of myths. The most significant myth is that one person can bring this idea to fruition. Organizational leaders imagine that they can simply observe this beauty unfolding because they hired the right Development Director. While this might be a little exaggerated, tell the truth—have you or someone on your team implied that something like this is possible?

This single-rescuer situation is not what we mean when we talk about creating a Culture of Philanthropy. Additionally, the knowledge and effort needed to create the culture definitely requires a group undertaking. Let's dive into what you need to know before you start your journey. I'll be defining terms and concepts that you'll see throughout the action chapters of this book so that you'll be familiar with the them when it comes time to focus on the *doing* part of changing hearts and minds.

"Philanthropy" and "Culture of Philanthropy" Defined

Philanthropy is defined in *Merriam-Webster's Dictionary* as "love of mankind." I prefer the more gender-neutral "love of humankind."

Here is the definition of *Culture of Philanthropy* that I ascribe to:

> *A Culture of Philanthropy* exists when organization-wide attitudes, actions and systems reflect an understanding, respect and responsibility for philanthropy's role in the success of the organization.
>
> *Philanthropy* is the generous way that community members can advance the cause, and can be expressed in financial gifts, volunteering, community engagement and in many creative forms of bigheartedness. This organization-wide commitment to building a culture that fosters philanthropy is reflected explicitly in the mission and reinforced through continuous engagement of all stakeholders. As a result, each person sees their vital role in assuring the long-term viability of the agency.

For me, these welcoming definitions of philanthropy and Culture of Philanthropy, are ones that invite us all to play, and they deserve to be shared. I have made an 8.5 x 11 print of the definition of Culture of Philanthropy, which you can download from our Book Hub at www.ChooseAbundanceBook.com.

Spread the word about this powerful revisioning! It's not uncommon for people to immediately think of the affluent upper 1 percent when the word *philanthropy* is mentioned. It is also common to imagine that all the money is held by rich, white males. That is not what we mean. While the 1 percent are welcome to the Culture of Philanthropy party, and, in fact, having the most privileged among us supporting our causes is very helpful, they aren't the main show. Our party includes *everyone*—the people who live next door to the organization, those who give their time or their financial assets, the staff and the board members. This is a true case where it takes a village.

Individuals may bring a variety of things to this metaphorical party. They may bring volunteerism, including expertise in legal issues, editing or writing, coaching and wisdom, needed items or money. I'll give you an example of one organization that started to reframe how they saw the individuals who were part of their larger community.

Most not-for-profit organizations are in the business of doing good in the world. And, of course, each organization serves a specific population. One client that I worked with provides services for adults with intellectual and developmental disabilities. When we discussed the definition of philanthropy as "love of humankind," it made them feel more comfortable inviting volunteers or funders to participate in their work. Who doesn't want to be part of making the world a little better for someone? They could quickly see that they were deeply committed to assuring that all members of our society, and specifically individuals with disabilities, were embraced in the folds of our community. Inviting participation in their work felt natural when framed as an expression of "love of humankind." This small mindset shift had significant impact on how staff engaged with donors and how they saw their role.

When we invite people to participate in our organizations, we have no idea what they bring to the table. The opportunity is to be open to who they are, who they're connected to, what their brilliance is, and how it can contribute to your work. You'll be amazed at what may surface.

The Complexities of Culture

Culture is challenging to understand. We seem to live in it like a fish lives in a fishbowl, but it's difficult to truly see it unless we are outside it. My husband and I lived in Los Angeles in the late 1980s. We often went to the town of Big Bear, located in the mountains high above Los Angeles, for vacation.

As we drove up the mountain, once we got to a high elevation, we could look down and see where the smog line was. We could clearly see the clean air above that smog line, but we could also see that everything below it was dirty—and that was what we lived in every day. We lived in a dirty fishbowl, but we weren't aware of that. It was just the environment that it was.

Organizations are like this, as well. You don't always see that you're living in a dirty fishbowl until you step outside of it or have an outsider point out what they're seeing from their perspective. From within the fishbowl, it's just the way it is!

I had this same observation as a young college student living in Austria. At first, I noticed what seemed obvious—the people around me spoke differently, they wore different clothes than I did, and they had different habits and different senses of humor. Then, after a few months of observing this, I suddenly noticed that back home we spoke differently, we wore different clothes and we had different habits and unique norms about what a sense of humor is. It was the first time I'd noticed my own culture. It isn't just "the way it is." I had been socialized, and had accepted the norms of my culture were just "the way it is."

Seth Godin, marketing expert and author of over 18 books. says, "People like us do things like this." That is his way of defining and addressing what *culture* is. In our organizations, if we aren't aware of or simply ignore the dirty fishbowl, we are keeping it stagnant.

Chapter 4

What Is Pushing Back Against a Culture of Philanthropy?

The bottom line for leaders is that if they do not become conscious of the culture in which they are embedded, those cultures will manage them.

—EDGAR SCHEIN

A Mindset of Scarcity: Becoming Aware

I'd like you to consider that we live every day in a mindset of scarcity. It is an intentionally constructed framework designed to have us think that we need more. It makes us feel dissatisfied, frustrated, and, at times, it can make us feel anxious. This framework is woven into our capitalism and has evolved over time. In this chapter, we will first explore how this mindset has unfolded.

Initially, at the onset of the industrial revolution in America, there was a need to build things for our survival. There aren't enough blankets to keep everyone warm? Let's figure out how to manufacture them more quickly instead of grandma making one at a time or having a sewing bee! This was repeated with several items necessary for human survival. We need our soldiers to have food when they are out fighting for our cause? Let's put things into cans. We need more housing? Let's develop a home that can be set up quickly! This was an amazing time as we worked out how to take care of more people (not everyone, but more of us).

Then, after some time, we started to have more than we needed. Wall Street's Paul Mazur, who worked as a banker at Lehman Brothers in 1927, said, "We must shift America from a needs culture to a desires culture. People must be trained to desire, to want new things, even before the old have been entirely consumed. Man's desires must overshadow his needs." ("Birth of Consumer Culture," businessinsider.com) This was the true beginning of marketing. How do we show people that they must have more stuff?

From the 1950s to our current time, the tenor and types of communications to this end evolved. Smoking appeared sexy on billboards, housewives began to look as though they were having the times of their lives waiting on their spouses and polishing their furniture with Pledge, and the most beautiful people apparently had more appliances, fancier cars and brighter, whiter children! Many social constructs were reinforced.

As we moved into the 1960s and 1970s, TV became one of the primary vehicles for instilling greater desire. It had a brainwashing effect. Sometimes, you couldn't tell the difference between a commercial and a TV show. Marketing within shows (product placement) became a vehicle to foster greater desire. Laura and Dick Van Dyke had the most contemporary things in their homes, as did the Brady Bunch with their mod California house. Some shows reinforced the luxurious life with bigger, fancier cars, furs and airplane travel! Disposable products became the norm.

The most creative work on television became advertising. How could a company reach their intended consumers? What shows had the best ratings in the demographic that would buy their products?

With the widespread use of the internet, a big foothold developed in the quest to stoke the desire for more. At first, most advertising came to your inbox, and then websites started to advertise and use cookies to track user behaviors and mine the resulting data. Products that you looked at previously would pop onto your screen when you were on a website. As you likely know, targeting individuals to buy specific items is a sophisticated science.

Today, we're constantly being bombarded with messages that we need more. The sheer volume of messages and advertising we receive is overwhelming. Guess how many times a day we get a message that we need more? Just guess. Okay, I realize it's hard to create an element of surprise here—especially if you read the below info when you came to this page!

> It is now estimated that an ordinary person gets exposed to between 6,000 and 10,000 images and messages *every single day*. These ads are meant to have

us feel dissatisfied, frustrated, less than adequate and wanting more (https://ppcprotect.com/how-many-ads-do-we-see-a-day).

This is huge, and it's all set up so that we'll purchase more goods. We get it on billboards on the highway, in the public subways, on trains and buses and in the streets of our cities, on social media, in online games, and in digital marketing. It's on the magazine rack and in the newspapers that we read or even walk by in our grocery stores.

It happens every time we open up an app or access the internet. As a not-for-profit professional, every time I use a search engine or a Doodle Poll to set a meeting with a team, I'm reminded that I looked at a pair of running shoes in the last week. Over and over again, we're reminded that we need more stuff, more pizzazz, more sleep, more sex, more love, more friends, a bigger or new or renovated house, or a fancier vacation. I get a reminder message that everyone else has a perfect lawn, that everyone else drives a luxury car—and I should too! Some of these are horribly blatant; one home-improvement magazine boasts that if I just renovate my kitchen, I will save myself "a lifetime of regrets"! Similar messages are made to help me improve my body to look like the supermodels that they highlight.

Now, add a pandemic. How about constant messages that invoke fear? In March of 2020, the tone of the messages in my inbox shifted from ones that instilled the need to purchase frivolous luxuries to panicky missives about how to survive—proof that even a crisis is fair game in the tactics of emotion-based marketing.

Our Culture's Impact on Organizational Staff and Board Members

What does this have to do with your not-for-profit organization? Let's play this out. You're an average human. You wake up and wish you had more sleep and more time for your family, and then, on your way to work, you're reminded hundreds of times about how you're supposed to own a number of things you can't afford, be fit in a way that you have no time to achieve, and be a superhuman. Is it any wonder we might feel a little inadequate?

Or maybe you work from home. If you're socially conscious, you inevitably check your email or read the newspaper first thing in the morning. What if you're shown how the world is going to hell in a handbasket, and there's barely anything that anyone can do about it—except fill out these ten surveys. Really?

Let's jump over to Facebook, where people are showing us their perfect lives. Why does she always get to be on vacation? I want that dog and picket fence! Is her dog really that sweet? Last I heard, it attacked the neighbor's dog! How does he have so many friends? I can barely maintain a handful.

Then you open your computer to get to work. Another fifty work emails since yesterday, and you still have a backlog of work from earlier in the week. That, on top of those thousands of images you received, reminding you that you need more.

Now, it's time to fundraise. Huh?

Again, what does all of this have to do with fund development? The constant reminders that we don't have enough do not put us in the mindset of what is possible, and they certainly don't make us feel magnanimous or inspire a lot of faith in our fellow human beings.

I was first introduced to this concept by Lynne Twist, who, in her book, *The Soul of Money* (W. W. Norton, 2017), introduces "Scarcity: The Great Lie," and its ability to dominate us. Reading her book was a true eye-opener. I recommend it highly. It is required reading for all of my students. I started to see myself as part of the culture clamoring for more. Once I could see myself as part of the culture, I was able to step away and consider its impact on me. I saw that, in fundraising, I was coming from this place where I felt there was not enough. But the fact that Lynne called it the "*Myth* of Scarcity" made me recognize that there was something else. Digging into our beliefs about money and fundraising is a good place to begin.

Noticing Scarcity Language

There are numerous cultural attitudes about money, wealth and philanthropy that can contribute to a mindset of scarcity. Let's unpack the scarcity language that exists in our culture about fundraising. When we ask people in our workshops what *scarcity language* we use in our culture, this is what they say:

- About money in general:
    - Money is the root of all evil. The verse is actually, "For the love of money is the root of all evil" (1 Tim. 6:10), but most times, we remember the abbreviated version.
    - Dirty money.
    - Money talks.
    - You are what you make.
    - If you've got it, hold onto it.
    - Wars were started over money.
    - Poverty and money separate us.
    - The top 1 percent rule the world.
- About the wealthy:
    - Filthy rich.
    - Stingy.
    - Miserly.
    - Watch out—the wealthy donors want to take over your organization.
- About people living in poverty:
    - Dirt poor.
    - They must be lazy.
    - They must be stupid.
    - They have nothing to contribute.
- About our relationship with money:
    - Feelings of guilt and shame.
    - She can't hold onto it.
    - I don't know what to do with it.
    - Living paycheck to paycheck.
    - I'm underpaid.
    - I deserve more.

- About fundraising:
    - It's a necessary evil.
    - Asking for money requires arm twisting.
    - That person can give more.
    - We can squeeze more out of 'em.
    - I don't know anyone with money.
    - Just don't ask me to help with fundraising.

This exercise starts to reveal and uncover the attitudes and mentality behind a cultural mindset of scarcity. When we are deep in the frame of a mindset of scarcity, it is difficult to be productive and forward-thinking. Do some of the above phrases ring true for you?

There also can be subtle attitudes we hold that are specific to our agency:

- Our mission is sweet and quaint, but it doesn't save lives like those other programs!
- That donor is so rich. What if I mess up? I'd better tiptoe around them for the sake of my job and the organization.
- Who would give a lot of money to this organization? I know the countless ways that we are less than perfect!
- I'm not comfortable meeting people I don't know.
- The economy is bad. How can I ask for money now?
- It's easier to stay in the office than go out and meet people.
- We don't want to involve people too deeply in our organization. They don't know what we do day-to-day, and it will take too much time to explain it.

Do these sound familiar? Do you hear language like this either in your head or in or around your organization?

Let's think about the basic steps of fundraising and unpack this further. Take a few minutes and think about what scarcity language you might hear in your organization as you go through what we're about to discuss—the Five Steps of Fundraising. What bullet points would you add below? Doing this exercise can be transformative—and especially so if you do it with a team of leaders. Try it!

Exercise

Take each of the Five Steps of Fundraising and Major Donor Work—Planning, Prospect Identification, Cultivation and Engagement, Asking, Stewardship—and examine what scarcity language might sound like in your organization. Be sure to touch on what you hear from both board members and staff.

1. Planning—setting clear goals. You think about what you aspire to do and how you will get there. During the Planning stage, scarcity language might sound like this:

- We don't have time to plan. We just need to raise money now!
- What good is an ambitious plan? We don't have the staff to implement it!
- We never seem to be able to raise more money than the year before.
- Let's not waste our time dreaming!

Does any of this sound familiar? What other things do you hear that come from a place of scarcity when you're attempting to set aside time to plan?

2. Prospect Identification—who you would like to know about your organization. What is the plan to connect with those individuals?

In the Prospect Identification stage, we might hear the following:

- I don't know anyone with money!
- That guy doesn't have any money. Have you seen what he drives?
- What good is it to bring on new donors? We don't have good relationships with our existing donors!

Does this resonate? Where might you feel stuck about finding prospective funders and taking the time to do a little research? Again, think about what scarcity language might be prevalent in your organization from both staff and board members.

3. Cultivation and Engagement—building relationships with individuals and having them learn about your organization. Regarding the Cultivation and Engagement stage, people might say any of these:

- We don't have the luxury to cultivate donors. We need to ask now!
- Everyone knows it's BS. Let's just cut to the chase and ask them for money now!
- Why would they want to get involved with us? I'm sure they're busy!

Do you have time to educate your donors about your mission and programs? Do you have buy-in to have them volunteer or visit your programs? What other disparaging or discouraging things do you hear in your agency about cultivating and engaging donors?

4. Asking—specifically, asking people to give money to your organization. Regarding Asking, we might hear something like:

- I'm afraid of the ask. What if people don't like me afterward?
- We don't have enough people on our board or staff who are willing to ask.
- The Executive Director is really uncomfortable with asking.

Do you have organizational board and staff leaders clamoring to do the asking? If not, what do you hear?

5. Stewardship—letting people know about the impact of their giving. Regarding stewardship, people might say:

- We don't have enough people to maintain a stewardship program.
- We don't have the resources to give our donors anything.
- I sent a thank-you note, isn't that enough?

Does this resonate? Are there other things that people say about stewardship within your organization that are rooted in a mindset of scarcity?

From this exercise, you can likely see there's potentially a lot of scarcity language that currently exists around fundraising in your organization. I would imagine that several things get done despite the language—and that might be okay. I'd like you to seriously consider that it's *not* okay. When we give in to scarcity language and let it dominate our work, we are settling for mediocrity, at best.

Dismantling Scarcity Language

Every step that you take in the direction of possibility has the potential for scarcity to push back. In fact, unless you are unpacking and dismantling the scarcity language in your organization, scarcity is winning the race.

The following exercise can be used by your team to explore the degree to which you have an organizational *thrownness* toward scarcity thinking. (*Thrownness* is a concept introduced by German philosopher Martin Heidegger [1889–1976], which refers to our inherited way of being that comes from our history and culture.)

If you are reading this book with some of your colleagues, try this out together. Or, if you decide to implement a Culture of Philanthropy Plan, it can be a fun way to launch into your work with a more comprehensive Culture of Philanthropy team. As you start to notice your language, you will find the humor in the way that this mindset can attempt to destroy possibility, and find delight in the opportunity to create another way of operating that is much more genuine and generative. But more on that later in this chapter…

Exercise

Take on being a Scarcity Detective over the period of a week:

1. Get a pile of index cards and hand out twenty-five to each of your colleagues.
2. Each time that you either hear yourself or someone else express a scarcity message, capture it on an index card. Put only one message on each card (no scarcity of cards, please!). You should not say who said it. You can even put down things that you think but don't say out loud. These all count!
3. Collect them all.
4. At your next team meeting (a week later), take them and shuffle them like a deck of playing cards.
5. Now have everyone read a random group of cards out loud, and have everyone listen to them.

Does your organization have a scarcity mindset? You may want to expand this beyond work and include attitudes and states of mind that come about on your way to and from work, or that might be influenced by what you see on media before or after work, and even what happens at home.

The idea is to *wake up* to the constant messaging that's coming at us. When we step back and observe

> the scarcity language and various ways that fear-based thinking rules us, we start to see our culture—these attitudes are, in fact, indicators of our culture.

We will be exploring in-depth the degree to which language and attitudes can help us gain greater philanthropic abundance or, in contrast, deter donors from engaging in and contributing to an organization's vision. We've found that, to make positive culture change, there is a *fundamental requirement* to first gain awareness and consciousness of the possibility that you and your organization could be trapped and mired in scarcity thinking. Only when you come to terms with this can your agency move toward a culture of true abundance.

It is as if there is something pushing back against a Culture of Philanthropy. This pushback is a mindset of scarcity, driven by fear. Note: As you work through these exercises, you may be thinking, *But wait. I see lots of good things too! Why is this author obsessed with looking at the negative?* Let me reiterate: Until we recognize the scarcity mindset that is in our way, it has control of us. It is very difficult to see the culture of your agency from within. But once you shift perspective to see the aspects of your culture that you no longer want to tolerate, then, and only then, do you have a chance to do something about it.

Another way to say this is *Revealing, unpacking, and dismantling the scarcity language (which reveals the scarcity mindset), is a fundamental and imperative step in building a Culture of Philanthropy.*

Chapter 5

Language and Its Ability to Advance or Crush Possibility

Watch your thoughts, for they become your words
Watch your words, for they become your actions
Watch your actions, for they become your habits
Watch your habits, for they become your character
Watch your character, for it becomes your destiny.

—HINDU UPANISHADS

Steve Zaffron and Dave Logan offer a powerful model that can be transformative to your organization. In their book, *The Three Laws of Performance* (Josey-Bass, 2011), they look deeply at language and its impact on results or performance. This is a critical link between the condition of the culture and the results that we get.

The **First Law of Performance** is *How people perform correlates to how situations occur to them.*

Zaffron and Logan assert that our thoughts, attitudes and how things are perceived by us dictate our performance. For example, if I hear that there are layoffs at the company where I work, my opinion might be that management is just a bunch of crooks, and I don't like this job, anyway. My performance would likely look something like this: I'd spend my time complaining to my peers, and I'd be apt to start looking for another job. On the other hand, if my perspective is that I'm really lucky to still have a job, I might start work early each day or try to show my worth. I'd spend less time complaining and more time working. In either case, you can kind of predict how it's going to turn out, right?

Let's look at this from a development point of view. Imagine you've received a $100,000 grant every year for the last five years. This year, you asked, and they declined. There are a variety of reasons this could occur. Let's think of what those ways could be, along with their corresponding predictable performance.

HOW DOES IT OCCUR TO YOU?

WE'VE RECEIVED A $100K GRANT FOR THE LAST FIVE YEARS, BUT THIS YEAR THEY SAID NO!	WAYS IT MIGHT OCCUR	CORRESPONDING LIKELY PERFORMANCE/ACTIONS
FROM THE DEVELOPMENT PROFESSIONAL'S PERSPECTIVE	I'm in trouble. What did I mess up?	Who can I blame? I'd better start looking for another job!
FROM THE DEVELOPMENT PROFESSIONAL'S PERSPECTIVE	That was a great wake-up call.	Let's talk to the funder to learn what we missed and to discuss future funding. In the meantime, we can make a plan to diversify funding sources.
FROM THE BOARD'S PERSPECTIVE	They're screwing up! They'd better not come to me for help with fundraising!	Time to ask the ED if there should be a staff change.
FROM THE BOARD'S PERSPECTIVE	I trust the leaders are doing something about this.	There is nothing that I need to do right now, but I'll be sure to check in with the ED.
FROM THE ED'S PERSPECTIVE	I knew that DD was no good!	It's time to finally fire the DD.
FROM THE ED'S PERSPECTIVE	I'm not worried. We have a well-oiled machine. But I want to be there for my team.	I'll check in with the DD and see if he or she needs anything from me.

5-1 How does it occur to you? *(Laurie Herrick, Rainmaker Consulting)*

As you can see from this chart, with just one scenario, we have six different ways that people might interpret the situation. We could easily go further and try to imagine how it would seem from the viewpoint of:

> The program staff—"I hope my program isn't at risk. Should I consider another job?"
>
> Or the mother of the Development Director—"You didn't mess up. What has the Executive Director done to mess up the relationship with the foundation? Frankie, you should consider finding another job where they appreciate you!"

We saw these perspectives quite a bit when, during both of the economic collapses of 2007 and 2020, a number of not-for-profit leaders backed off and were afraid to fundraise. They saw these as frightening times. They didn't call their donors. They didn't want to be pushy or inappropriate.

Another group of leaders got on the phone and talked with their funders. They saw their donors as partners in making the mission come to fruition, regardless of the state of the economy. They connected with them over their shared intentions, their fears of what was going on in the world, and with their desire to make the world a better place. If these leaders were appropriately donor focused, they checked in on the donors, they didn't make an initial call to ask for money. Listening was a key component of the most effective of these conversations.

Now put yourself in the shoes of these donors. If you were the donor in this scenario, and one of the organizations you care about and give your money to reaches out to you to check in, reassures you, and gets you in touch with their cause—and another organization drops you like a hot potato—where would you invest your precious resources to make a difference?

We have an illusion that how things appear to us is exactly how things appear to others. At every moment, we each have our own unique way of looking at things. We are bound and determined to form an interpretation of just about everything. And we are often surprised when someone responds and acts differently than we do to a given set of circumstances.

Photographer Rick Smolan put it well when he said, "What amazes me is that you can have ten different photographers in the same room, and you see ten different rooms. You realize how much of it is the person's perspective, rather than the situation itself."

So how can we figure out what is motivating someone who responds or acts differently than we do?

According to the **Second Law of Performance**: *How things occur for people, arises in language.*

In other words, you can readily tell how things are perceived by someone from what they say. What is so enlightening about this is that if you listen to language, you can see where someone is headed. If I say I could never run a marathon, what do you think my chances are? You'll notice that we can easily apply this to both the individual and to your organization.

The reason this is so important is because building an extraordinary organization and achieving your mission *require* you pay attention to language—your own language *and* the language of others. Language is a critical indicator, the canary in the coal mine of what is to come. This is why I sometimes use *scarcity mindset* and *scarcity language* interchangeably. Scarcity language is an indicator of one's scarcity mindset. Both of these indicate your probable future.

The authors of *The Three Laws of Performance* call this effect that our language has on our future the *Default Future*. The Default Future is what is very likely going to happen if nothing unexpected comes along. It's where the train is headed. They suggest that every family, team, organization and person has a Default Future.

A few years ago, I was preparing with the executive leaders of a social service agency for a work/life balance training for approximately forty members of their leadership team. I described *The Three Laws of Performance* and proposed the idea of using this as a tool for their staff. One of the women at that meeting said, "My gosh, I see my future right in front of my eyes! Neither my husband nor I have time to take care of ourselves or spend time with our kids. I can clearly see that as our kids get a little older, we're going to be out of shape and not able to be actively involved with them. We're going to wake up, and they're going to be grown up, and we'll be lucky if we make it to the time that they decide to have children of their own!" Sadly, this is a very common example of scarcity language.

Now, if you take a few minutes and consider what people say when they use scarcity language about fundraising, it makes perfect sense that they would have difficulty raising money. Think of the Five Steps of Fundraising and Major Donor Work we went over earlier in Chapter 4. Is your organization riddled with scarcity language? Did many of those scarcity-language sentences sound familiar?

This is a chance for you to stop and look at the language your organization actually uses and see what train you're on. Are you headed in the direction you intend? What is your Default Future? Can you predict where you are going when a board member calls fundraising a necessary evil, nondevelopment staff consider fundraising to be beneath programs, the development professional can't find time to meet with funders, and the CEO has excluded development from the leadership team? It's not pretty.

You might be growing tired of this scarcity conversation. Do you find yourself saying, "When is she going to get to abundance? I'm an optimist!" Here is where it's critical that you sit in the discomfort of looking scarcity thinking in the eye. Stepping over it does you no good. If anyone in the organization—from the janitor to the CEO—is using scarcity language, it will likely infect and spread throughout your organization. You need to eliminate it from your organization's vocabulary. Do not swerve past this too quickly. As I said earlier, I've found that making positive culture change has a fundamental requirement to first gain awareness and consciousness of the probability that you and your organization could be mired in scarcity thinking.

One of the things that Zaffron and Logan emphasize with this: if you are intent on truly making a change of trajectory, you have to get to a place where you are completely unwilling to have your Default

Future happen. You have to get to *Hell No!* You have to be disgusted at where you're headed, as this will motivate your team to make the appropriate change happen. In fact, we cannot move on to the Third Law of Performance until we sit in this one for a while. If you aren't totally motivated and committed, everyday life will take over, and fires will need to be put out, and you'll find yourself in the same place a year or decade later.

I cannot emphasize this enough:

Culture change is difficult and not for those seeking an easy solution. Only when your leadership team is deeply aware of the cost of a culture of scarcity thinking will they be motivated to build something stronger and more powerful.

Guidepost

Getting to Hell No!

I've worked with countless groups that have hired a series of consultants without getting the change they desired. One group in particular told me one fundraising consultant after another had been engaged, but the board was just unwilling to budge and embrace fundraising. The CEO told me, "They just weren't motivated—or maybe they aren't a fundraising board."

He asked me to lead a retreat on building a Culture of Philanthropy to truly transform the board's engagement in development. During the retreat, I shared about the concept of a Default Future. They were currently funded almost exclusively from restricted state and federal grants. There was no public- or private-sector fundraising to speak of. They had no money to supplement a program or be responsive to their clients' or staff's needs. They had hired development people in the past, but none had worked out. I asked them to really look at what their Default Future was. I asked them questions, and they shared a little about what that future might be. I pushed them to look deeper.

The CEO asked that we take a few-minute break. During the break, he came to me and said we needed to stop the conversation and move on. I said no. He looked at me, somewhat appalled. *No?* I had been asked to move this board to action (which other consultants had failed to do previously), and his suggestion we move on had me believe that he, in fact, had been in the way of the board fully embracing the needed change in their agency.

A scarcity mindset takes many forms. Sometimes, it's a CEO not wanting to upset a board. Sometimes, it's the board that really wasn't brought on to think about development. Sometimes, it's a board that depends on the CEO to protect them from the consultant. Regardless of what form it comes in, the bottom line is that scarcity thinking does not support a Culture of Philanthropy. They are polar opposites.

Imagine if, instead, the board dug deeply into what was not working and understood they weren't on a path to being a sustainable organization. What if they identified the weak points where they needed to step into a greater development role? What if they got to *Hell No*? What if they took a stand? What if one or more of the business leaders on their board threw their metaphorical hats over the fence and committed to building a Major Donor Program by sharing their passion for the cause with their circles in the community?

Sadly, it isn't what happened. It was a day-long retreat that many would say was interesting but didn't result in much change. I was able to keep going a little

> bit, but we didn't dig in nearly as deep as I thought was needed.

Most organizations have something very strong pushing back against a Culture of Philanthropy. Sometimes, there are multiple things. Without first unpacking the problems, taking them apart and identifying what the ingrained norms are, you'll never reach your potential as an organization.

> *Only when you face the ingrained scarcity mindset, recognize its toll on your organization's ability to fulfill its mission (the Default Future) and get to Hell No! can you then Choose Abundance.*

Chapter 6
How to Make Culture Change

Some people don't like change, but you need to embrace change if the alternative is disaster.

—ELON MUSK

So how do we begin to make cultural change within our organizations? Fortunately, Robert Gass, founder of the Social Transformation Project, has created this model Wheel of Change to help us better understand how to positively transform our agencies. Visual reminders are powerful tools, and you can download a printable version from our Book Hub at www.ChooseAbundanceBook.com. This framework will be used throughout the rest of the book. (You'll notice I begin to capitalize each part of the Wheel of Change: Structure, Behavior, Hearts & Minds starting at this point of the book. I do this so you recognize how many opportunities you have to build a Culture of Philanthropy with all three of these domains every day.)

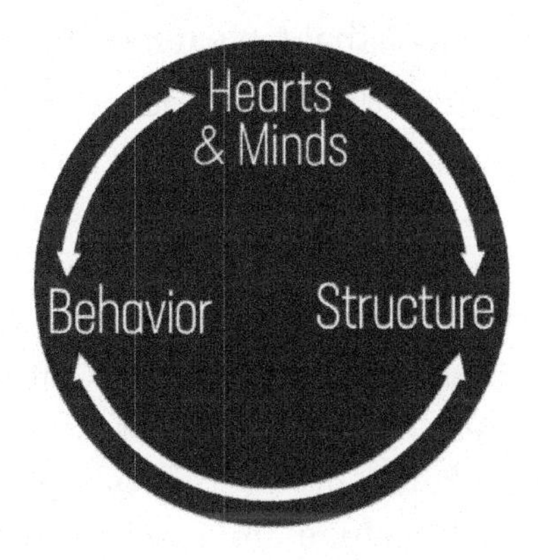

6-1 The Wheel of Change

(Robert Gass of the Social Transformation Project)

The Wheel of Change Model suggests that we need to work three different domains simultaneously in order to impact an organization's culture. When attempting to enhance our development efforts, we are often drawn to the Structures, such as a database, the staff roles on the organizational chart or a strategic plan. We are also focused on our Behaviors, like getting the board to get more involved in development, asking for the gift, hiring a new development professional, or publicly acknowledging donors in an annual report. The one area that is most likely to be overlooked is the third sphere—Hearts & Minds. This is where attitudes, beliefs and feelings lie. Steve Zaffron and Dave Logan in *The Three Laws of Performance* use the word *occur*. This is part of the Hearts & Minds sphere. How something occurs goes to someone's perspective, feelings, etc. As we discovered in the exercise at the end of Chapter 4, some of these are articulated, and some of them are quiet and in our minds. But whether silent or shouted, attitudes, beliefs and feelings deeply impact our success.

The Hearts & Minds aspect of culture is invisible unless you're looking for it. It isn't that the Structures and Behaviors aren't important. They are very important. *However, hiring a Development Director on top of an organizational mindset of scarcity or with the deep-seated belief that your cause isn't worthy is a waste of good money.* I have seen countless organizations that have done this exact thing.

In fact, the beliefs, attitudes and mindset are the foundation for your organization's success. Let's say you have an organizational mindset that sounds like this: "We are merely an arts organization, who would fund us when people are hungry and need to be fed?" As an organizational leader, you believe that the mindset needs to be challenged in the current staff and board. What if the organization doesn't focus on addressing it, but instead hires someone to solve their fundraising issues? The mindset stays the same, and the staff and board are reluctant to help or empower the development person because they don't believe their cause is a priority.

> Scarcity thinking and scarcity language are the constant force pushing up against your desired Culture of Philanthropy.
>
> —Eric Phelps, Rainmaker Consulting Principal

This mindset will hinder your organization's fundraising success.

Exercise

Take a moment to reflect on the Structures, Behaviors and Hearts & Minds that are prevalent in your organization.

Structure—Structures run throughout every organization. Think of the various examples of Structures in yours.

- Is there an organizational flow chart showing the various staff positions?
- Are there silos?
- Are there weekly meetings?
- How about a Structure for clocking in?
- Are there structural protocols for how to report to the state or federal government? Or structural mandates for foundations that have given your organization grants?
- Do you have particular Structures to assure safety of clients, members and employees?
- How about the Structures associated with development? Is there a database? Is it an important tool that tracks relationships, or does it manage financial transactions only?
- Who is a part of the leadership team? Is development included?
- Who talks to whom?
- Who reports to whom?
- Is there a mandate for staff to be "in their seats"? Are there rules for when people take breaks?
- Are there Structures that people do not often comply with? Ones they love or hate?
- Do people show up to meetings on time?

All of these Structures are indicators of the culture of your organization. Take a few minutes and list examples of Structures that exist in your agency.

Behavior—Similarly, there are Behaviors that reveal a lot about your organization. Take the time to write these down.

- Do people chat and have lunch together?
- Do some people intentionally stay outside of the main social network? Are some people just not welcome?
- Who gets hired and promoted and who doesn't?
- Do leaders include staff in decision-making?
- To what extent do the board members know the staff?
- What gets rewarded and what does not?
- What is the approach to professional evolution and learning?
- Are there opportunities for board members to meet clients or have a firsthand experience of the work you do?
- Do people communicate directly with someone if they are upset about something, or do they talk behind people's backs?
- Does the Executive Director work closely with development?
- Does the Executive Director meet with donors?

Now, look at these, which combine Structures and Behaviors.

- What is your performance evaluation Structure? What does it reveal about Behaviors that are most valued?

- What is the budget Structure and process? What does it reveal about valued Behaviors?

Again, list the various Behaviors that are part of your agency. Notice the changes in Behavior, which may have happened in more challenging times. Did nondevelopment staff and board members in your organization step up and call funders?

Hearts & Minds—Hearts & Minds has to do with people's attitudes, thoughts and opinions. This is where scarcity and abundance thinking live. Spend some time looking at the Hearts & Minds within your agency. You likely saw in the previous chapter where a mindset of scarcity dominates your organization.

Keep in mind that this is a very sneaky domain, and it isn't obvious from the inside. Think about the dirty fishbowl metaphor I mentioned previously. We get hints of a culture riddled with scarcity when someone says something, but often not directly. When we think about it, we just know that is the agreed-upon way of thinking and doing things. Again, as Seth Godin says about culture, "People like us do things like this!"

Make a list now of the Hearts & Minds that are prevalent in your organization as indicated through people's words and actions:

- Is fund development perceived to be a necessary evil?
- Do people believe that there is a scarcity of resources?
- Is there a sense that asking people to volunteer would put them out?
- Are there organizational values stated somewhere? Do people seem to embrace them?

- Is there trust of the leadership?
- Are donors or board members thought to be unapproachable or "above" the program staff?
- Are the development staff perceived as below the program staff?
- Do staff people feel heard?
- Does the board feel empowered?

As you make a list of these three domains that exist within your organization, you began to see your culture. Are these healthy traits? Are they aligned with the organizational values?

You can also try this with a group of team members. Have everyone do this as a reflection exercise then share their thoughts in a group. Identify places where your culture is aligned with and misaligned with a Culture of Philanthropy.

I teach a class about building a Culture of Philanthropy, and, at one recent session, a participant asked this question: Am I the problem or the solution? I appreciated the authenticity and vulnerability of the question. And, most importantly, I was deeply impressed with their understanding that it might be a little of both—and an opportunity to choose. The more you are able to look authentically at your role in holding a scarcity mindset in place, the more likely you will succeed at building a Culture of Philanthropy. This success is dependent on you both recognizing and calling out your own and others' scarcity mindset.

Guidepost

Recognizing Your Own Internal Scarcity Dialogue

I work with an organization where a small team of us tend to get along very well, and while we have different opinions, we listen respectfully to each other. Recently, a newcomer joined the group and, a few days later, mentioned to me, "I notice that people are really *eyerolly* with each other."

I thought, *Huh! I've never noticed this.*

I started watching and listening and realized she was right. There was a lot of eyerolling going on, and we were not generous with each other! I also started to become aware of my own internal opinions and self-dialogue. During meetings, I heard myself say inside my head, *There she goes again! Okay, time for so-and-so to pitch in their two cents. We know what that guy is going to add to the conversation—he's a broken record!*

While we all liked each other, we had been working together long enough to have each other pegged, and we often dismissed our colleagues' contributions to the conversation. All at once, I saw the scarcity in my *listening*. At times I was listening more to my inner conversations than to what others were saying. I thought I knew where someone was going before they finished their sentence.

It was a wake-up call for me. Attentiveness toward us is often generous in the beginning—like a *honeymoon stage*—but after a while, people think they know us, so they begin to assume how we might respond. If there is something they don't particularly like about us (or we don't particularly like about someone), listening happens through that filter. In this case at my workplace, it had taken an outsider to call it out in order for me to see it.

I'm sharing this inner dialogue so you can recognize your own silent scarcity thinking. It may be silent, and yet, it still may be limiting your possibilities because you "already know how this will turn out." *The mindset of the people within your organization is the*

> *area that, when targeted for positive change, can create the most powerful transformation.* It's also the domain that we are most blind to, our own biggest "dirty fishbowl." And I don't say that lightly.
>
> To dig into this, you have to be authentic and consider that you may have overlooked something very important: your role in enabling the current culture. My goal is to shine a light on this domain that we often overlook: our blind spots. The more willing you are to hunt down and look honestly at your blind spots, the more value you'll get out of this book. Once we dig into the scarcity language around our organizations, and we see it as part of the culture (in the Wheel of Change), we can see how this perpetuates.

So, how do we see that which we cannot see?

One thing you can do is begin to pay careful attention to your inner conversations, those musings that rattle around in each of our heads, judging and opinionating on everything and everyone. Try to notice when your opinions are full of generosity or when they lean toward being critical and stingy. If you are being generous, you are apt to give people the benefit of the doubt. Notice when you think you *know* how someone will behave, or if you hear a self-righteous internal thought when they do something you *knew* was what they would do.

This translates to how we listen to new ideas, not just individual people. Does someone introduce a new idea, and people remark, "We already tried that before!"? These automatic naysaying comments and the disparaging judgments we make are both signs of a culture of scarcity.

Our judgments, opinions and thoughts are all made up. And, as many a Zen master has said, and I paraphrase, *we can't exactly stop our inner dialogue*. But we can own it and consider an alternative interpretation...one that empowers our organization and a Culture of Philanthropy.

Lastly, as you've been reading this, you might be thinking, "Oh, I really hope so-and-so reads this section! Maybe I'll tell them that they have to stop being so judgmental!" Warning: don't do it. This section is for you. All of us have scarcity thinking from time to time. Pointing fingers at the scarcity thinking of others is not nearly as effective as owning and admitting your own. And when you own your personal scarcity thinking, by acknowledging it to your peers, but still share your commitment to a larger vision of a Culture of Philanthropy, you end up empowering others to do the same.

Chapter 7
Choosing Abundance

It could be said that a great fund-raiser is a broker for
the sacred energy of money, helping people use the money that
flows through their lives in the most useful way
that is consistent with their aspirations and hopes for humanity.

— LYNNE TWIST, *THE SOUL OF MONEY*

Once you have an understanding of the scarcity thinking that is prevalent in our society and in our organizations, how it manifests scarcity language, and that what we say or repeat in our heads leads to limited possibilities and outcomes, you can then—and only then—start to create something new. You now have a choice. When I fully grasped this concept, it resulted in the beginning of a profound shift in understanding my role as a development professional. As my very humorous and spot-on Rainmaker colleague, Eric Phelps, has said to me multiple times, "Laurie, once you become a pickle, you can never go back to being a cucumber!"

This heightened awareness of what is possible makes room for the **Third Law of Performance** in *The Three Laws of Performance: Future-Based Language, or Generative Language, transforms how situations are interpreted by people.*

In other words, if it occurs to you that anything is possible, it will change your Behavior and your actions. As you can see, this includes all three parts of the Wheel of Change—your Heart & Mind says something is possible, and your actions and Behaviors change, and you build a Structure of support to make them stick!

When I truly understood that Generative Language can create a new future, I felt as if I'd been sleeping and suddenly woke up to a new possibility. Instead of money as a barrier to what I was committed to, I saw money as a conduit to the world that works for everyone. The limits started to fade away. Paying attention to and studying scarcity thinking opened me up to its nemesis: *Abundance Thinking*!

Money is a resource that can bring new possibilities into existence. It can wake up the best that humans have to offer. And it can disrupt the status quo. Money can be a path to the world I am committed to. If I can begin to have other people understand the same thing, they, too, can begin to harness money as a possibility for the things we value and are committed to in the world.

Well, there truly is a lot of money available in the United States to support your work:

TOTAL GIVING IN UNITED STATES IN 2019 \$449.64B

\$309.66B + **\$43.21B** = **\$352.87B**

INDIVIDUAL GIVING | CHARITABLE BEQUESTS | (79% OF TOTAL GIVING)

FOUNDATIONS GIVE **\$75.69B (17%)**
CORPORATIONS GIVE **\$21.09B (<5%)**

Source: Giving USA 2020 Report on 2019

7-1 Total Giving in the United States in 2019
(Total Giving Platform, 2020 Report)

You'll notice that the focus of this book is primarily on individual giving. This chart makes it clear why: 79 percent of total philanthropy in the United States comes from individuals. Many are surprised to see just how much money is given each year in the United States. People are generous, and they like to make a difference with their resources!

If you recall, we discussed associations between scarcity mindset and money. Now, let's begin to look at the abundance of money and resources in our culture. When we ask people in our workshops what abundance language we use in our culture, this is what they say:

- About money in general:
  - Money makes the world go around.
  - Money can impact social justice, leisure, health, mobility, travel, fitness or any other meaningful cause.

  - o Money can provide us with possibilities for people.
  - o Poverty separates us—money can bring us together.

- About the wealthy:
  - o People who are wealthy want to make a difference.
  - o People being philanthropic has created a tremendous amount of good in the world.
  - o There is an opportunity to partner with people who have money in abundance and create some good in the world.
  - o There is an opportunity to build strong relationships with individuals who are committed to the same thing that we are.
- About people living in poverty:
  - o The term *poor* is misguided. And especially when we define people as "the poor," it focuses on money as the sole defining attribute. We all have attributes or assets in abundance.
  - o We all have important things to contribute to our society.
  - o There is an opportunity to partner with people who have ideas or skills in abundance and create some good in the world.
  - o "There are no haves and have-nots. We are all haves, and our assets are diverse. In the alchemy of collaboration, we become equal partners; we create wholeness and sufficiency for everyone." (Lynne Twist, *The Soul of Money*)
- About our relationship to money: We can create a healthy relationship to money, not one born out of fear and scarcity.
- About fundraising:
  - o It's a way to strengthen your agency by partnering with people who have a variety of assets, skills and

resources, and empower them to use those things in support of your organizational vision.

- It's an opportunity to partner with people to make the world a better place!
- Inviting someone to give is a *mitzvah**. When you invite them to give, you give them a chance to do good work in our community!

  * The literal meaning of the Hebrew word *mitzvah* is *commandment,* but the generally accepted understanding is that of *a good deed*. The emphasis is on *deeds*—not on positive thoughts or wishes, but on conscious acts of empathy and kindness.

Exercise

Infuse development work with a mindset of abundance. Let's go back to the basic steps of fundraising and think about abundance thinking in this context. Take a few minutes and think about what abundance language you might hear in your organization as you go through the following basic fundraising steps if you shifted to a different mindset. What bullet points would you add below? Doing this exercise can be totally transformative—and especially so if you do it with a team of leaders—try it!

1. Planning—At the Planning stage, you set clear goals. You think about what you aspire to do and how you will get there. During the Planning stage, abundance language might sound like this:

- What an opportunity! We can build an organization with our highest vision!
- While we may not currently have the financial resources to fulfill our organizational vision, I feel confident that, if we articulate what we

have in mind, people will be enrolled and will help us.

- Once we are clear about where we're headed, people will want to be part of what we're up to!

What other things might you hear at the Planning Stage if your organizational mindset was steeped in abundance?

2. Prospect Identification—Who would you like to learn about your agency? What is the plan to connect with those individuals? In the Prospect Identification Stage, we might hear some of the following:

- Let's think of who we know and get to know them. We have no real idea of what resources (of all kinds) they might have in abundance.
- Let's not judge what resources people have. Until we sit down and chat, we don't have a clue what they might like to contribute to our cause.
- Let's be mindful to stay in touch with our existing funders, and as we bring in new folks, be certain to take care of them, as well.
- We have so many connections in our community. Let's talk to them and see what their interests are in our agency. Perhaps they have ideas and resources that we are unaware of that they might want to share.

Can you imagine having your board and staff steeped in abundance thinking? Think about how powerful that could be! Sometimes, the best resources are right under your nose, but because you wouldn't normally go there, have that conversation, or even be open to it, you overlook them. When you are steeped in Generative Language and creating something that previously looked impossible, new opportunities and possibilities arise.

3. Cultivation and Engagement—This is about building relationships with individuals and having them learn about your organization. Regarding the Cultivation and Engagement stage, people might say things like:

- Of course, people would want to learn more about what we're doing here. It's the best kept secret!
- Let's invite people in to share their wisdom, their ideas, their connections and their time to help fulfill our mission.
- Wow, how exciting! People are busy, but they still want to be a part of what we're doing!
- It's awesome to see how lit up our volunteers get when they see that they make a difference in the lives of our clients. It feels like we're giving them a gift when we invite them to be involved.

What other things do you hear people say about cultivating and engaging donors that come from a place of abundance?

4. Enrollment—When we get to the Asking stage, we might want to shift to using different language. I think it is more powerful to think about *Enrollment* versus *Asking*. And it is wonderful to invite people to *invest* in your work. You then might hear—and think:

- Of course people would want to invest in our agency. It's going to make a tremendous impact!
- Board and staff are happy to be sharing their stories about what happens day-to-day in our agency.

- The Executive Director has gotten more comfortable with inviting people to be a part of our work—it ends up forming a greater partnership between us and community members.
- I totally see how inviting Joe to invest in our agency was a gift to him. I watched him light up. He feels part of something big and meaningful in our community.

What are other ways that you could frame the possibility of inviting people to invest in your work?

5. Stewardship—This is letting people know about the impact of their giving. Regarding Stewardship, people steeped in abundance thinking might say the following:

- Stewardship is the most important thing we can do. Our current donors are our best assets, and we must show them what a profound difference they are making. Asking board members to make Stewardship calls to our investors is a great way to show people that they made a great investment in our work!
- People don't need organizational bling or tchotchkes from us, they need evidence that what they gave made a difference. A thirty-second video made with a cell phone that demonstrates that a gift made a difference is more worthwhile than any coffee mug or t-shirt.
- The more connected we are with our funders/investors, the more they'll feel confident about what we're doing—and the more candid we can be about what our challenges are.

Do these statements resonate? Are there other things that people say about stewardship within your organization that are rooted in a mindset of abundance?

I'd like you to consider that the Myth of Scarcity is exactly that, a myth. If you have blinders on, you won't see the reality. There are hundreds of people already connected to your agency who could bring abundance your way. Later on, I'll discuss how to access those individuals, but know that this myth could be blocking your vision. It could be like wearing dark glasses after the sun goes down. Once you start to wear the clear-lens, magnifying abundance glasses, you'll discover humans who want to contribute their time, connections, skills and wealth. Sometimes, this wealth will literally be money, and sometimes, individuals surrounding your agency will bring resources that you could not have imagined. This is the time to *Choose Abundance.*

Consider what Seth Godin, entrepreneur, best-selling author and speaker has to say about money.

Insights from the Field

Seth Godin
(Blog post, March 26, 2014)

Your Story About Money

Is a story. About money.

Money isn't real. It's a method of exchange, a unit we exchange for something we actually need or value. It has worth because we agree it has worth, because we agree what it can be exchanged for.

But there's something far more powerful going on here.

We don't actually agree, because each person's valuation of money is based on the stories we tell ourselves about it.

Our bank balance is merely a number, bits represented on a screen, but it's also a signal and symptom. We tell ourselves a story about how we got that money, what it says about us, what we're going to do with it and how other people judge us. We tell ourselves a story about how that might grow, and more vividly, how that money might disappear or shrink or be taken away.

And those stories, those very powerful unstated stories, impact the narrative of just about everything else we do.

So yes, there's money. But before there's money, there's a story. It turns out that once you change the story, the money changes too.

Chapter 8
The 5 Points of Possibility

Every day, we write the future. Together, we sign it.
Together, we declare it. We share it.
For this truth marches on inside each of us.

—AMANDA GORMAN, "BELIEVER'S HYMN FOR THE REPUBLIC"

If you've ever worked in sales, you've probably heard the phrase *points of pain*. This refers to the problems or challenges your prospective customers are having. The point of pain is the thing that keeps people up at night. A salesperson typically speaks to the point of pain in order to get potential customers to realize how much they need a product. The recommended sales approach is to demonstrate how you can fix the customer's points of pain, and they will want to buy. Well, I've been there, done that. I'm much more inspired by *Points of Possibility*.

Since 2003, I've been teaching people how to use the tools that you will learn in this section. At the end of the first course I taught for development professionals (called GIFT), participants shared their takeaways. Their initial insights and breakthroughs seemed random and disconnected. After looking more deeply, I discovered that these takeaways fell into five distinct buckets that I have named the 5 Points of Possibility.

As you begin to plan the rollout of your Culture of Philanthropy, you can constantly hold these five points in front of you to guide your way. They are a key part of my overall implementation model, and I will use these throughout the rest of this book. These powerful points belong on your bulletin board! Go to our Book Hub at www.ChooseAbundanceBook.com and download your 5 Points of Possibility Poster!

1. **Culture of Philanthropy Is Integral to Our Mission**
2. **Everyone Shares Some Responsibility for a Culture of Philanthropy**

3. **We Build and Maintain Deep Donor Relationships and Partnerships**
4. **Community Engagement Is What We Do**
5. **We Recognize Every Contribution of Service, Items or Money as an Expression of Philanthropy**

Point of Possibility 1: Culture of Philanthropy Is Integral to Our Mission

This Point of Possibility is the one most fundamentally grounded in the Hearts & Minds from the Wheel of Change. While you could literally use the words *Culture of Philanthropy* within the mission, it has much more to do with values—the attitudes, beliefs and feelings of everyone throughout the agency. It means the leaders of the agency believe everyone has something to contribute. It's here that we must remind ourselves "culture eats strategy for breakfast," as stated by Peter Drucker. If the Hearts & Minds aren't there, no strategy will fly.

What if a Culture of Philanthropy was part of your organization's mission? What would it look like? Imagine if, as you embarked on a Strategic Planning Process, a Culture of Philanthropy was at the top of your agency's priorities. You could examine the values associated with the desired culture, and you would set corresponding goals.

Each year, you would revisit your goals to build community partnerships and strengthen donor relations. At board meetings, when reviewing organizational benchmarks, board members would check to see if plans and actions were consistent with this vision of a Culture of Philanthropy. Would there be a mandate to include supporters and stakeholders in key decisions? Remember, you don't need to rush and do these things. Just imagine what it would be like in its most functional and fully embraced form.

A warning with this Point: one organization I know of was very enthusiastic to work with me because of my experience building a Culture of Philanthropy. When I saw that they had Culture of Philanthropy as a key tenant of their strategic plan, I was so pleased.

I came to understand the first step they'd taken was to push all staff to give a financial gift. There was a lot of upset about this, and, as I conducted an assessment, I learned that the Hearts & Minds aspect was not at all aligned with a Culture of Philanthropy. In fact, they had a culture of distrust.

When the frontline staff make a fraction of what the execs make, and a) the staff expressed in a strategic-planning survey that they felt underpaid and underappreciated, b) they didn't hear anything back about their feelings and what the commitment of the leadership team was, and c) the staff didn't agree to a request to make a financial contribution (it was more of a demand disguised as a request), it should come as no surprise they would feel disparaged and unheard. And, most likely, they would be really peeved to have the development professional knock on their door.

Putting a Culture of Philanthropy into your mission statement or near the top of the list of your guiding principles is a great idea. However, you have to be clear about what it is and what it isn't. What are the values consistent with this statement? What are the corresponding Behaviors associated with these values? Further, look at what is pushing up against it, especially in the domain of Hearts & Minds. A Culture of Philanthropy is not a mandate to give. Avoid these three fatal mistakes:

- Failing to be introspective, starting with the top leaders of the organization and continuing throughout the agency.
- Failing to enroll people on every level of the organization by having authentic and honest conversations about what's working and what's not working.
- Failing to have complete buy-in from the top leaders in creating a Culture of Philanthropy.

Even without literally writing a Culture of Philanthropy goal into your strategic plan or naming it in your mission statement, you can have it be at the heart of the values of your agency. This is a place to start. From there, you can establish practices to reinforce it.

In the Guideposts (or case studies) throughout this book, I share stories of leaders and organizations that have been actively and intentionally working to build a Culture of Philanthropy. I hope you will be inspired by their paths, their lessons and their breakthroughs. You will perhaps notice one organization, the Harry & Rose Samson Jewish Community Center of Greater Milwaukee, is featured a number of times. This is because, several years ago, I led a course for development professionals called GIFT that had three participants from this agency in it.

The development professionals in the course were able to do some great work within their organizations, but I began to notice a disconcerting trend: there was only so far they could go in building an organizational Culture of Philanthropy before they would hit a roadblock. Either their CEO wasn't buying into it or their board was not engaged.

In the example of my students from Milwaukee, they did a great job enlisting their CEO, Mark Shapiro, in the idea of building a Culture of Philanthropy. But there was not yet an organization-wide Culture of Philanthropy. It wasn't quite in their DNA. The following case study tells how Mark began his journey in transforming his agency. (And, I promise, you'll hear more from Mark and his team later on in the book, as well.)

Guidepost

Taking the Leap

Mark Shapiro,
CEO of the Harry & Rose Samson
Jewish Community Center of Greater Milwaukee

In every CEO's life, there's a moment where you are standing at the ledge, and you know you have to take a leap of faith. Creating a Culture of Philanthropy and embracing it as a change of our culture was just that moment. Our agency was succeeding in many ways, and we were clearly on the cusp of great fundraising potential. We brought in a consultant to teach our board how to ask people for money—the feared task of "the ask." Our presenter was fantastic, and she energized the board. She was polished and a great presenter, and our board was engaged for the entire two-day facilitated discussion. Moments after she left, though, we noticed something—people just weren't ready to ask. If there was one part of fundraising they feared the most, it was just the moment of asking people for money. We forgot to lay the foundation and begin to change the culture of our organization and the board's role *before* we got to the hard part.

I began to recognize that neither the climate nor the culture of our agency was ready for this. Our board just hadn't bought in to the idea of asking people for money, and we were definitely putting the cart before the horse. Many of our board members had no relationship with our donors, and, quite frankly, some of them weren't funders themselves.

Flash-forward two years, and we welcomed Laurie into our board meetings to begin to change our culture. We started the evening with a glass of wine, which led to a second one, and all we did that night was tell our stories. Laurie listened and heard every one of our officers tell her why they loved the JCC. A few tears were shed. I heard stories I didn't know about from my own board members. Over those next few days, we really began to embrace the idea of changing culture and creating a new Culture of Philanthropy with our board, our senior staff, our program teams and, honestly, anybody who would listen!

After a few days of discussing, we realized the next best step was to create a time-limited Task Force to set the course for our process. Of course, everyone was thinking about starting a Committee, but we realized our Task Force needed first to set the foundation for how we could create long-lasting change.

I personally became so attached to this idea I was able to convince Laurie to allow me to begin to work with her and design a curriculum where we could train the entire agency in our vision for a Culture of Philanthropy. I realized we needed a bunch of people at the table, and other organizations could actually benefit from learning this, peer to peer.

There were many breakthroughs that came out of this experience of building a new culture. One of the most telling is the example of Lenny, the director of Albert and Ann Deshur JCC Rainbow Day Camp. Rainbow is a traditional day camp and is part of our larger Jewish Community Center operations. We serve about 350 kids each day, and it sits on a pristine 110 acres of land, making for an idyllic setting for a day camp. This is a place where kids get to simply be kids. They make lasting friendships, explore new skills, they learn values and they get an opportunity to be with counselors full of life and love and adventure. Rainbow is one of several programs of the Harry & Rose Samson Family Jewish Community Center and is supported by the Culture of Philanthropy staff and Committee of the JCC.

In our course, Lenny noticed on his own that he had been coming from a place of scarcity thinking, specifically in the areas of fundraising and development. He went on to share, if he were being completely honest (and he did get more honest throughout the course), asking for money was about trying to pry something out of someone's hands. The whole idea of asking people for money had always rubbed him the wrong way.

When we introduced the idea of seeing our funders as *investors* vs *givers,* this resonated deeply with Lenny. The idea that people were investing in him and the campers connected in a new and exciting way for Lenny. He started to see he was not alone in his passion for the camp and for the impact it had on kids. He quickly discovered there were so many people who wanted to be a part of what he was doing and to contribute their abundant resources.

We all have different things in abundance; some have wisdom, some have extra time, some have firsthand stories about organizational programs, some simply have money to invest, and some have connections. We began to connect with many new investors and often found the investors happened to have an abundance of money. In *every* case they wanted to use their money to help camp improve. What isn't to love about that?

Lenny's camp has been having a capital campaign for the past eighteen months, and you can bet he has been the most welcoming to our guests visiting to see firsthand the programs happening on our campgrounds. The campaign is doing brilliantly, and it's largely because Lenny welcomes people, shares his stories and passion and makes special time to learn about his guests' stories too.

Point of Possibility 2: Everyone Shares Some Responsibility for a Culture of Philanthropy

There are countless ways different individuals on staff and on the board can partner with your development staff and own some of the success of building a Culture of Philanthropy. You will find ideas that you can adopt scattered throughout this book, including the chapters in Part 4, where we focus on distinct roles. Before we dive deeper into roles in a Culture of Philanthropy, there are a few more things to consider.

- What if there were a true partnership between the Executive Director and the development staff?
    - What would that look like in your organization?
    - Would you meet weekly?
    - If so, what would you do together? The healthiest organizations I've seen have had weekly development team meetings where there was a focus on customized, individual donor strategies, development planning overall and deployment of staff to work on specific projects.
- What about impacting the Hearts & Minds agency-wide?
    - Would there need to be some training so that some of the opinions, thoughts and attitudes about development changed?
    - Would the board have a new Culture of Philanthropy Committee? Would they embrace training on fund development and donor relations? Would they have a Culture of Philanthropy report and mini training at each board meeting?
- What would the roles be for different staff in your agency around development?
- Would program staff start to have a process for gathering firsthand stories of success in your agency?

Following is an example of efforts that united a whole organization, working from the frontline staff through the board and executive leadership.

Guidepost
Riverside Industries Creates Mission Moments

I was hired to consult with Riverside Industries, an agency that empowers people with intellectual and developmental disabilities to live rich and full lives. The Executive Director, Char, was all in. We did a strategic plan and then agency-wide Culture of Philanthropy Training. I shared with her the importance of everyone being a part of a Culture of Philanthropy, and she embraced it. I did seven trainings with the board, the van drivers, the program directors, supervisors and direct care staff.

Early on in the process, I asked about stories of success. Char asked me, "Do you mean *Mission Moments*?" I loved this! It was the first time I'd heard that term. And being a consultant who is all about adopting powerful language, I embraced it! As I did the trainings with each group of staff or board members, I asked them to reflect on a moment when they saw some sort of breakthrough with one of the program's participants. What happened? Who was there?

Char stepped into the light, really illustrating how good leadership can make a difference. At each staff meeting, Char would begin with an inspiring story of one of their program participants, either one she had heard about from a staff person or experienced herself. She then asked each of the staff team leaders to do what she did and be gatherers of moments when it was apparent that they were delivering on their mission. When did a participant light up and have a personal breakthrough during one of the programs? What did a parent say about how much it made a difference that their son or daughter was able to go to their program each day? What was said? Who was there? How did they say it?

They were asked to start their team meetings sharing this. Why? It reinforced what was working. It made everyone aware of what mattered in their day-to-day work. And it established a Structure so that it would happen habitually.

Char did the same thing for the board meetings. This had a beautiful grounding effect. People would show up at board meetings coming down from the busyness of their days. Having a story of success, a Mission Moment, right at the beginning reminded them why they were there. Char encouraged them to share their own stories about Riverside Industries or simply borrow hers. It became an opportunity to spread the word while simultaneously reinforcing the commitment of the board member. Brilliant!

The following exercise provides you and your team an opportunity to discover the power of Mission Moments.

Exercise

Create Mission Moments. Keep a small journal with you to capture moments that illustrate the difference your organization makes. At first, you might have a few notes that just remind you of what you witnessed, but then fill it in. Get details. Read the tips in this book to learn more about how to create a great story. It's especially powerful if this starts at the top—the Executive Director or the Board Chair. But, of course, it requires people on the frontline helping you gather these stories. Start out with a Mission Moment at any team or board meeting. It will ground people and clarify why they are volunteering or working with the agency.

Have Mission Moments be part of your organizational culture. Do something fun like have a contest for the most moving story each week or each month. It will bring the successes to the forefront, encouraging more abundant thinking. Who wouldn't want to work with us, volunteer with us, contribute their resources to us? We're doing such good work!

Point of Possibility 3: We Build and Maintain Deep Donor Relationships and Partnerships

Let's first talk about what deep donor relationships and partnerships are—and what they are not. A partnership implies a type of equality, two or more people embarking on something together. This is a healthy approach. The term *donor-centric* has been used quite a bit in the field. While for some that means donor partnerships as I have just described, others believe it means we should put the donor on a pedestal. This is not a healthy approach. For this very reason, I do not use the term donor-centric. The donor-as-the-almighty should not be the center of your organization's universe. This is not a true partnership, as it lacks equity.

With this Point of Possibility, it's imperative that you keep your personal and organizational values top of mind. If you approach your donors like they are the all-knowing, all-powerful, and you are less than, you will be relinquishing your power, diminishing the partnership, and quite possibly taking actions that the donor sees as important, but your agency does not. This is also known as *mission drift* or *following the money versus the mission*. Remember that, as a staff person (and especially if you are the CEO), you are the content and program expert. It is good to learn from others, but don't be swayed by someone who is holding you captive with their money. These types of relationships place too much value on money, and they often lack authenticity.

You as an organizational leader have assets—your knowledge and wisdom, your dedication and your past experience in the field. Your donors have other assets—their commitment to do good, their connections, their money and their wisdom. When you get to know your donors and see them as investors in your shared vision, you will have achieved a powerful synergy.

As many of us work to create a more just and equitable world, we can struggle with this dynamic, as the majority of the wealthiest individuals in our Major Donor portfolios are also the most privileged. This is where your leadership comes in. By standing in authentic partnership with your donors, including those with financial wealth, you have an opportunity to change the world and shift the power dynamic by helping them see the value of investing in a more just community.

If we look historically, some people of privilege stepped up and were important allies of the right for women to vote and for slavery to be abolished. Those breakthroughs were advanced due, in part, to the education and participation of members of the privileged class who believed in and took the risks needed to advance these important causes. One of your jobs is to use your leadership role to enroll people of privilege to invest in positive change.

Further, building deep and authentic partnerships is about community engagement and inviting a broad and diverse group of people to invest in your cause. Who should be part of your community so that they can weigh in with their unique perspectives?

Once your Hearts & Minds are in the right place, you can begin to integrate the concept into your agency:

- What would need to be established to deepen donor partnerships?
- Are there Structures that would need to be built in order to track donor conversations and personal history with your organization?

- Would board or other key individuals help with stewardship, showing donors that their investment in your agency made a difference?
- Who could you imagine doing what?
- How often would donors be showing up at your location?
- What would they want to share with you? Would you have in place detailed individualized donor relations plans for your top 10 percent of donors (as we describe in a later chapter)?
- Would the Executive Director, development staff and key board members feel comfortable calling and connecting with donors?
- Would funders come to expect that?

Later, I'll show you how to integrate the answers to these questions into your overall Culture of Philanthropy Plan.

Guidepost

Lessons from an Orchid

Mark Shapiro

I've been blessed to have some really great mentors. When I first got my job as the CEO of the JCC, it was really nerve-racking for me. I came from the Jewish camping world. I really didn't know anything about fundraising. I remember, within the first couple of weeks, I had to solicit someone for a $1,000,000 gift. I'd never asked anybody for a penny, let alone $1,000,000. The meeting ended up slightly successful, as I ended up with about half of the gift—but, more importantly, it really set me on a path to realizing I still had a long way to go in learning about development.

One of my favorite lessons came from a gentleman by the name of Bert. Bert and his wife, Audrey, were consistent givers to our community, and there was one day when we were working on our community hall at the JCC. The two of them had made a substantial capital gift to the organization, and, quite frankly, they didn't like how the decorating was done. Audrey said that the decorations and light fixtures made the room appear antiseptic.

I recognized we had very special donors here. Normally, when someone donated a substantial amount of money building out a space, and they didn't like how it looked, they would tell you to fix it. They wouldn't give you the money to do it. They would just tell you to do it. Bert decided he was going to fund us fixing the space to the way he felt it ought to be, and Audrey was coming by regularly to help think about specific colors and design themes.

One day, Audrey was working on this project, and Bert came along. Bert and I were talking for a little bit, and he asked me to come for a walk with him. I was still young in my career, and Bert was a pretty intimidating guy. He was a prominent lawyer, and he didn't talk very much—kind of the opposite of my personality. I always felt like I had to fill the empty space with a lot of chatter.

As we were walking, he rather shockingly shared with me that he had just been diagnosed with cancer, and it was a very poor prognosis. He confided he had just shared this with his family in the last couple of days and his condition was terminal, and it was going to be fast. I was stunned. I had lost my own father to cancer years before this, and I'd witnessed somebody going through what Bert was likely going to be going through. He then grabbed the back of my arm while we were walking and asked me if I would take care of a couple of things for him when he was gone.

He said, "I'd like it if, every year on Audrey's birthday, you'd send her an orchid."

And I said, "Of course I will!" But I really didn't understand what was behind it. I suspected it was just a favorite flower of theirs, but I had a feeling there was more to it. I asked him what the significance of the orchid was.

He said, "Besides the fact that it's Audrey's favorite flower, I actually think I want you to get an orchid, too."

I asked for clarification. "You mean for myself?"

And he said, "Yes."

I said, "If you don't mind me asking, why?"

He said, "Mark, almost more than anyone else I know, you need an orchid."

I knew this was likely an insult. This wasn't like a *you're a magnificent human being, and everything in your life is in perfect order, so you should go reward yourself with an orchid*. This was some form of a slam on how I was young and petulant and talked too much—and I should go and get an orchid!

Slowly but surely, Bert said this: "Nothing teaches patience more than caring for an orchid. You have to slow down. You have to understand the orchid. The orchid doesn't have to understand you. These flowers are magnificent and will stay forever if you care for them exactly the way you should. You can't overwater them, but you can underwater them.

"You have to understand each orchid has its own way it wants to be cared for. When the flowers are out in their beauty, it doesn't mean everything is okay. If you don't keep paying attention to it the way it wants, in a matter of days, the petals will fall off. When that happens, it doesn't mean the plant has died. It's just a matter of caring for it as if it were full of life and vibrant, and soon, it will reward you with another flower.

"Sometimes, you have to cut your losses if you don't take care of it for a while, if you forget about it—kind of like a donor. At some point, cut off the stem, have no expectations and wait a while. Keep nurturing it as if it were flowering for you, and, sooner or later, a new stem will come out, and the next stem will start to grow, and it will have little buds. It takes a long time until it actually blossoms. It could be weeks or months, and, sometimes, it can take forever. But you have to keep caring for it as if it's already giving you the biggest gift you've ever had."

I think every Development Director should have an orchid in their office reminding them of what it takes to cultivate deep relationships. This story has really impacted me, and I can tell you our Development Director has an orchid in her office as a reminder, even when everything is in full bloom, we still have to take care of our supporters.

Even when they are MIA, we still take care of them—even when they are so quiet that we wonder if they're still alive! And, sometimes, we have to cut our losses and keep nurturing, regardless of how things appear, and they will likely come back. Orchids are very forgiving flowers, but, at the same time, not very forgiving of mistakes—like a lot of funders we know.

This gift from Bert had a lasting impact on me. I was very blessed. We spent the next almost year really cultivating a real friendship, and I learned things I'd never known about him. I owe Bert a lot. The orchid has taken a very important place in my life since then. I probably have twenty orchids in my house.

Bert taught me we always need to make sure we understand how our donors like to be cared for. We might not always get it perfectly right, but if we pay attention and listen well, they will tell us their needs, just like the orchids.

Point of Possibility 4: Community Engagement Is What We Do

What would it look like to have people in your surrounding community feel as if they were key stakeholders in your agency? Would movers and shakers be clamoring to be on your board? Would volunteers become a more significant part of your organization?

Guidepost

North Lakeland Discovery Center, Birch Bark Canoe Ride Leads to Donor Connections

David Sharken

Rainmaker Consulting was hired to work with an environmental education center as they launched their first-ever capital campaign for a new, large building to house their programs, get their staff out of a cold office trailer, create a year-round community center and establish a small endowment fund. As the Rainmaker consultant, I strongly encouraged their leadership to invite all the staff and all the board members to a morning orientation on how to build a Culture of Philanthropy. A number of them attended.

Several months went by, and one of their staff educators was leading a birch bark canoe ride. While the group canoed, the staff member recalled my main message of "get to know your stakeholders." She struck up a conversation with one of the attendees.

She learned he was a seasoned architect and building developer. Then, she mentioned the strategic vision of creating a new facility. They had an engaging conversation!

Fast-forward a few months. That gentleman has donated close to $10,000 of intensive, program-centric building design. He has enthusiastically worked with staff to redesign the facility with programming, client experience and staff needs in mind. And he and his wife are ready to make a contribution in the five figures.

How did this happen? Board members and staff were introduced to the idea of simply connecting with individuals on common values and offering an engagement opportunity in a shared vision for the community. In this real-life example, a line of curious inquiry from the staff person to the program participant led to a partnership, which transformed the organization and the individuals involved.

Look for connections in your community. Identify ways to collaborate, share ideas, partner and be generous with organizations and individuals who overlap with the work of your organization. Find people who are committed to the same things that you are. Then, get to know them and find out how they would like to partner with your agency.

Point of Possibility 5: We Recognize Every Contribution of Service, Items or Money as an Expression of Philanthropy

An organization dedicated to building a Culture of Philanthropy is one where everyone who comes to the table is understood to have some ways in which they are resource rich. They may be endowed with a particular skill, a connection, a passion, certain items or money. In a Culture of Philanthropy there is a deep-seated desire to discover what that individual feels they have in abundance, and then to team up with them to advance your shared vision. I've met people who are stereotypically called rich, and I've met people who are stereotypically called poor. Both types of individuals are not types at all. They are unique human beings with unique gifts. And both have things they feel abundant about and things they feel scarce about.

As someone committed to building a Culture of Philanthropy, your task (as a development professional, board member, Executive Director or staff person) is to discover the unique richness of the member, volunteer, participant, donor, vendor or stakeholder that is connected to your organization. If an entire team of you do this, you will build a powerful and diverse community engaged in fostering your mission and your agency.

This Point of Possibility is steeped in Hearts & Minds. It is an intentional attitude. It's about being curious and being genuinely interested in discovering people's greatness. While we might have a stereotype or assumption buzz through our head about someone, we don't let it affect our actions. We commit to something larger, more generous and magnanimous.

It is a common misconception that you should focus your energy in finding people with tremendous financial wealth. Part of this is a mindset caught in scarcity—we don't have time for development, let's just find a rich financial savior! While people with financial wealth are welcome at the Culture of Philanthropy table, an organizational culture that welcomes a diverse array of human resources will benefit exponentially. An obsession with money being the highest value devalues the trove of talents and treasures that can be equally important to your work.

Here are a few reasons why overly focusing on just the money and people who you imagine to be wealthy are not particularly helpful to building a Culture of Philanthropy.

- No one wants to be valued exclusively for their money.

- If you only focus on who you perceive to be wealthy, you miss out on all the gifts (money and otherwise) of other members of your community.
- If you have one or a small handful of Major Donors who represent the majority of your fundraising from individuals, you do not have a diverse portfolio of individuals giving to your agency. The loss of one funder could be devastating to your organization.
- Building strong, deep donor relations means knowing what passions and resources—besides money—people might like to share.
- When an organization is obsessed with money and not focusing on other aspects of the donor's skills and interests, there is a tendency to hold the top funders as holy and all-powerful, and therefore, the staff take on a role of being subordinate, or passive. This is not a healthy relationship.

If you get to know your existing funders and what makes their hearts sing, you will establish stronger and more authentic partnerships. There are countless experiences I've had that illustrate the range of people's generosity:

- The architect in the Guidepost earlier in this chapter who gave his services for free.
- My colleague Kathleen, who doesn't want to be on a board or a fundraising committee, but volunteers to write a number of handwritten thank-you notes to donors each month for organizations she's passionate about.
- A group of at-risk, young women who read their poetry at a fundraiser at a women's foundation, who, when there was an invitation from the front of the room for all to make a meaningful gift, decided to pool their money and put it in the contribution envelope. Not only was their poetry reading a powerful and critical contribution to the program, but their financial gift (a little under $20) was most likely the largest stretch gift made in the room.

- A consulting colleague who gives his fundraising coaching and training to Acupuncturists Without Borders for free.
- My friend Peter, mentioned in Chapter 2, who figured out how he could make a significant financial contribution to RESULTS. He's now contributing his time and energy to Climate Restoration—renovative solutions that have the capacity to turn around climate change.
- An agency in New Jersey that has enlisted a man—who is a self-described handyman—to make lawn signs, to be painted by another group of volunteers, promoting their upcoming campaign.
- A donor who has a beautiful yard and garden, who has, for many summers now, hosted a garden party for top funders and volunteers, to honor and appreciate their giving and support.
- A board member who loves to put on sophisticated, intimate gatherings for an alternative educational program, and who works with the Executive Director to make them mission-based, compelling events.
- Countless teachers and students who are part of a New England craft program called Snowfarm, who contribute seconds of beautiful art pieces for the annual fundraising seconds sale. Also, amateur student glass blowers (like myself), who contribute their time to teach people how to blow a glass ornament at the annual sale.
- A $10/month donor, who also connects the agency with a foundation that she knows.

The 5 Points of Possibility will lead you to these transformative outcomes:

- Valuable community partners
- Increased donor loyalty and retention
- Greater board and staff engagement
- Larger gifts
- Abundant resources!

In all of the cases I listed, it took a staff person or board member who was dedicated to finding out what the individual had in abundance that they were willing to share with the organization. See Terry Axelrod's Treasure Map in Chapter 9, to learn more about the people already surrounding your agency. And in Chapter 16, learn how you can have a conversation to get to know people, learn what they already have in abundance and what they might want to contribute to your organization.

You've learned a few concepts in this section, including the 5 Points of Possibility, Abundance Thinking and Generative Language. The place where these three intersect and are applied are where a breakthrough in a Culture of Philanthropy will happen, where those outcomes will come to fruition.

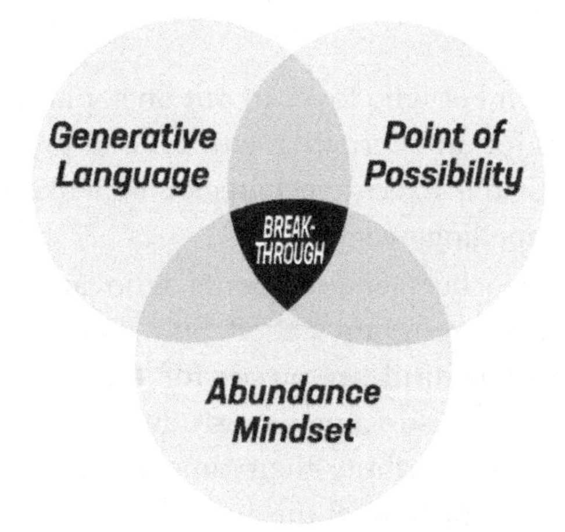

8-1 A breakthrough in fundraising occurs when the Points of Possibility, an Abundance Mindset and Generative Language intersect.
(Laurie Herrick, Rainmaker Consulting)

Now that you are armed with knowledge of the problem, recognize your organization can benefit from culture change, and know the terms and concepts necessary to take actionable steps, we'll move to the part of the book that tells you exactly how to move toward the vibrant, flourishing Culture of Philanthropy of your dreams.

Part III

Implementing a Culture of Philanthropy Agency-Wide

Chapter 9
The Choose Abundance Model

If two or three persons should come with a high spiritual aim and with great powers, the world would fall into their hands like a ripe peach.

—RALPH WALDO EMERSON

The potential for progress increases exponentially when there's a team of you working to make change. In this chapter, we focus on making an agency-wide commitment to change. And it all starts with one person—that would be you—taking a stand, then building from the inside out. You *and* a team of people who are committed to this transformational process of building a Culture of Philanthropy will lead to fundraising success and mission fulfillment.

Large, systemic change throughout an organization is very difficult. It requires layers of communication, input and buy-in from different groups. It requires creativity, training, risk taking, vulnerability and innovation. It requires delving into the Hearts & Minds.

Building a Culture of Philanthropy for your entire agency is one of the most significant, yet most difficult, things you will ever take on. It will not happen overnight. In fact, it will take years to fully implement. It isn't for the weak of heart. It takes serious bigheartedness.

At the same time, every step you take forward will be useful and powerful and will advance your agency. Building it will test your leadership skills (regardless of your position). As we've discussed, in order to make long-term, institution-wide, permanent change, you need to take several steps, which you will be empowered to do by the close of this book. And, if you persist, you'll be known for forever altering the trajectory of your agency.

An important note: your agency may have other prior or emerging commitments to make culture change. You may be in the midst of making powerful systemic change to have your organization include more diversity, equity and inclusion (DEI), for example. If you are also committed to building a Culture of Philanthropy, you can use this time and this model to integrate your highest values into this process.

The steps of the Choose Abundance Model that follow focus on the specific goals of a Culture of Philanthropy. I encourage you to integrate your organization's aspirational values and goals into this process.

The Choose Abundance Model for Implementation

1. **Throw Your Hat Over the Fence.** Take a stand for a Culture of Philanthropy.
2. **Find and Enroll a Committed Listener.** Someone who will be your champion.
3. **Create a Culture of Philanthropy Task Force.** A team of leaders that includes the CEO, Development Leader and Board Leader, at a minimum.
4. **What Is So?** Conduct a Culture of Philanthropy Assessment.
5. **Educate, Educate, Educate.** Establish shared language. Have everyone on the same page regarding what a Culture of Philanthropy is and what it could mean for your organization.
6. **Hell No!** Create impetus for a Culture of Philanthropy.
7. **Design Your Preferred Future.** Do this as a team.
8. **Create Your Implementation Plan.** Use SHMART goals with 5 Points of Possibility.
9. **Communicate and Enroll Next Layer of Stakeholders.** *Within* your organization—let people riff on what that means for them in their role. Be sure to share wins widely!
10. **Community Engagement.** Expand your vision to those *outside* of your organization.
11. **Track Successes.** Report back to the whole group and institutionalize.

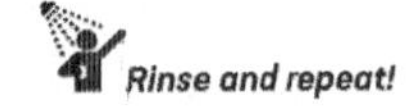

9-1 The Choose Abundance Model to Build a Culture of Philanthropy

(Laurie Herrick, Rainmaker Consulting)

Frankly, of all the downloads I suggest in the book, this is the most fun (www.ChooseAbundanceBook.com). I think you will also find it useful to have around and reference from time to time to assure you are continuing on your Culture of Philanthropy path.

While there are 11 steps in this model, it is not apt to be a completely linear process where you move from Step 1 to Step 2 to Step 3, then you win the prize—you achieve a Culture of

Philanthropy! You may need to work on more than one step at a time, or you may skip over one and circle back to it. (While 11 steps may seem a little unconventional, for fun, you can watch the Spinal Tap video "It Goes to Eleven" on YouTube to see why it's important to have 11 steps.)

As you embark on this process, you may discover you are already well down the path on your Culture of Philanthropy journey, or you may find you have not achieved very many of the steps. That's okay. Take a look and see if a step you skipped over is worth exploring. You may find that you go forward, then you need to go back and take actions in a prior step. Culture change is not a straight and easy path, or everyone would be doing it.

Let's add The Choose Abundance Model to your set of tools.

Step 1—Throw Your Hat Over the Fence

As I shared in the introduction of this book, throwing my hat over the fence by taking a stand for a million-dollar donor for RESULTS was a significant step toward me actually achieving that goal. Whether you are in a position of authority or not (I was not), what matters is that to begin institution-wide culture change, one visionary individual needs to step up. That person sees what is possible and isn't content with either mediocre or subpar. They stand for something big—the health and well-being of the agency and fulfillment of the organization's vision. You may be crystal clear about your vision. If so, advance to Step 2. If you aren't crystal clear, or you want to make your vision even clearer, try this exercise.

Exercise

Your Vision

Sit in a quiet place and meditate on the following.

What about this idea of a Culture of Philanthropy is so compelling to you? Why do you want it? Think about your organization, your cause. Why do you spend your time doing it? What is it about the cause that resonates for you? Why is that important? When you get an answer to that "why" question, I suggest you ask yourself *why* multiple times until you drill down to something that moves you deeply. Maybe it even brings you to tears.

Take a few minutes to really appreciate the work your agency does, the difference it makes and the possibility it holds. Write down your thoughts about why your work is meaningful to you.

- What would it look like if it was fully funded—what would be manifested in your community, or, perhaps, the world?
- What would be different if your organization had what it needed to fulfill its mission?

Jot down what that would look like.

Now, envision your organization with a Culture of Philanthropy.

- What are some examples of organizations that are highly functional and inspiring to you?
- Have you seen some examples in this book or in your community?

Start writing down what you like about those organizations.

- What are their strongest attributes?
- Do any of these attributes already exist within your own organization? Try to think of any ideals already in existence in your organization that would be useful to expand.

Remember, this is an imagination exercise. There are no wrong ideas, and nothing is impossible.

- What opportunities do you believe there are for your agency now that you've been reading about a Culture of Philanthropy?
- Is there an area where improvement would cause a breakthrough?

As you do this imagining exercise, think through the 5 Points of Possibility from the last chapter. Inevitably, some exciting things bubbled up as you learned about them, and you saw some amazing possibility for your organization. Write those possibilities down. Highlight those items that are apt to be the most impactful. Here they are again to spark your imagination.

The 5 Points of Possibility:

1. Culture of Philanthropy Is Integral to Our Mission
2. Everyone Shares Some Responsibility for a Culture of Philanthropy
3. We Build and Maintain Deep Donor Relationships and Partnerships
4. Community Engagement Is What We Do
5. We Recognize Every Contribution of Service, Items or Money as an Expression of Philanthropy

It's also likely that, as you do this exercise, you can imagine some blocks and barriers. Don't focus on those. If they come up, list them on a separate piece of paper. You'll have an opportunity to address these items at a later point. Don't let perceived obstacles get in your way or cloud your vision.

Now, look at what your stand is. This is a powerful opportunity. Will you take a stand to create a Culture of Philanthropy in your agency? Will you throw your hat over the fence? Even with the potential barriers, will you partner with the organization's leaders to build a more sustainable agency? Not just piecemeal, but agency-wide?

Your vision, your leadership and your intention will help you establish your stand. Write down what your stand is. Start it like this:

> My stand for this agency is to ______________, which would impact ______________, ______________ and ______________________.

Step 2—Find and Enroll a Committed Listener

Once you have a clear stand, the next thing to do is to find someone who will be your champion. Again, referring to my story with Lynne Twist, she encouraged me to find someone who would be my Committed Listener, someone who would encourage me, partner with me, and believe with me that my stand was possible. Peter was someone who encouraged the best in me. He didn't just agree with everything I said. In many cases, he pushed back. But he did it in a way that lifted up what was possible. Our conversations were steeped in Generative Language.

Find that person who can be your Committed Listener. Be sure it is someone who sees the greatness or potential in you, yet isn't afraid to disagree. Talk to them about your vision and your intention to positively transform your agency. Tell them about your insights, your stand, and this process of building a Culture of Philanthropy. Ask them if they'll work with you on this. They need not be staff or a board member. They could be a particularly close friend, someone who knows you well and believes in you.

If they agree, then set up guidelines for how you will work with each other. Agree to be authentic, share challenges and not hold back. It is great if you can agree to be able to share your doubts, your scarcity thinking and your frustrations *without being taken too seriously*. Doubts will likely surface, and there will be moments when it seems impossible. Your Committed Listener will be best when they hear you and feel your pain, but then don't buy into it. They believe in your greatness, remember! Not your smallness.

Here is a sample conversation between you and your Committed Listener. (Scene Background: You've taken on building an agency-wide Culture of Philanthropy and have been working on it for a few months—but today you feel full of doubt and trapped in a mindset of scarcity. You need help, so you call your Committed Listener—CL.)

You: Committed Listener, I need to be heard because I feel like this plan to build a Culture of Philanthropy is going nowhere!

CL: Great, go ahead!

You: I have brought up a Culture of Philanthropy to a few people, but everyone seems too busy to talk about it. I asked Jennifer if she'd meet with me about it, and she did, but she seemed entirely distracted. I also have the issue that I have so much work on my plate that I hardly can focus on this. In fact, I got handed a deadline for raising a lot more money over the next few months, and I feel like I have to go ask for money when the donors aren't ready, which is completely opposite to a Culture of Philanthropy! I don't know what to do!

CL: I hear you. That must be very frustrating! What else do you want to say about it?

You: I asked Bob if he would be part of our Culture of Philanthropy Task Force, and he said yes, but he won't return my calls. I feel like I'm fighting an uphill battle.

CL: I hear you. What else do you need?

You: Nothing. I'm just frustrated.

CL: Okay, what next step would help you feel good about moving forward?

You get the point. Say what you need to say until there is nothing left to say. You might need to repeat something a couple of times until your CL totally gets it. Then, commit to your next action. Note that the CL did not indulge you. They heard you but did not add to the misery by adding their own scarcity thinking.

Your Committed Listener may choose to be part of the next circle, actively part of a team that is pushing this idea forward. This would be ideal. They could also be your go-to person outside of the inner circle who helps you navigate this project. Either choice is fine.

I've been asked if it's possible to do this sort of project without a Committed Listener. I suppose it is possible. But just like throwing your hat over the fence and taking a stand, acquiring a Committed Listener involves taking a bold risk. It also builds your enrollment muscles; you have to articulate your vision and make a request of someone. When you set yourself up with someone who is there to encourage you, you have a far greater chance of success. The goal of making cultural change is a formidable one. Having someone to champion you when things are stalled or become frustrating, can be a significant asset.

Step 3—Create a Culture of Philanthropy Task Force

A group of leaders with an aligned, meaningful intention have the ability and opportunity to alter the course of your organization. Once you have a clear vision and you have a Committed Listener, you need to build a team with a few key internal leaders. You need an inner circle, a Culture of Philanthropy Task Force that will give you feedback, enhance your vision and help lead the agency to its next phase.

Who is in the ring of this inner circle? Who are the important individuals who should be brought in right in the beginning? There may need to be different approaches depending on whether you are the top executive or if you are a junior staff person or board member. It's vital that you get the upper-echelon leaders on board.

Your Culture of Philanthropy Task Force should include key staff leadership and key board members. *In repeated instances with our clients, we've seen that, for maximum results, you will want to include the Executive Director or CEO, your highest development professional, and a top board member.*

It will be even better if you have multiple people from those different areas, and also a few program staff members. If there is an active development committee on the board, the chair of that committee would be an ideal member. If you don't have a development professional at all, enrolling someone who is deeply committed to development success and who will take on key development responsibilities will be important. If you have someone who is involved with marketing, this person would be a brilliant addition to the team.

There might be an opportunity for specific funders or volunteers to be part of this circle. In fact, it's possible that you might have someone like Peter, the donor who I shared about in my story in the beginning of this book. There could be individuals in your organization who are eager to be part of a visionary conversation, and who would cement their loyalty to your organization if they were invited to be part of this forward-thinking venture of building a Culture of Philanthropy.

While I've mentioned a wide range of different individuals who could be part of the team, choose no more than six or seven people from the list of potentials. You might be more comfortable having individual conversations first or setting up a think-tank type of meeting with the group of them. Share your vision. Let them know you are seeking a team of people to reimagine your organization with you. Tell them why you chose them. Why are they so key to the success of this? Then, tell them you have a process that you'd like them to take on with you. And share with them that the way to make culture change is to take a stand, together.

The members of your Culture of Philanthropy Task Force need to agree to embark on a long-term journey with you. You want individuals who are willing to do some hard work together. It matters that they are deeply committed to your organization. They should be open-minded learners, willing to be vulnerable, and share authentically. They will get to know each other well, and they will be part of an organizational transformation that is both unpredictable and unprecedented.

Kevin Oakes, in his book, *Culture Renovation* (McGraw-Hill Education, 2021), refers to three different types of individuals who you want to be sure to engage in your vision: *influencers, energizers* and *blockers*. Some may make sense to include in your Task Force, and some may be appropriate to bring in later on in the process, like at Step 9 as you expand your team. My take on how you might want to use them specifically in your creation of a Culture of Philanthropy is this:

- **Influencers**—These are the people who have a lot of influence. People listen to what they say, because they have either informal or formal authority.
- **Energizers**—These are people who adopt ideas and get to work on them. They are great models, and they should be sought. When they get in action, their good work should be highlighted.
- **Blockers**—These are the naysayers, the individuals who tend to enroll people in "it's impossible." You have to pay attention to them.

You should be mindful of who you bring on to your Task Force and how they might contribute to your vision. It's great to have people who have a lot of influence over certain groups in your community, people who can energize and inspire others by modeling appropriate actions. Regarding the blockers, you need to have early conversations with them and find appropriate roles for them. Do not avoid these individuals, as they can be destructive if they are ignored. They may have something important to offer, and you want to be open to learning from all perspectives. However, be cautious about blockers or naysayers on your cabinet/team who may disrupt your momentum.

Guidepost

Laurie Herrick

This invitation to be on your Culture of Philanthropy Task Force should be an *enrollment conversation,* not a sales pitch. I learned this valuable concept when I was a volunteer on a weekend-long ropes course. I had been in the course, and then started to volunteer for it. Ultimately, I graduated to the role of rappel send-off. This meant that I was the person standing at the edge of a forty-foot cliff, encouraging people to back off (with lots of safety equipment) and rappel backward.

Frightened course participants would timidly walk up to me. I'd double check all their safety equipment. I'd explain how it was going to go. I'd look them in the eye and tell them to lean back. Early in my experience in this role, I had a fair number of balkers, people who basically said, "No way. I'm not doing it!"

On one particular day, I was at an all-time low. More people than ever refused to step into the abyss, forfeiting their breakthrough experience. The woman coaching me, Dana, was wonderful. She was cheering me on, but to no avail. That evening, a group of us, including Dana, went to a local pub. I was in a bit of a cranky mood, frustrated with my results.

It was nearly impossible to get the bartender's attention, but when I did, I ordered a club soda. He rolled his eyes at my choice, and then got me a tonic water. Yuck. Not what I had in mind. I tried to get his attention again. I expressed my frustration with this exercise in futility to Dana, who quickly caught the eye of the bartender and asked him in her sweet and kind voice, "Would you mind helping my friend out?"

Needless to say, he quickly corrected the order, and within a few minutes, not only did I have the club soda that I wanted, but he had assigned Dana the role of being his assistant, and she was behind the bar getting snacks for all of our group. When she came back to me, I noted to her how amazing she was with people. She had turned a total jerk into a nice guy!

She laughed, looked at me, and got serious. "There is an important lesson for you here, Laurie. Here's what you're missing. Every conversation is an enrollment conversation. Either you are being enrolled or you are enrolling someone. You got enrolled in this guy's schtick. He's playing the tough bartender guy who doesn't know the difference between a club soda and a tonic water. You got enrolled and annoyed with that. I enrolled him in helping me out. I didn't get enrolled in his tough-bartender-guy routine.

"This is just like the rappel. Instead of you enrolling people in 'You're fine, lean back,' you're getting enrolled in what you imagine is going on in the course participant's heads—'Oh, my God. I'm gonna die!'"

She was spot-on. It was the difference in taking on possibility versus fear. I definitely was enrolled in people's fear on the rappel. This was a huge breakthrough for me. It instantly changed my effectiveness in helping people have a powerful experience. It took heightened self-awareness, for one thing. I started paying better attention to my internal narrative, recognizing the difference between what was going on right in front of me versus my opinion about what someone was thinking. I started to see that I could be among the naysayers, or I could create a new possibility with what I said.

On the ropes course, with Dana's coaching, I found a way to enroll people in the breakthrough available to them. Instead of participants submitting to their fear and balking, they could take powerful actions, despite their fear. This translated to their lives, of course, where, through the ropes experience, they got to see how they could take on things that are scary in a more powerful way. (It turns out that this is also very useful in donor relations.)

As you have your conversation with both your Committed Listener and potential members of your Culture of Philanthropy Task Force, start to pay attention to who is enrolling whom. A great way to see this, if you are a parent, is with your children. I'm sure you can think of times when you were enrolled by your child in a delightful way—and times when you were enrolled in their less-than-flattering ways. If you're enrolled in the delightful possibilities that they are, you're madly in love with them. If you're enrolled in their bad behavior, well, then it's likely you want to throttle them (metaphorically, of course).

What if you could switch gears and choose what you get enrolled by? Think of the opportunity in getting enrolled in a greater potential than you can imagine for someone instead of getting hooked (as I did with the bartender) into how annoying they can be. The former certainly has a greater chance of producing positive results. But, more importantly, by enrolling the bartender in his greatness rather than enrolling others in "this guy is a jerk," I'm actually taking a stand for the world being a little bit kinder and better. Complaining to others just reinforces the worst aspects of humanity—the jerkiness of the bartender, myself as a complainer and gossip, and a separation of us vs. them.

The bottom line with this is that you have a choice in what you get enrolled in and what you enroll others in. When you hear things like, "We tried that," or, "Nothing will ever change," don't get enrolled. As you saw back in the section on *The Three Laws of Performance,* there are so many different perspectives for any one scenario. Hear people's concerns. Everyone needs to be heard, even the blockers. Then, choose an interpretation that empowers you and your project to create the possibility of a Culture of Philanthropy in your organization.

> Rosamund Stone Zander and Ben Zander, in their book, *The Art of Possibility,* (Penguin Books, 2002), define enrollment this way: "Enrollment is the art and practice of generating a spark of possibility for others to share." They go on to say, "The practice of enrollment is about giving yourself as a possibility to others and being ready, in turn, to catch their spark. It is about playing together as partners in a field of light."

Once you enroll your team your Culture of Philanthropy Task Force, then it's time to move on to the next steps.

Step 4—What Is So

Take the Choose Abundance Culture of Philanthropy Assessment at www.ChooseAbundanceBook.com and get your baseline. It's only up from here!

Inevitably, when you were having your enrollment conversations with your Culture of Philanthropy Task Force, you came up against obstacles to creating a Culture of Philanthropy. Remember, if this was easy, everyone would be doing it. Building a Culture of Philanthropy is not for people looking for the easy way out.

And while I said it's important to hear everyone's perspective and not get enrolled in disempowering interpretations, it's critical that you also face the reality of what is so. What is working well within your agency? What isn't working very well? Where are you excelling or failing in your quest to have a Culture of Philanthropy?

Exercise

You and your Culture of Philanthropy Task Force should, independent of each other (no cheating!), take the following free Choose Abundance Culture of Philanthropy Assessment.

Go to the Assessment on our Book Hub at www.ChooseAbundanceBook.com to measure the baseline for your organization. You will receive a report that shows your team's results. Together, look at those results and consider the following:

- **Where are the scores very inconsistent?** Take the time to talk with your team about why there are varied opinions. This is an opportunity to recognize the need to educate people more broadly. The same goes if a number of individuals choose a middle-of-the-road option, indicating indecision, lack of knowledge or neutrality. For example, if your board members are unaware of practices you have for Major Donor engagement, there's an opportunity to have this be part of board transformation down the road. Make a note of the things that need to be covered in education of board or staff members.
- **Where are the scores particularly good?** Take this as a way to acknowledge what you've done really well. Woo-hoo! Celebrate it. You are doing well in these areas! Be sure that you capture this information so you can share it as you build support for this project.
- **Where are the scores particularly poor?** Use low scores as an opportunity to make change. You don't have to move into action yet, but

start to see things that could be easy wins. Also, if you score low on something, ask this question—if not, why not? Is leadership not supporting something? Is there an attitude (perhaps given your organization's constituency) that money or people with wealth are bad? Does someone refuse to invest in a relationship-tracking fundraising database? Make a note of what needs attention.

- **Culture change balance.** Do you give more attention to one of the parts of the Wheel of Change, ignoring the others? Again, make a note and share it with the group.
- **Balance in the 5 Points of Possibility.** The fact that you are taking this on means that you are committed to organizational change. Look through the lens of the 5 Points of Possibility. Is there one of these domains that is particularly problematic? Make a note and share it with your team.

Preparing this material for sharing with your team is very important. You ultimately want to relay the current reality so that they too get to *Hell No!*, that place where they are unwilling to accept the Default Future. You want to strike the balance of both understanding the current reality and predictable future and comparing it to your vision. Which one do you want? You should also have some ideas begin to bubble up that could bring a Culture of Philanthropy forward.

Step 5—Educate, Educate, Educate

You and your team need to get on the same page on what a Culture of Philanthropy is and what it is not. You can have them read this book, and you can conduct a training. But be certain that people on your Culture of Philanthropy Task Force understand that a Culture of Philanthropy is not just about finding the elusive rich person to save your organization. See the training designed for larger groups in Step 9.

Step 6—Hell No!

As mentioned in Step 4, you need to use the Choose Abundance Culture of Philanthropy Assessment to show the contrast of the current reality versus your vision. As the quantity of self-help books in the world will show, it's difficult to change habits and make substantial life change. Many things need to be in place to assure success. One is an understanding of the high contrast between your Default Future and your newly invented vision for the future.

Exercise

Have your Culture of Philanthropy Task Force read the sections of this book on *The Three Laws of Performance* and scarcity language. Meet with your leadership team to create your Urgent Action Statement for a Culture of Philanthropy. The urgent case for action emerges in the answers to the following questions:

- What is the Default Future of our agency?
- If we don't take action now, where will we end up?
- If we don't act now, what risks will we be exposed to?
- If we don't act now, what opportunities will we miss?

This case for action doesn't need to be perfectly wordsmithed. It's important to work on it as a group because doing it as a team and formulating it together creates buy-in. It is an opportunity to move from one person's initial vision of a Culture of Philanthropy (Step 1 of this model) to an approach that has team agreement and alignment. Choose someone to facilitate a brainstorming session where there are no wrong answers, and the group looks at the questions above. It's critical that this exercise is well-managed, people freely give their input, and it stays on track, avoiding distractions and side comments.

Use a white board or flip chart to answer each of the four questions above and capture everyone's thoughts. Do one question at a time (without the other questions visible to the group) until people feel their ideas have been captured. Be certain to save your pages. Next, the facilitator should start a new page entitled *proposals*. The proposal should be a statement that expresses one of two things.

> "We propose that avoiding the risk of _______ is urgent."
>
> "We propose that we act to seize this opportunity of _______ immediately."

As you write your Urgent Action Statement, be as specific as possible. Agree to open yourselves up to talking with your team with a deep desire and commitment to finding the most powerful suggestions together. Really listen, as opposed to arguing for your ideas. Work together on the Urgent Action Statement for a Culture of Philanthropy, and keep going until each and every person says, "This speaks for me!" When this happens, you've reached a state of alignment. Once you've done this, you have an *Urgent Action Statement for a Culture of Philanthropy.*

One note about the word *urgent* in the Urgent Action Statement: The reason that Zaffron and Logan use this term is to motivate your team to get to work, *now*. I see it as a time to choose a pathway to abundance thinking and a Culture of Philanthropy. At the same time, you have to recognize that this change, while urgent, won't happen fast. Remember that culture change takes time.

An example of an Urgent Action Statement for a Culture of Philanthropy is this:

> "We propose that avoiding the risk of depending on a small number of Major Donors is urgent."
>
> "We propose that we act to seize this opportunity of Building a Culture of Philanthropy and building deep donor partnerships and relationships immediately."

Step 7—Design Your Preferred Future

Next, you should have a follow-up meeting with your Culture of Philanthropy Task Force where you start to sketch out what you want. This is your opportunity to create a *Preferred Future,* not a *Default Future.* This will be based on creating the possibility you envision in your organization. It also requires examining what it will take from each of you to make it a reality.

Exercise

Set Effective Goals

Before you come to this meeting, each of the team members should prepare a written response to this exercise. Write it in the form of a letter.

The valuable process described in these first two paragraphs is discussed by Rosamund Stone Zander and Benjamin Zander in their book, *The Art of Possibility* (Penguin Books, 2000).

1. Imagine it's now a year from now. You've just spent a full year working as part of a team, doing a brilliant job building and strengthening a Culture of Philanthropy at your agency. You've done this because you've made a shift in how you do business; your way of operating, your mindset, your M.O. Date your letter a year from now. It should start with "Dear Team, my part of building an extraordinary Culture of Philanthropy was..."

In this letter, report on all of the *insights* you acquired and breakthroughs you accomplished as if they are already in the past. It should not be written with future-based language (e.g., no phrases like *I hope to, I intend to* or *I will*). It's about looking back at your time together working on this project. This is not about your team. *It's about you.* I want to know how your molecules will have shifted in order to cause this organization-wide breakthrough.

You may, if you wish, mention specific goals accomplished, but I am especially interested in the attitude, the feelings, and the worldview of this person you've become. When you get to the meeting initially, keep these letters private. You will circle back to them in a little while.

2. This next part of the exercise requires one of your Culture of Philanthropy Task Force members lead a brainstorming discussion on how you might build a Culture of Philanthropy. There are no bad ideas. The suggestions that people make are not final decisions. They are simply ideas. Put the first of the 5 Points of Possibility up on a white board.

Point 1: Culture of Philanthropy Is Integral to Our Mission

Have your team all bring up things that would be exciting to have at your agency related to this first point. It could be to continue or enhance something you're already doing. It could also be a new idea that you've read about in this book, or that you bring from your experience with other organizations. Remember to not get attached to any ideas. Just be open to what comes up from the group. Be sure to include all three parts of the Wheel of Change—Behavior, Structure and Hearts & Minds. The facilitator's job is to encourage creativity and be certain the ideas all get captured.

When you've exhausted your ideas, move on to the second of the 5 Points of Possibility. You should take ten to fifteen minutes to gather suggestions for each of these next four Points. Try not to get overwhelmed, as there will likely be more good ideas than could possibly be implemented. Here are the rest of the 5 Points.

Point 2: Everyone Shares Responsibility for a Culture of Philanthropy

Point 3: We Build and Maintain Deep Donor Relationships and Partnerships

Point 4: Community Engagement Is What We Do

Point 5: We Recognize Every Contribution of Service, Items or Money as an Expression of Philanthropy

3. Give each team member a different-colored marker or ten sticky dots of a unique color. Each person on the team should star their top ten choices chosen from all of the suggestions by going to the list and adding their stars. The facilitator should complete this part of the exercise by circling those suggestions under each of the 5 Points of Possibility that seem to be the priority of this group. Talk about why they are important, and if someone feels that the item they starred (which got little or no support) is important, then give them time to discuss for a few minutes. At the end of this exercise, you should have some key first steps you will take on.

4. Now, we'll look at what we have to do to be able to make these things happen. As a group, this is a time to share the letters that you prepared ahead of time. It's critical we understand that it isn't the other person who needs to shift. All of you, as team members, have to be open to shifting your own Behaviors and Hearts & Minds in order to make this change happen.

Be great listeners when people are sharing their letters. Notice if, when someone is speaking, you are thinking about your letter, or if you are genuinely present in listening to theirs. The better you are at listening, the smarter your colleagues will become, and the greater your understanding of your partners will be!

Insights from the Field

Listening Is Difficult

Seth Godin

Hearing happens when we're able to recognize a sound. Listening happens when we put in the effort to understand what it means. It not only requires focus, but it also requires a commitment to encountering the experience, intent and emotion behind the words. And that commitment can be scary. Because if we're exposed to that emotion and those ideas, we discover things we might be avoiding.

---

5. After everyone has read their letter, have the group share their feelings. What insights did you each have? Did anyone learn from other people's letters? What would it feel like to really accomplish these things?

6. Next, discuss the following questions about your partnership and leadership team (list ideas on a flip chart or white board and capture them):

- Who would we need to be to make this vision happen?
- If we want to avoid our Default Future and create a new future, what conversations need to stop? Who will take on leading this change?
- If we want to avoid our Default Future and create this new one, what new conversations need to be generated? Who will take on leading this change?
- What organizational conversations that we already practice should we embrace and continue, as they support a Culture of Philanthropy?
- To what extent do we agree to follow through?
- What would be an accountability Structure that could genuinely work for this team?

Take the outcomes of this exercise and capture them so that you can later incorporate them in your plan.

The next exercise is designed to help you gain awareness of potential obstacles. You can do it immediately after the previous exercise.

Exercise

This exercise requires people be very authentic with each other. It's the kind of activity that can make a tremendous difference in the success of your intentions. The facilitator should come prepared with a stack of index cards (fifteen or more per person on the team) and several similar pens if you want to preserve anonymity.

Have the organizational leader (CEO or Board Chair) talk about the need to be authentic in this process. He or she should share about their own blind spots and discoveries that have occurred for them while exploring how to build a Culture of Philanthropy. This sort of sharing will expand communications to ensure success. It will require everyone being open with each other and being vulnerable. Some of the organizations that I've worked with read Brené Brown's book, *Dare to Lead* (Random House, 2018). Brené studies the importance of vulnerability in the evolution of great leaders. If this is something that your team or your executive leader wants to take on, it can be extremely transformative to the group.

And issues like these—communication problems, areas that need transformation—are always going to pop up. Consider them growing pains. Next, you'll use your group time to collectively anticipate these roadblocks to a Culture of Philanthropy in your organization. The following exercise will help acknowledge possible obstacles so that overcoming them can take the form of plan and action. This will allow for more forward momentum—waiting to address potential problems until they block the way, opens up the chance for future excuses to stop your organization's efforts toward culture change.

1. Each person should find a quiet space to do this alone. Imagine now that it's a year later, and this intention to build a Culture of Philanthropy totally bombed. Write down what, in your imagination, would have caused this to fail. Do not add your name—keep all reasons anonymous. Put one reason for failure on each index card.

2. Have everyone come back to the room in fifteen minutes and hand the facilitator all of their index cards. The facilitator should shuffle them up and have everyone get a mixture of responses to read out loud.

3. As a group, take the time to discuss each of these perceived barriers to your success.

- Are there barriers that you hadn't thought of previously?
- Are there multiple cultures at play?
- Is there a culture of distrust?
- Is there a culture of learning?
- What other subcultures are there that might be worth discussing? An easy way to get to the bottom of that question is to think about the mindset.
- Where might the mindset be dysfunctional?
- Are there key individuals outside of the exercise group who you need to be part of this conversation?
- Are there challenges that you could resolve by having a conversation with someone?
- Perhaps an enrollment conversation?

- What about other small fixes now that might avert disaster later?
- Remember the blockers. Is there someone who might throw things off?

4. Now that you've examined how important your group's dynamics are, discuss what agreements you would need to make to be certain that this is a success.

- Do you have a way that you want to conduct yourselves?
- Are there key people who are imperative to the success of this project?
- What is your accountability Structure?
- Do you need to set up regular meetings?
- Is there someone who will take a stand for driving this?

In Step 7, we've looked at the alternative to the Default Future, the Preferred Future. We've examined how we personally need to shift to make this happen. We've scrutinized how the organization needs to operate differently to make this happen. We've thought through some of our wildest dreams of how it might be stronger, better and full of resources. We've even looked at what might get in the way. Now, we are ready to start the Implementation Plan.

Step 8—Create Your Implementation Plan

To start implementing a Culture of Philanthropy Plan requires first a Commitment Statement, and then SHMART goals. (No, that isn't a typo. The normal well-known acronym is SMART goals, and it refers to Specific, Measurable, Attainable, Relevant, Time-Bound. My friends at the Springfield Mass JCC noticed something missing in the SMART goals model. It was the Hearts & Minds. SHMART was the outcome—a newly invented word, which we say is influenced by Yiddish and a Bostonian dialect!)

Exercise

Begin Your Implementation Plan

What is your stand, your commitment regarding a Culture of Philanthropy? This is different from your Urgent Action Statement for a Culture of Philanthropy. That was designed to get you in touch with your Default Future so that you get in action. Your Commitment Statement is your North Star. It will set your direction and guide your way.

Write on a white board, "We are committed to fostering a Culture of Philanthropy at our agency by: ______________________________."

This Commitment Statement should be the vision that you need to get started. It will go at the top of your Implementation Plan to inspire your work and keep your intention alive. Fill in the goals that have come from the exercises earlier in this chapter. Each of your team members should take on goals that engage their own constituency group in building a Culture of Philanthropy. For example, board, executive leader, or development staff. And since Hearts & Minds is more in the domain of *being* rather than *doing*, be certain that each of the groups is actively pursuing something in the Hearts & Minds.

Be sure to include goals that will be significant indicators of your success, or Key Performance Indicators (KPIs). Examples of KPIs that I encourage you to use are specific numbers for:

- Donor retention
- The number of board or staff members involved in development efforts (all aspects of development, not just asking)

- The number of Major Donors giving to your organization each year
- The number of meaningful personalized conversations with Major Donors
- The number of volunteers involved with your organization

The timeframe for this plan should be multiyear. By showing goals out two or three years, you're acknowledging to everyone that this will not happen overnight. A common way a Culture of Philanthropy fails is if there isn't recognition that this will take time. You will need to have patience. You may want to use project management software to plan out and document milestones or goals.

A couple of notes as you work on this plan. Be sure that you're finding the sweet spot between things that are attainable and ones that make a difference. First, be certain that you have some easy wins; they build confidence. But be clear that easy wins that are frivolous don't build confidence. They feel like a disempowering waste of time. Choose initial items that will be both impactful and easily achievable.

In trying to make major cultural change in your agency, leadership and accountability Structure are key. Be sure that those are among your goals. Who is accountable to whom? Who will keep your goals top of mind?

You can write your goals into a plan of your own design, or you can go to our Book Hub at www.ChooseAbundanceBook.com and download the Choose Abundance Implementation Plan. You'll see that the download with that title (CA Implementation Plan) is a blank plan, and one I've filled in is called the Choose Abundance Implementation Plan *Sample*. The latter has examples so you can see how this chart could work. I strongly recommend that you do not have as many goals as I do in the sample plan. I give plenty of examples to show variety—but there are too many to implement. Feel free to take these ideas and create a plan that best serves your agency.

Once you download the Plan, begin to fill it out. Here is some advice on how to make this tool work for you.

- Choose actions that excite and empower your team.
- Don't take on too many goals. (The filled-out chart gives numerous examples. A total of three to five goals should be plenty to get you going.)
- Be certain that there are some meaningful, easy wins.
- Be sure to track successes as they come along.
- Be certain that you include some visionary long-term goals.

Step 9—Communicate and Enroll Next Layers of Stakeholders

Step 9 is about rollout of your plan and buy-in on multiple layers. The idea here is to start to build momentum by enlarging your circle of supporters. With any project starting from scratch, you have to essentially put ten times the effort in to get one outcome to fruition. Once you achieve one outcome, work on multiple others. This will produce what Jim Collins in his book, *Good to Great* (HarperBusiness, 2001), calls the "Flywheel Effect." At a certain point, from the outsider's perspective, it will seem like effortless change. But from the perspective of those in the inside, you will have had to put in a Herculean effort to get the flywheel moving before momentum takes over. By expanding your team in an intentional way, you're making the ratio more favorable to your commitment to culture change. With your team, determine who the next layers of individuals are that you need to enroll to assure success.

There is the obvious next layer, the staff and the board. A training for these individuals (or multiple ones) is a very useful way to teach about a Culture of Philanthropy and get everyone on the same page. You'll see that it is a top priority in the Implementation Plan *Sample* that I've included at www.ChooseAbundanceBook.com.

If you're truly committed to organization-wide change, the CEO or Executive Director should be at each training—and ideally the development professional, if there is one. At Riverside Industries (as mentioned in the Guidepost in Chapter 8) there was a large staff. I ended up facilitating seven trainings with the board, the van drivers, the program directors, supervisors and the direct care staff. (More than a hundred people were trained in total!) At every single training, the CEO and Development Director were in attendance.

I strongly urge you to engage all staff and board members in the basic concept and action steps toward building a Culture of Philanthropy. Put simply, *train them, engage them and empower them to act.* Let's not be shortsighted. Why bring all of your board and staff together on this approach? Seriously, why ever would you not?

Culture of Philanthropy Training

As a way to gain a comprehensive understanding of a Culture of Philanthropy, read this book as a team. If you do this prior to a training, your team will be so much further ahead. Along with a prior homework assignment of reading the book or not, here's an outline for a basic Culture of Philanthropy Training (you'll notice that it is a simplified parallel of the outline of this book):

I. Welcome and Introductions
   a. Why We are Doing This—include stated vision (CEO)
   b. Why We Need Your Help (CEO)

II. Purpose of Training: To Build a Culture of Philanthropy Throughout Our Organization

III. Fill Out the Choose Abundance Culture of Philanthropy Assessment and Set Aside (Facilitator/trainer should facilitate through section IX)

IV. What Is a Culture of Philanthropy?

  a. What do we mean by *Philanthropy*?

  b. What does this concept of Culture mean to us?

V. Scarcity Thinking

VI. Culture Change Model

VII. Generative Language and Creating the Future We Want

VIII. Review Choose Abundance Culture of Philanthropy Assessment Results in small groups. Where are you aligned?

IX. The Implementation Plan—Share the plan as it exists now. Are there ideas that could be added to this plan from the constituency groups?

X. What things might you take on in small groups (departments, board, etc.)?

XI. Set up a support Structure to assure success.

Step 10—Community Engagement

In Step 10, you should go beyond your staff and board in order to think about your larger community, consistent with Point of Possibility 4: Community Engagement Is What We Do.

To better understand your greater community, complete the following exercise, which is designed to identify both groups and individuals with whom you can connect. In this context of building your next level of buy-in for a Culture of Philanthropy, you will first see how many people surrounding your agency are already allies. From there, you will easily identify individuals who should be around the table as you build this Culture of Philanthropy. This exercise is so useful and powerful that you should do it twice; once with your leadership team to think about your rollout of a Culture of Philanthropy, and later as a board and staff training for people to think about who could be supporters of your agency (and be educated on why they should be compelled to be part of your agency).

This exercise was designed by Terry Axelrod. I recommend her book, *The Benevon Model for Sustainable Funding: A Step-by-Step Guide to Getting It Right*, which you can find online. For now, I'm going to walk you through her Treasure Map Exercise.

Exercise

The Benevon Treasure Map Exercise

Reprinted with permission of the author of ***The Benevon Model for Sustainable Funding: A Step-by-Step Guide to Getting It Right, Second Edition,*** Terry Axelrod, 2017, Seattle, WA

You might want to empower the team members to learn this process, so they can then lead it with others. For example, this training could be conducted with either your board, a group of volunteers, or a group of stakeholders for your organization.

The facilitator should have a flip chart or white board. A bigger format will work best. The facilitator should have at least four different-colored markers that are thick enough that everyone can see the writing from a distance, but fine enough that you can write detail.

The premise with this Treasure Map is that there are a number of individuals already surrounding your organization. There is tremendous value in understanding who they are, what their passion is, what they have in abundance to contribute to your good work, and what they get out of engaging with your organization.

TREASURE MAP
GROUPS AND ORGANIZATIONS

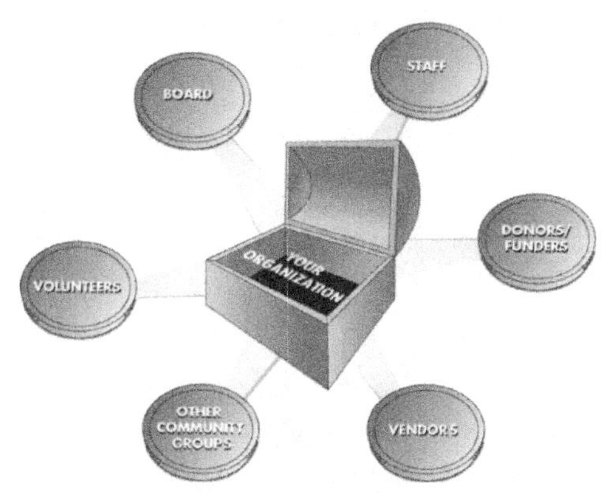

9-2 Groups and Organizations
(Terry Axelrod, The Benevon Model for Sustainable Funding, page 77)

1. Start by putting the name of your organization in the middle of the page.

2. Next, let's think about the various groups that surround your organization. What are some examples? Let people brainstorm.

What are the different groups and agencies that surround your organization? Put them around the outside like satellites surrounding a planet. Start with groups like your board, staff, volunteers, donors and funders, vendors and different groups that you interact with regularly.

3. Now, with a different-colored marker, list the resources that each of these groups has in abundance. Why? Because this is an abundance-based model of fundraising, and it presumes that people will naturally want to give what they have plenty of.

People want to say yes, and it's easier for them to say yes if you're asking them for something that they have in abundance. For some people, you may not know what that abundance is. That's okay. Later in this book, I'll show you how to find out more!

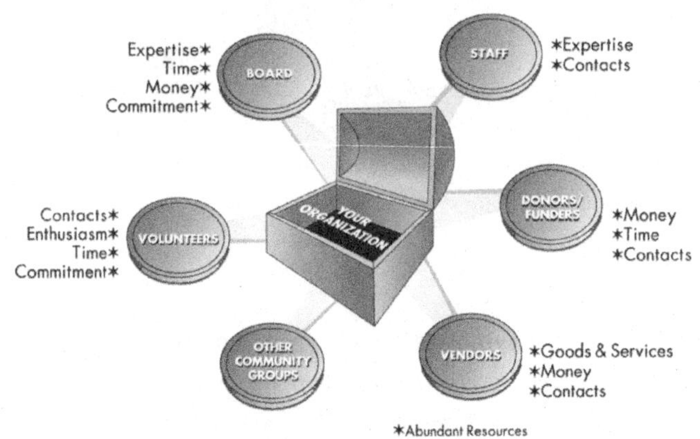

9-3 Abundant Resources

(Terry Axelrod, The Benevon Model for Sustainable Funding, page 78)

Like this image from Terry Axelrod's book, start to list the abundant resources of your board, staff, volunteers and so on. Take the time to do this with each group surrounding your organization.

4. Now, let's go to each group again and ask what their self-interest is. Self-interest is a good thing in the way that it drives our actions. We have self-interest in reading this book (to learn something or accomplish a class assignment and get an *A*), or taking a class (to get paid higher or develop your skill), or going to work (to get paid, to make a difference). Self-interest can be positive, and it can be negative. It can be noble and inspiring or selfish and manipulative. People may give to a program because of a tax write-off, or to look good to their friends, or because they are deeply committed to social change. It may easily be a combination of these things.

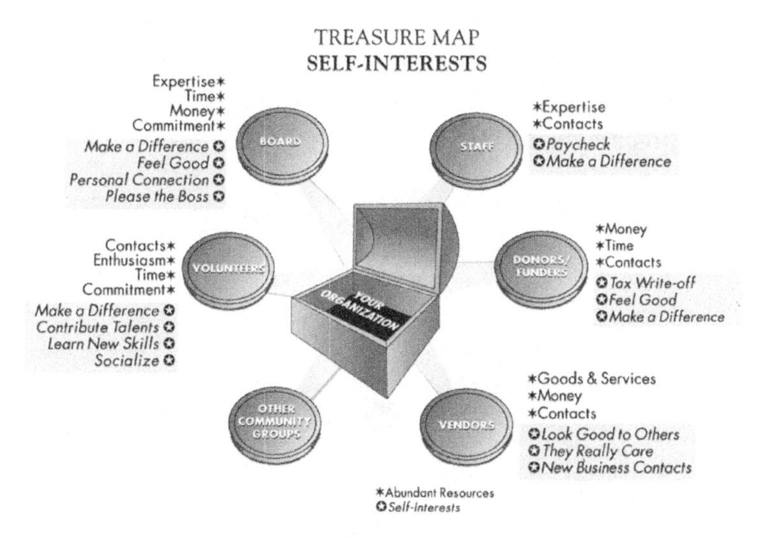

9-4 Self Interests

(Terry Axelrod, The Benevon Model for Sustainable Funding, page 80)

Self-interest is more complex than it appears at first. If you really take the time to identify the self-interests of each group on your Treasure Map, it will simplify your work. You will have more compassion for the folks who come to your organization, and you'll want to recall the self-interest that led to their involvement in the first place. By exploring and understanding their self-interest, you will engage them more deeply, and they will be drawn to be committed lifelong funders for your organization. Use a different-color marker to write below the list of things your groups of people have in abundance and identify what their self-interest might be. Go ahead and do that with all of your groups.

5. Next, we're going to add Fantasy Groups. Who is not yet on your map—but could make a tremendous difference in your organization? Whose involvement would leverage a whole world of support and credibility? Typical examples are corporate executives, celebrities, the media, or local religious or political leaders. Be creative coming up with dream-team categories.

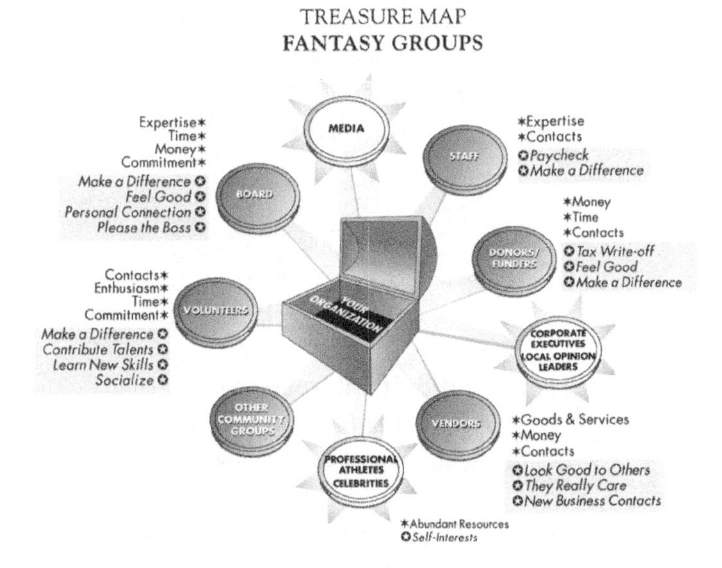

9-5 Fantasy Groups

(Terry Axelrod, The Benevon Model for Sustainable Funding, page 81)

Who in these groups knows people from other groups? Do staff members know business owners? Are there volunteers who might know people in the media? You will see instantly how fast news travels. You could probably draw lines between these groups that already talk to each other, but it would make a big mess of a beautiful Treasure Map. If only a handful of new people were to learn about your organization, where else might the word spread?

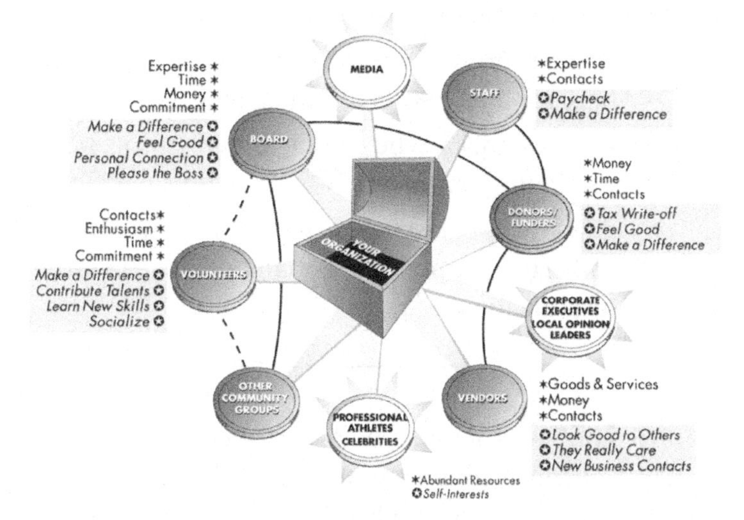

9-6 Who Talks to Whom

(Terry Axelrod, The Benevon Model for Sustainable Funding, page 82)

6. Now, take a look at your completed organizational Treasure Map. Start to think of the people in each of these groups. Who comes to mind through this process that should be part of the next layer of your Culture of Philanthropy Plan? Most likely, you'll come up with some names that you want to reach out to immediately. Determine as a group who it makes sense to bring into the fold of your Culture of Philanthropy vision. Who is the right person to reach out to them? What would be the forum for this conversation? Be intentional about the waves of engagement.

There may be people who easily come to mind, but you have no idea what they have in abundance! This is an opportunity to sit down with people to get to know them. (See how to conduct a Discovery Meeting in Chapter 17 to learn how to get to know what people have in abundance!) We've heard all sorts of things that have come out of these types of meetings.

- A microbrewer who was honored to offer her beer for a reception for an agency
- A designer who contributed pro bono marketing materials
- A natural salesperson who took on making calls to people on behalf of his favorite organization

---

In Step 10, you've explored a wide range of potential people and communities you could connect with. It's likely that you thought of some great individuals—some who are influential, some who know lots of other movers and shakers, and some who are the key individuals whose buy-in could make or break you. Ideally, they are *possibilitarians*—individuals who are receptive to creating something that gives birth to new possibility.

You may have also found some people who are typical naysayers, or blockers, as discussed in Step 3. Are they anyone whose influence is particularly important to the success of this plan? Think before acting. What would be wise?

If, in fact, someone does come to mind who you think needs to be at the table, but there's a group reluctance to include them, perhaps hold out on including them for now. Capture this information and include them at a later time, once you have some successes under your belt and there is greater community buy-in.

Once you have educated and enrolled an expanding team, it's now time to let people riff on the possibilities that you've created together. You want to embrace people's ideas, so long as they align with what you've already designed in your Implementation Plan. Have your plan with goals handy for current and future meetings. Have this newly expanded team fully educated on your plan. Have them find their place within it.

Step 11—Track Successes

As mentioned above, referring to your plan will help align your actions with your vision. Put Structures in place to your Culture of Philanthropy, and make goals and intentions top of mind. Conduct a quarterly review (put in the board and staff calendars) using the Choose Abundance Culture of Philanthropy Assessment to determine your progress. When there is an unexpected or intentional success, let people know about it. Be gentle with failures. They will happen. They are proof that you are standing for something big and significant. Keep things going, regardless of stumbles along the way.

You move to this stage specifically when you have people's Hearts & Minds enrolled in the possibility of a Culture of Philanthropy. Without buy-in, the attitudes won't be there, and the Behaviors will be half-hearted. That means that it is important to give people a chance to share their doubts, their skepticism and their fears. Some of these might bring up a legitimate obstacle that requires action. Other concerns that may surface will only require a good listener.

Over time, you can move from less to more permanent Structure. For example, at the Harry & Rose Samson Family Jewish Community Center, initially there was no appetite for a new board committee. Instead, they established The Culture of Philanthropy Task Force. Two people co-chaired this group, and they created a plan for how, if they achieved particular benchmarks, they would form the Culture of Philanthropy Committee. (See Chapter 14 to see how this all came together.)

Once they had a Culture of Philanthropy Committee, checking in on their Implementation Plan was a natural topic. Board members as well as staff had Structures and Behaviors that they were accountable for. It became easy to see the progress and keep moving forward.

Part IV

The Ideal World: What Does It Look Like?

Chapter 10
Roles in Building a Culture of Philanthropy

The great leaders are not the strongest,
they are the ones who are honest about their weaknesses.
The great leaders are not the smartest;
they are the ones who admit how much they don't know.
The great leaders can't do everything;
they are the ones who look to others to help them.
Great leaders don't see themselves as great;
they see themselves as human.

—Simon Sinek

No matter how good you are at taking the right fundraising actions, if you have an organization that suffers from scarcity thinking, your ability to succeed will be stunted. Point of Possibility 2: Everyone Shares Some Responsibility for a Culture of Philanthropy, is one way to have staff and board step into roles that fast-track fundraising success. This is not simply because more people are helping the fundraising professional, but because there are greater understanding and heightened opportunities for collaboration when we are aware of each other's roles. It ends up advancing everyone's departments. You will see in this section how different roles can support development while not overburdening *anyone*. But let's first look at the cost of simply leaving development to a single development professional (or even a small team).

For example, as a board member, you can encourage the Executive Director to hire a development staff person, but if everyone breathes a huge sigh of relief that, at last, they are off the hook, and someone is handling this "evil necessity," that development person will not succeed. Not only will the development person be working on a monumental project all alone, but the environmental mindset of scarcity suggests that there will not be funding (or the funding *priority*) for the right tools to get the job done. There will be a shortage of understanding of the damage that limited resources have on development efforts, donors will likely not be appreciated properly, and the development professional will likely hate their job. It is difficult to love a job that is under-resourced and that most people look down upon.

In a Culture of Philanthropy, there is a whole team of people who embrace development and make it happen—the Executive Director, the program staff, the board of directors, administration, operations, marketing and a development committee. While you may be able to make some progress by teaching a single staff person or board member to embrace fundraising, you'll still be pedaling uphill. You will always be pushing up against scarcity thinking.

I saw this again and again through my work at the Harold Grinspoon Foundation, when I taught seven-year-long cohorts a professional development course called GIFT. Each GIFT cohort had about fifteen fundraising professionals in it. They were able to make some decent advancements in strengthening a fundraising program, but they kept running up against barriers when it came to getting the board and other staff to buy in to and support their efforts. Most of the individuals in this program were from small- to medium-sized agencies. They often had no development staff assisting them, or perhaps one development associate. Many struggled to get a decent relational fundraising database.

One of the most significant challenges they had was making time to focus on a Major Donor Portfolio, where they needed to design a customized plan for each of the top donors. This was known to have the highest ROI (return on investment) for their agency, yet the board and Executive Directors kept insisting that the development professional coordinate galas, order food for board meetings, and do minutia that wasn't development focused, much less intent on building healthy donor partnerships! Further, we kept running up against limited board engagement with development and Executive Directors who were unwilling to support their development staff in making that happen. There were many more examples like these.

We tried to include the board and executive leaders in the development person's course, but they hadn't signed up for it, and they didn't understand the context of building a Culture of Philanthropy since they hadn't been there in every classroom session. In fact, after a number of years of frustration, we asked the participants what they needed, and their answers became the impetus to create a new course that included mandatory participation of a development professional, a board member and the top executive. They were allowed to include two more people if they desired. This felt risky, as it was possible that it was too much to ask of volunteer board members and top executives.

I asked Mark Shapiro, the CEO of the Harry & Rose Samson Jewish Community Center of Greater Milwaukee (who has been mentioned a number of times so far in this book for his breakthrough results at their agency), and he helped design a multi-month program that we named the GIFT Leadership Institute (GLI). With this model, we began to see agency-wide buy-in in a way that we had not previously. The course requires a team approach: the CEO, a development professional, a board leader and program staff all must be part of the course. In fact, many of those groups that have been in the program have continued building their Culture of Philanthropy, and we've provided ongoing coaching and support. While all of the agencies in that program are still on their Culture of Philanthropy journey, we have seen wonderful breakthrough results.

Guidepost

Fundraising That Feels Like Magic

How can building a Culture of Philanthropy feel like making magic? What would it take to have funding magically appear in your organization? Consider this story that a development friend told me.

She worked for a large museum that had just embarked upon a $75 million capital campaign. As part of the training, the development department presented the organizational story to more than 500 staff as to why it was so critical to fund the museum campaign. These staff included guards, porters, the curator, program and frontline ticketing staff. It really paid off, as you'll see.

Toward the end of the campaign, they were baffled as to why one of their community leaders, a famous philanthropist in their city, had been unresponsive to requests for a meeting. One day, the mother and granddaughter of this gentleman came to visit the museum. A savvy ticketer at the membership desk noted their names and alerted a nearby porter, who ran up to development to tell them that the family of this philanthropist was in the house.

Those family members got the tour of their lives! Programs worked with exhibits to release the best of the on-floor explainers to engage the two. They received a tour behind the theater as well as the planetarium. They went to visit the curators, who were restoring an old clock. You get the picture.

The very next day, my friend was sitting with the president at their usual morning meeting. They got a call from the philanthropist's executive assistant, who asked, "On your board, what is the largest category for giving?"

"A million and up," they replied.

By the next week, they received a check from this family in the amount of $2 million.

So, what was the magic that had this $2 million fall from the sky? In fact, there was no magic in this. There was a cohesive culture—interdepartmental intention, planning, training and multiple conversations. Notice that this would not have happened if all of these individuals had not been trained.

- The development team was responsible for training staff in sharing the essential story of the museum.
- The front desk (the ticketer) had the wherewithal to know who was coming in the door.
- The porter readily went to development to share the news of the philanthropist's family arrival.
- The curator played an important role by including the family in the day's activities.
- And, most importantly, they saw themselves as a team, not separate silos. They all had value, and they all owned their responsibility.

Lastly, did you notice the question that the philanthropist's office asked? They wanted to know what the largest category of giving was for the board. If their board's highest level of giving had been $1,000, then perhaps the philanthropist would have given $2,000 instead of $2 million! The museum's board had to be actively seeking stretch gifts.

While this story is about a very wealthy Major Donor, the fact is that, if you have your team trained well, everyone who walks in the door should be championed like a Major Donor. They should be listened to, appreciated, respected and honored. Having this as an organizational framework and commitment will lead to resources that you can't even imagine. As Lynne Twist says, *"What you appreciate, appreciates."*

Successful fundraising comes from having every volunteer and professional member of your team trained and aware of how important a role they have in supporting your development team. Now you know—even if it feels like magic, it was the integration of their development team through the fabric of the museum that led to this donation, and the same integration can give your organization many similar success stories.

While we will look at roles in this section, first and foremost, there has to be an agreed-upon leader for this change. That leader has to have the authority within the agency and the support of the team members to take on this leadership role. The leader has to embrace the idea that everyone has a role in development. It is also important that there be ownership by all the other agency team leaders (development, program staff, board, executive team, and volunteer coordinators.)

As you look through the following chapters, you might be inclined to just read the chapter that has your job title.

Don't.

Just like your nonprofit is made up a of an array of people with diverse skills that combine to create the tapestry that is the organization, so too do individual roles weave together in ways that need to be understood. It is vital to the steps outlined in this book that you move through each section, regardless of whether or not you hold the particular title. Understanding each arena is critical to sustainable change.

For example, based on the size of your agency, you may be responsible for helping make the case for support, even if you aren't the development professional. Or you may be a program director and share a story of impact or a Mission Moment with marketing or development staff to distribute more broadly. I've arranged the chapters by typical roles, understanding that different sized agencies divide tasks differently. Don't let this be a deterrent to learning more about what is involved in other roles. When you learn what others are doing, there's an opportunity to support their success by sharing your insights. Remember Point of Possibility 2: Everyone Shares Some Responsibility for a Culture of Philanthropy.

When you learn about the various roles and tasks involved, you'll be better poised to fully own what it will take to make this culture change a success—and maintain that success in many situations.

We will examine how each role within your organization can embrace a Culture of Philanthropy, whether in a strong and healthy economy or during a major economic depression or a recession.

Chapter 11

A Dream Development Team

A High-Functioning Structure to Support a Culture of Philanthropy

When you shift your conversations and explore the greatness of your team members, you're likely to become a person who creates opportunities for their strength to show up on the job.

—JOHN YOKOYAMA, *WHEN FISH FLY*

Let's talk about development department setup and hiring. If you're reading this book, it's likely that you are part of an organization, and most likely, there's already a development effort, if not a development department. If you're a small agency, it's probably a smaller department—or you might be so small that you don't have any staff at all that are 100 percent dedicated to fundraising. If you're part of a larger agency, you might have a larger department with multiple roles. I recognize that there's a broad variety of circumstances among the readers of this book. I've run into a number of larger social service agencies that have relied on state and federal grants for years. While they might have a larger budget, many do not have an individual giving program. There might simply be a part-time grant writer, or a consultant with experience writing large state and federal grants.

Regardless of your agency's size, if you're intent on having a Culture of Philanthropy, it makes sense to examine, and perhaps recreate, the framework of your development team—which includes staff (the development department) as well as board and other volunteers. The Structure laid out in this chapter is one that is *ideal*. If you don't have the resources to build this sort of ideal development team, you will need to be creative. Map out the various tasks required to do the work you are committed to; identify what positions you have or can afford to have. Then, start identifying roles that you do not have the resources to hire, and imagine how board members and volunteers could begin to fulfill those responsibilities.

Take a few minutes to complete this exercise.

Exercise

Create a High-Functioning Development Team

Begin by filling out this form:

What are the financial needs of your agency annually? $___________

How much needs to be raised annually (beyond state and federal grants and any fee for service)? $___________

Are these numbers based on history? (Y/N) _____

Does this amount cover full implementation of your program? (Y/N) _____

If a higher number is needed to fully serve your clients, write that number here. $___________

What was raised last year? $___________

Is this year different for any reason? (Y/N) _____

If yes, note why _______________________.

____

How was last year's money raised? (Give the breakdown. For example, individual donor work, grants, direct mail, etc.) _____________________

____

What was the staff and board development team configuration? ____________________________

____

What would be the ideal staff and board development team configuration? ____________

____

Now, take a piece of paper and sketch it out. Make a flow chart. It should be something that looks like this, but include your idealized team.

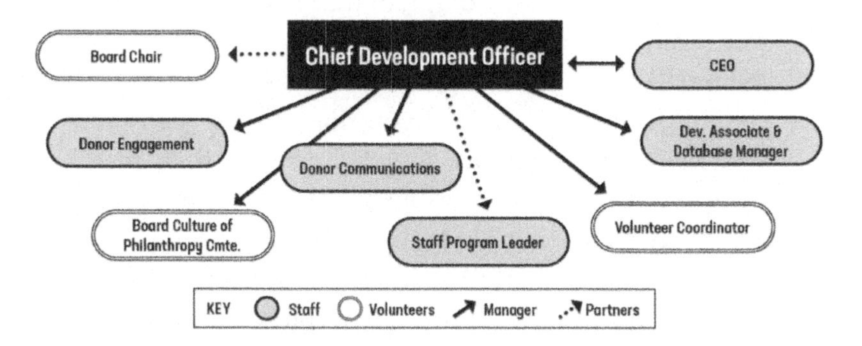

11-1 Development Team Flow Chart
(Laurie Herrick, Rainmaker Consulting)

Let's look now at the different roles and how they might work together. In this scenario, the top development position is Chief Development Officer, because we want to be sure that the highest position development person sits on the organization's executive management team. If your agency is too small for Chiefs, Development Director might be the proper name.

I've made two-way arrows between the Chief Development Officer (CDO) and the CEO because there should be a two-way management Structure here. The CEO should be working very closely with the CDO, and the CEO should support the CDO in his or her goals, including oversite of a detailed Major Donor Portfolio. Likewise, the CDO should be supporting the CEO in her or his Major Donor Portfolio goals. They should partner around goals and individual strategies in weekly meetings. There should be a strong-yet-comfortable accountability Structure in place. This dynamic is an important distinction of a Culture of Philanthropy. The CDO also has a fair amount of management of an entire team of development professionals and volunteers.

You'll notice in the diagram that I've intentionally put some volunteer roles in here. Most likely, given the goals that your organization has, one person cannot do it all alone, and you may not be ready to add new staff positions. Not to mention that, in a culture with a heightened awareness of abundance, you likely have community members who would love to support your work! Whether you are staffed with paid positions, operate on an all-volunteer basis, or work with a mix of both, you'll need to make sure that every role is committed to creating the same culture. Every role should be factored into that commitment, and each role contributes to the goal—unified momentum toward change.

If you're leading the development effort, you are the director of a metaphorical orchestra. Each of your team members has a role, and your job is to help them find the one that makes their heart sing. Inspire them to find their part, and help carry the tune toward a successful, resource-full, harmonizing agency.

Each of the different roles within an agency has the potential to either build and boost a Culture of Philanthropy or get in the way. Within each role I hope that you'll see potential for strengthening and reinforcing your vision. It's the way that you can roll out Point of Possibility 2: Everyone Shares Some Responsibility for a Culture of Philanthropy.

New ways of thinking can be challenging, and defining team roles inside a Culture of Philanthropy Plan is no different. I created a chart to get you started. Remember, Culture of Philanthropy work is about everyone, and the chart includes activities for nearly every role in your agency. Download it from the *Choose Abundance* Book Hub, at www.ChooseAbundanceBook.com. The chart illustrates the vast number of tasks involved in each step of donor engagement. You might use this chart with your culture change team or a board Culture of Philanthropy Committee.

Chapter 12

The Executive Director/CEO

The Critical Role of Leadership: How to Inspire and Drive an Organization-Wide Culture of Philanthropy

Anyone who claims to be a leader must speak like a leader.
That means speaking with integrity and truth.

—KAMALA HARRIS

As the Chief Executive of your agency, you have a tremendous responsibility in leading the Culture of Philanthropy charge. At the same time, it is a wonderful opportunity. Let's focus on the responsibility, first. And in case you are not the Executive Director, read on. Remember, leadership lives at every level of the organization.

If you want an organization-wide Culture of Philanthropy, you have to be willing to walk the talk. This means that you have to show up at trainings, reinforcing your commitment to your desired culture change. You have to be open to learning.

Dr. Carol Dweck, a highly influential American psychologist and professor at Stanford University, suggests that we have belief systems that can either limit or empower our success. Forefront in her work is the model of the Growth Mindset and the Fixed Mindset. The idea is that if you have a Growth Mindset, you are open to learning and you see that you have potential to change and develop as a human being. If you have a Fixed Mindset, you see yourself in a particular way. *I am as I am, and I'm not going to change.* Your belief that you aren't going to change will keep you in a state of not growing.

A powerful distinction she makes is that *we have choice about which mindset we take on.* If you adopt a Growth Mindset as a leader, you are open to seeing your blind spots. You embrace mistakes as opportunities for growth, and you inspire learning in others. If, by contrast, you shy away from anything that makes you feel uncomfortable, it is not likely that you will be able to move and inspire others to take the leap into anything that has them feel vulnerable.

Vulnerability is core to having a Growth Mindset. In fact, some people shy away from a Growth Mindset because it requires a willingness to be open. Some of us have been taught that to be a leader we have to be all-knowing and always confident. Vulnerability is not part of the 1950s business leadership model. However, as a leader seeking a radical step forward for your agency, you have a responsibility to model Behaviors that will allow for personal and organizational transformation. And transformation is not for the person seeking an easy way out. For those seeing an organizational breakthrough, personal transformation is the most effective path to getting there.

Let's not step over that Dr. Dweck says we *can choose* to adopt either a Growth or Fixed Mindset. We may lean toward one or another, but we have a choice. Similarly, we control whether we choose a scarcity, fear-based mindset, or one of abundance.

So how does a leader step up and into this type of transformational leadership? It starts with self-awareness. Listen to your inner narrative and notice when you have a tendency to resort to a scarcity mindset. When you go there, jot down your thoughts. Sometimes, seeing them in writing is enough to distinguish them from your higher vision, and you can more readily choose what you are more deeply committed to.

If your scarcity monologue feels overwhelming, it's time to share it with your Committed Listener. As described in the scripted sample conversation with your Committed Listener (Chapter 9), share about your fears and scarcity thinking with someone who will hear you but not take it on as a truth (it is just your mind's rather disempowering opinion). Talk it out until you get to a place where you see the opportunity to break through and can focus on what is possible within the framework of a Culture of Philanthropy.

Once scarcity thinking stops having a hold on you, you have a teaching moment. You can share your process of shifting from a scarcity to an abundance mindset. While this may feel vulnerable, it is a powerful way to show your commitment to growth and learning, and it shows your willingness to stretch yourself, something that you are inevitably asking others to do. If you are not used to sharing this type of thing with your colleagues, start with your Culture of Philanthropy Task Force. By showing your commitment to growth, you will be encouraging them to do the same.

Guidepost

Making Room for Abundance Thinking in a Sea of Scarcity

Beth Spong

Over the last fifteen years, I've worked with a number of smaller social change organizations doing extraordinary grassroots work. One was working with domestic violence, another with mothers in prisons, another on reproductive justice, and a fourth focusing on providing support for mothers experiencing postpartum depression. Each of these organizations was doing brilliant work addressing the root causes of social injustice. Yet all of them were doing it on shoestring budgets.

One day, I was working with one of the Executive Directors, and I asked her about her inspired vision for the organization. I wanted to hear how her words would resonate for donors and potential partners in our community. Before long, she was expressing her frustration with our society and our community. I tried to steer her back to her vision. The conversation once again went south. I could feel her pain, but I wanted to hear her talk about what was possible.

After a while, I came to see that many grassroots social justice organizations are entrenched in a culture of being against something. Being against racism, against sexism, against poverty, and against the "machine" of our society that perpetuates injustice and racist, sexist, homophobic practices. I fully support being against these "isms." And, when you see your role as railing against the dominant culture, you become expert at articulating what you are *against*, rather than what you are *for*.

There is an unspoken agreement in many social justice organizations that the dominant culture and institutions are "bad." Scarcity beliefs take it further on that trajectory.

- People with money (those with the most influence over the culture) are bad.
- Money itself is bad or corrupt.
- People and institutions with money are holding the "isms" in place. They are the enemy.

From inside this scarcity mindset, it can appear that taking the righteous route means remaining on the side of justice and poverty. Not having sufficient resources becomes an act of solidarity with the marginalized people or groups these nonprofits seek to help. This scarcity mindset often keeps causes and organizations in poverty and prevents them from successfully achieving their missions.

A big part of our work is encouraging groups to claim their big vision—what they are for and what they believe is possible. This means having them recognize that their words are indicators of where they are headed (their Default Future). The first step is self-awareness of the degree to which you have a scarcity mindset and use scarcity "against something" language. This is deeply personal work, but it is necessary. And it is a game changer.

> I was once asked why I don't participate in anti-war demonstrations. I said that I will never do that, but as soon as you have a pro-peace rally, I'll be there. —Mother Teresa

To shift our organizations, leaders need to first recognize their own scarcity thinking, and then shift from being against something to being for something. Then, and only then, there is a newfound capacity to shift from what is impossible to what is possible. Once you begin to articulate what is possible, you start to see the abundance surrounding your agency. Your language will attract more people who support what you stand for. You will discover partners, who you may previously have thought to be the enemy, who will share their resources to align with your inspired vision.

This is the moment of breakthrough.

The Importance and Influence of Top Leadership

As the top executive, you need to be self-aware and recognize when you're caught up in a scarcity moment.

Remember:

Scarcity is pushing back against your intentions to build a Culture of Philanthropy. Scarcity is likely showing up for your staff as frequently as it shows up for you! Every time that we call it out and name it, its hold on us loosens. It doesn't make you small to admit that scarcity has crept in. In fact, it makes you stronger to name it and slay it!

We have to ground ourselves before we can positively impact others. Starting with the Hearts & Minds, you can either breathe possibility and abundance or fear and smallness into your organization. If you make a mistake and squelch someone's possibility with your own scarcity thinking, clean it up, which we later discuss how to do.

One additional responsibility you have as the top executive leader is to be constantly identifying Behaviors, Structures and Hearts & Minds (mindset) within your organization that do not currently align with your vision of a Culture of Philanthropy. Whenever you embark on any long-range planning, be certain that all proposed changes are checked against your Culture of Philanthropy Plan.

Culture is a construct. It is part of the internal architecture of your agency. You get to utilize your authority to build it, reinforce it and protect it. I've heard of culture within a business described as the personality of the CEO. While I think it is more complex than that, I think it is worth considering. To what degree does your personality support, advance or diminish a Culture of Philanthropy? As a leader, you have a say in what sort of culture will exist. Stepping back for a new perspective, use the Hearts & Minds, the Structures and the Behaviors as a lens for your organization.

I worked with an organization that had a person in the C Suite who established a culture of fear and distrust through his behavior. This was done by talking about people in derogatory ways behind their backs. He established an "in crowd" and an "out crowd." In meetings, he could be lovely, articulate and seemingly respectful. Afterward, he would privately exert power over people who were not present by revealing his perception of their shortcomings. It was petty and quite toxic. The CEO saw it but was unwilling to name it or discuss it. In fact, she promoted him.

As an outside consultant, I observed the degree to which this leadership trait impacted the whole organization. It was not a safe space for people to ask for what they needed to do their jobs well. They didn't feel empowered, and throughout the agency, there was distrust of the leadership. Their Indeed Company Review reflected the environment.

Brené Brown talks about the different types of power as a fundamental way to better understand leadership. The main distinction in different types of power is between power *over* and power *with*. Leaders who believe that power is finite and scarce resort to power *over*. Leaders who exhibit power over, utilize manipulation, shaming and control. It is driven by fear (scarcity). By contrast, leaders who use power *with*, exude trust, empowerment and partnerships. Leaders who use power *with* are coming from possibility, the opposite of fear.

Brené also shares in some of her podcasts about her business model, where the values have aligned corollary behaviors. For example, an organization that has a value of transparency has a commitment that "the meeting happens *in* the meeting, not *after* the meeting." This means that you don't say what you think afterward privately to someone. You share what you think in the meeting itself, even if you have doubts or disagree.

In my story above, the organization had a top-down, power-over dominant culture. While they would hire consultants to try to bring about positive culture change, the unwillingness to name the dysfunctional culture of shame, gossip and control kept it in place. There was no possibility of building a Culture of Philanthropy when we could not discuss the dominating culture.

You may want to examine your existing culture if you find yourself spinning your wheels. Is there a culture of racism, classism, ableism, sexism or homophobia? How about distrust, a lack of transparency, or sexual harassment? If there are toxic cultural norms, you might have bigger institutional issues that need to be addressed.

Consider this:

> The culture of any organization is shaped by the worst behaviors the leaders are willing to tolerate.
>
> —Steve Gruenert and Todd Whitaker

Do not step over the inappropriate bad behaviors that may be prevalent in your agency.

Insights from the Field

Affirmations and Appreciations from the Executive Director

(courtesy of Zemo Trevathan)

Everyone has their own leadership style, and affirming when someone gets it right will get you far in building a Culture of Philanthropy. The first reason is that acknowledging someone is a generous thing to do; it is aligned with abundance and not aligned with scarcity.

The single most critical type of conversation we need to have for a culture to stay healthy and productive, at least in terms of frequency, is the conversation we have with someone else to let them know that they are seen and appreciated.

Research by the Gottmans at the University of Washington has quantified this frequency: for a relationship to stay healthy (gottman.com/blog/the-magic-relationship-ratio-according-science/): It takes five times as many "positive" conversations as "withdrawals" (requests, criticisms, disagreements). Now, the specific context for this research was personal relationships, but there's plenty of experience to suggest that ratio holds true in any partnership-oriented relationship between people, such as being teammates within an organization.

Your mandate for sustaining a healthy, productive, philanthropic culture: make sure you give people strokes (thank-yous, appreciations, affirmations, acknowledgments, smiles, warmth) five times as often as you ask for something or hit them with something that is perceived by them as an energy drain. Following are two simple pointers about how to do that skillfully.

Pointer One

Affirmations must be sincere to be meaningful or impactful. Don't ever affirm or thank someone because you think you have to, or because you're about to give them some critical feedback and you think they need the boost of a "positive" first. Affirmations work when you are telling the truth.

Don't generalize. Affirmations are most effective the more specific they are, so the recipient knows that you were actually paying attention, and that the appreciation you're offering is meant for them specifically. Instead of saying, "Thanks for all the help on that project last week," try saying, "I noticed you stayed long hours a couple different evenings to help us get that project done last week. That kind of extra effort really makes a difference."

Pointer Two

Link the behavior you noticed (or the quality of the person you're noticing) specifically to the positive impact that it had. This could be in the form of positive feelings you had as a result of their efforts (personal impact on you). Or it could be in the form of the difference their contribution made to the company, to the vision, to the future.

Phrase it like this: "You staying late those couple afternoons helped make the difference in getting that grant submitted on time. You just helped make the future of our organization brighter, and I appreciate it. Thank you."

Or, "Knowing that you have done that and would do it again gives me a deep sense of being partnered and supported. I feel so much more at peace as a result of your commitment to going the extra mile. Thank you."

Do this five times as often as you criticize, disagree or ask for something!

Exercise

Affirmation Appreciation

Zemo Trevathan

(The Aligned Team. http://www.thealignedteam.com)

Make a list of people who you admire, people who have made a difference to you or your organization. Think about both people whose character or qualities make a difference and anyone whose actions or behavior have made a positive difference recently.

For each person on the list, ask yourself, "Have I fully affirmed/appreciated them for this quality/action? Have I expressed the difference it makes (to either me or the organization)?"

If there are any people on your list you have not thanked (or not thanked recently), commit to delivering an affirmation, and give yourself a "by when" for each of these conversations.

Notice if you have a tendency to be stingy about appreciating people. If you do, what is that about? Does it make you feel small to have others look good? Or does it make you feel important if you keep others small? If so, consider that it takes a bighearted, generous person to pass out authentic appreciation to peers, employees, family and our leaders.

If you aren't in the habit of it already, make it a point to specifically appreciate someone on your team. Put it in your daily to-do list. Watch for moments of strong team leadership, or kindness, or insightfulness. If you are mindful and appreciative of how your staff and board are being generous, coming from a place of abundance, or if they are advancing your Culture of Philanthropy, it will do much to ignite the culture change you desire. It will also be a good source of inspiration and possibility for you!

Tied closely to affirmations is listening closely to members of staff and board who seem burned out. Does your staff get sufficient breaks? Do they have time to take care of themselves and their families? Take the time (again, a sign of generosity) to listen to your team. Don't assume or impose what would be good for you. Hear what would be *great* for them. Be creative about trying to get them what they need. Your aim is to discover what they need to be able to be their best selves and be able to partner with you to fulfill your mission.

Customer Service Is Part of a Culture of Philanthropy

It may seem that a section on customer service is coming from left field. Believe me, it isn't. Customer service is how your organization shows up to the public. It is the *experience* that your clients, your stakeholders and your neighbors have when they interact with your staff. Customer service is a great indicator of organizational culture. As you read in the story about the museum, how people are greeted when they call your agency or walk in the door has impact.

I belong to a YMCA. When I walk in the door, sleepy-eyed, at 5:45 in the morning, Milly, the receptionist, says good morning to me! She knows my name. She knows everyone's name! And she's lovely. She asks how I am. If it's a Friday, we know it when we walk in the door because she's dressed up in bright colors and has fun dance music on. As soon as I arrive there, I feel like I've arrived home. It feels great.

She does a similar thing when I'm leaving. She calls everyone sweetheart and tells us to have a wonderful day.

Let's think about businesses that we sometimes call for customer service. First of all, a robot-voiced answering machine is rarely something memorable—at least not in a good way! By contrast, what about those businesses or organizations that you call and a person answers the phone? When you tell them your name, they listen, they make you feel comfortable and they empathize with you. They feel your pain, and they want to help. There's a big difference there.

As an Executive Director, the higher degree to which your team makes noteworthy, positive experiences for people coming to your place of business, the more likely those people are to support you. By contrast, if you have staff that are abrupt, if they are condescending to clients, if they try to pretend that no one walked in the door, or if they are other than gracious to everyone, it will be in the way of your success. As you evaluate how well your organization does in customer service, be sure to look at all three aspects of the Wheel of Change:

Structure

- If someone calls your agency, does a person answer, or do they get an answering machine? What happens when someone comes in the door? Is there a receptionist there that greets and welcomes people?
- Is the person who answers the phone or greets someone as they come in the door able to make decisions, or are they there strictly so that other staff are not "bothered"? Is there a way to have that frontline person empowered to handle key functions to make it a positive and efficient experience for the "customer"?
- Is it easy for donors to get answers to questions about their contributions? If someone wants something fixed on their donor record, is it easy to do? Does this type of request typically get lost?
- Is it easy to give online? How many steps does it take to complete making a contribution? I encourage you to test this.

As recently as yesterday, I tried three times to give to an organization, and it failed each time. One has to be pretty committed to make a gift happen when they enter all of their personal contact information three times, and each time a whirling icon comes up and the transaction never completes.

- Do phone calls get answered quickly? Do thank-you notes go out quickly?
- If you have multiple programs at your agency, are records easily accessible in each area, or do members/participants have to refill similar forms for their membership, or to give, enroll in your services, or to buy tickets?

Behavior

- Do the people who answer the phone have the resources they need to get answers to someone calling?
- Are they trained to greet people and give their full attention to anyone who calls on the phone or walks in the door, or is it tolerated that they ignore people when they arrive?
- Are they cheerful and welcoming?

Hearts & Minds

- Do the frontline people have great attitudes?
- Do you have van drivers, people who work with vendors, teachers, or professionals who interact with your members/participants or their family members?
- Are they trained on how to act kindly?
- Are they given breaks so that they can rejuvenate?

I hope you'll see that there are myriad ways you can have people feel great or frustrated as soon as they approach your organization. Look at the best (for-profit) businesses you know, and see what you can borrow from them to help visitors, clients, donors, board members and anyone who interacts with your agency have a powerful experience. I can't help but think of our local Apple store. From the second you approach the store, they're deeply committed to you having an amazing experience. What if our not-for-profit frontline staff were as committed to creating a memorable and lovely experience?

Getting Good at Fundraising if You Aren't Already

Some Executive Directors, and you may be one of them, didn't come to their job with experience in fundraising. In fact, you may, in the back of your mind, believe that fundraising is a distraction from your more important work. If you're a reluctant fundraiser, I can't blame you. Fundraising gets a bad rap. With so many dominating narratives about arm twisting and the evils of money, it's no surprise.

I'd like to help you reframe what fundraising is and why it's such an honorable and meaningful career. And, as the head of an organization, your leadership in development matters profoundly. Your Hearts & Minds has the potential to advance or tank your agency. Seriously.

Warning! This part might not be easy. But I invite you, as a leader of your organization, to dig deep and explore. This is your Growth Mindset opportunity! (Incidentally, this process can be useful for board members and staff, as well.)

In our society, talking about money is taboo. It's tabooer (yes, that's a word!) than just about anything! You would never walk up to a stranger—and certainly not a friend—and ask how much savings they had, or how much money they made, of if they had inherited wealth. There are a few reasons that the topic is so off-limits. One reason is that we have so many different negative conversations in our culture about money.

Certainly, if we are all judging ourselves and each other about how much we have or don't have, it would follow that it could provoke a reluctance to ask people for money. Also, a lot of us inherited very personal baggage around money. When we start to talk about fundraising, it can bring up all sorts of other things, like our personal issues with money, which we can be ashamed of or embarrassed about.

Perhaps we had expectations that we would earn a certain amount of money, or that we would live a particular lifestyle. Maybe we have wealth that we inherited that we feel we don't deserve. Maybe we feel that we deserved money that we did not receive. All of this shame and embarrassment can get in the way of our ability to talk freely about money, and, ultimately, our ability to fundraise.

Exercise

This is a private sort of exercise. While you may decide to share it with others at some point, write it for yourself and be totally authentic. Put your phone or computer out of sight. Set aside a half hour to do this, and don't let yourself get up for that whole half hour. Hold yourself to a rigorous self-chat where you reflect and write down the internal conversations that you have about money that are unproductive.

1. Think about your childhood, about growing up, and think about your lasting attitudes and opinions about money. Do you have thoughts about people who have money? What are they?

____

____

____

2. Do you have thoughts and opinions about people who don't have a lot of money?

____

____

____

3. Do these interpretations come with judgment and meaning?

____

____

____

4. What expectations did you have of yourself earning money?

____

____

____

5. Did you achieve what you wanted?

____

____

____

6. Do you feel fairly compensated for your work?

____

____

____

7. Do you sometimes feel badly about your economic class? Why? What are your thoughts about this?

____

____

____

8. Do you have debt or financial matters that you're embarrassed or ashamed about? What are they? Go ahead and write them down.

____

____

____

9. How do you feel about larger donors? Do you feel glad to have them around your agency? Why or why not?

____

____

____

10. Do you like talking to them? Why or why not?

____

____

____

11. Do you like calling them? Does it make you nervous?

____

____

____

12. Is it easy to prioritize Major Donor work? If you're avoiding it, why?

____

____

____

Dealing with personal money issues is not easy. While this exercise is not going to erase years of frustration, it can be very powerful. I, too, used to have some of these feelings. And I experienced firsthand that when you start to write down and acknowledge your thoughts and feelings of scarcity about money and resources (versus ignoring them or stifling them), you can then start from scratch and create a new framework; you can choose a framework steeped in abundance thinking.

Think back to Chapter 5, where we discussed the Default Future. If you notice and observe in yourself that you have attitudes and feelings of scarcity about resources, you can see how that might influence your performance. For example, if in the preceding writing exercise, you noticed that you truly think (or have an underlying suppressed opinion) that fundraising is about arm twisting, or that people with money are stingy, or that funders will take over your organization if they are involved, then it's fairly evident that what would follow, your Default Future, would be to have an aversion to fundraising. Your actions (or lack thereof) would follow. The end result would be that you're unsuccessful in it, and your agency is unsuccessful, as well.

As with any task, if your attitude isn't great about fundraising (Hearts & Minds), and if you don't take the actions (the Behavior), and you don't follow a Structure (the third element in the Wheel of Change), you won't complete the job. Or, at best, you'll complete it poorly.

As the leader of an organization, if you find in this exercise that you have a tremendous amount of baggage, including strong feelings and opinions based in fear and scarcity thinking, you might be doing more damage than you think. It's possible that your mindset is undermining your leadership, and it's getting in the way of your agency achieving its mission.

Considering this possibility is difficult, I know. But the only way out of it is to confront it. It's exactly like noticing the scarcity thinking that we did in the exercises earlier in this book. Once you see it, it's like noticing the dirty fishbowl that you're living in. Only when you notice that it's murky do you have a chance to clean it up!

If you're realizing at this point that, in fact, there is a prevailing mindset of scarcity in your agency, it's critical that you confront it, talk about it and work through it. Attempting to build a Culture of Philanthropy on top of this culture is an exercise in frustration. It will fail. A classic problem that I've seen multiple times over the years is executive leaders having a fear of fundraising and supporting a prevailing organizational mindset of scarcity (by surrounding themselves with fundraising naysayers like themselves). Then, they hire a development professional to solve their funding woes.

I know that I've said this in a few different ways so far in this book. I want to be clear. I've seen this development mistake more frequently than just about any other. Hiring someone to do the job that no one respects will not work out. They won't have the resources they need to do their job. They won't get support from the Executive Director or the board. They will be essentially left alone to do the heavy lifting. Very often, they won't even be included in leadership meetings. This means that they won't be on top of the programmatic opportunities that donors would want to invest in.

In some cases, I've even seen examples where the Executive Director won't allow the development professional to talk directly to donors. This isn't just my experience. The Haas/Compass Point study called "Underdeveloped" that came out in 2013 shows this sort of thing happening over and over across North America. While many years have passed since that study came out, my experience shows that the issues remain the same.

Changing Your Perspectives

So, the question is, how do you turn something like that around? This is a case where the Hearts & Minds needs to be addressed first, and then the chances that the Behaviors and Structures will fall into place increase substantially. You have to first acknowledge what your Default Future is and be willing to say, "Hell No!" You have to recognize that you have been more committed to listening to an old, worn-out, and disempowering narrative, and that old narrative is holding you back. You have the chance now, in a simple declaration, to outgrow it.

This new narrative could create a different future for you and for your agency. Once you acknowledge the disempowering narrative about money, if you're ready to move forward, getting training is the easy part. There may be moments where the old narrative haunts you, but setting up a reminder of what your higher commitment is will help bring you back on track.

It is exciting when someone genuinely asks the question, "Am I helping or hindering a Culture of Philanthropy?" That takes bravery and true leadership to authentically explore that query.

Finding abundance isn't limited to tending to our fears and issues around money and fundraising. Recognizing our views on humanity is also important. For example, if you feel that people are good and generous, that gives you a perspective that's useful in donor relations. You assume the best in people; that they want the same world you do, one that works for everyone, with no exceptions.

Notice if you have opinions about particular donors. *Should* that person give more? As soon as you hear yourself say or think the word *should,* you know that you have opinions or attitudes about their capacity. On the other hand, do you make judgments like "that person could never give"? Once again, notice where your opinion might not empower you or your supporter. I use *empower* intentionally. It is empowering to be thought of as someone who has something to contribute. It's disempowering to be thought of as someone who has nothing to contribute.

If you don't see a lot of evidence that people are generous, seek this information out. Remember that drama sells, which is why there's so much of it in the news. The great news is that this doesn't mean that this is the only thing happening in the world. While there's plenty of bad news, there are also outstanding acts of generosity.

Your job as the leader of the agency is to find these bright spots and share them with your team. Seek out news and articles that confirm the kindness and the greatness of humans. Read *Yes!* magazine, or blogs such as Seth Godin's, or David Byrne's blog, *Reasons to Be Cheerful.*

If you aspire to have an agency that has an abundance of resources, you need to be generating possibility on a daily basis. This may seem especially daunting if you work in a field that addresses some of the most negative challenges that affect our society. It's also quite daunting if you're having to make staff cutbacks due to an economic downturn, or if you're suffering personal challenges.

Even if you aren't typically in a scarcity mindset, we all fall into it at some point. When you do have these feelings, find someone who will listen to you, allow you to express your fears and your thoughts or attitudes and just hear you and not buy in to your narrative. This would be a good time to go to your Committed Listener, if you have one. We all have moments when we need support in rising above the fear and advancing toward our highest vision.

Remember that we get to make up what interpretation we adopt. Choose an interpretation that empowers you, your team and your organization's mission, and then move forward creating a more powerful conversation for possibility. Then start articulating and repeating this narrative. Once again, below is something from Seth Godin, author of eighteen books and an award-winning blogger on marketing and culture. This is the only way for you, as a leader, to be the source, to truly generate a new, resource-full future for your agency.

Insights from the Field

The Repetition of Stories

by Seth Godin

(https://seths.blog/2019/01/the-repetition-of-stories)

It's not difficult to maintain a grey cloud and a sullen outlook. The event is long over, but the story remains.

A proven approach is to keep repeating the narrative that led us ever deeper into this memory hole. As with a missing tooth, we probe that spot, over and over, examining it from all angles, again and again, in order to keep the story fresh.

On the other hand, forgotten stories have little power.

And the same approach works for a feeling of optimism and possibility. What happens to us matters a great deal, but even more powerful are the stories we repeat about what happened. Repeating stories (to ourselves and others) about good fortune and generosity makes those stories more powerful...and it manifests them.

Reframing Philanthropy: People's Generosity

If you or your team (either staff or board members) have been reluctant fundraisers, I invite you to consider this—fundraising is simply enrolling people in the possibility that you see your organization addressing. Do you work for an environmental organization? Then fundraising for your agency is about gaining buy-in for a pristine, bountiful and more just planet. Do you work in a school or learning institution? People who give to your organization believe in an enlightened, educated and informed community. Do you work with populations that are discriminated against due to race, ability, gender, gender identification or orientation? People who invest in your work are committed to social justice.

When you ask someone to give to your agency, you are inviting and allowing them to partner with you and advance your work. You are letting them join a team of people who are advancing justice, environmentalism, health or education. For you to accomplish your organizational goals, you need these partners. Asking them to partner with you is a gift to them. It's giving them a way to make an impact in the world. And it's a gift to you, giving you the opportunity to fulfill the mission, or at least get closer to fulfilling it.

I believe deeply that everyone has something to contribute to the world. When you find someone who is committed to your cause, you get to discover what they have in abundance that they want to contribute. You may have approached this individual because you believe they have money in abundance, but someone who is committed to your cause likely has ideas and opinions about how to make the biggest impact. They may have other things like skills, or connections or influence that would come in handy. Or they might have access to something that your organization needs, like furniture, or computers, a particular skill or a rental space.

I understand that some of my readers may now be thinking, *Yeah, and some of those ideas those funders have are misguided, and they have no idea what it is like to run this agency!* Of course, you're correct. Some people will come to you with crazy ideas. Some will be pushy and feel like if they give, you have to do what they want. Some will offer to give you something that you simply don't want, like a beat-up couch or outdated computers!

Yes, funders like this exist. Your job is to listen and consider what they have to say. Perhaps there is a brilliant idea, or a skill that you need on your team, or a connection to a community member that you want to make. Equally important is that you state what you need and want, and you don't take advice, material things, or direction that doesn't serve your mission. You have to be direct and kind about this.

While there are some donors who come to an agency with an agenda, or with misguided ideas, I've found that most donors are eager learners who want to help you do your meaningful work.

As you gain comfort with this idea, you will start to see that you and your funders are partners in generating a greater possibility in the world. Once you adopt this perspective, you will be surprised at what comes from viewing supporters through this lens. If you need more help with this, review Chapter 8, Point of Possibility 3: We Build and Maintain Deep Donor Relationships and Partnerships.

How to Create Your Own Portfolio of Major Donors (And Still Do the Rest of Your Job)

Once you get your head, heart and mind in the right space, the rest will follow. Whether you're a new and reluctant fundraiser or a more experienced one, the one action that will move you from beginner to accomplished is building a portfolio of Major Donors. Why? In the sales world, it is said like this—*your best customers are your existing customers.*

To get a new customer is extremely expensive. To keep an existing customer is a great investment, as it will pay off exponentially. That customer will likely increase their buying from you over time, and they will tell their friends about you if their experience is extraordinary. *When you build a customized Major Donor Portfolio, you're committed to partnering in a way that's intent upon providing extraordinary experiences for your donors.*

But wait! What if, as you're reading this, we're in tough economic times? Should you still try to do this now? Yes! At the beginning of Chapter 1, I mentioned the Chinese proverb about planting a tree. While the best time to have planted it was years ago, the second-best time is today. If your agency is in the midst of uncertainty, your very best investment of time and resources is in working with those who are already connected to your agency, deepening those relationships so that they remain loyal. It has the best return on investment (ROI), and it will provide the best net revenue.

Building a Major Donor Portfolio is not the same as periodically connecting with some of the agency's top donors. Disappointingly, many organizations only connect with their funders when they need money. They see the relationship as one-way. This is the donor-as-ATM syndrome. A slightly better organization reaches out to donors randomly and when they think of it. If you want to build a Culture of Philanthropy, you need to build a Major Donor Program where some key staff and perhaps some board members build customized Major Donor Portfolios. It's a very intentional and detailed process. See details on this in Chapter 17.

A key part of the process is having the Structures in place to be successful. One Structure that is often overlooked is the database. Please don't make this mistake. If your organization has existed without a functional fundraising Customer Relationship Management (CRM) database for more than five years, I'll take a leap and say that your organization is being stifled by a mindset of scarcity. Here's what it signals to me:

- Donors are not viewed as important assets.
- Your development staff is not worth investing in.
- Fundraising from individuals is not a focus of your agency.

Your database should not only be a tracker of monetary transactions. It should be a true Customer *Relationship* Management system. It should be the place where multiple people within your agency can track donor connections, communications, family information, desires regarding stewardship and acknowledgments, favorite programs and passions, and next steps. This single tool is a technological necessity for building a Culture of Philanthropy. It will have a significant ROI.

If you invest in a good CRM you are indicating that:

- You are committed to building deep donor relations.
- You care about the people who contribute to your agency.
- You are invested in development and the potential for people surrounding your agency to help realize your mission.

Both Partnering with and Managing Your Development Team

Your development team—whether one or a whole cadre of people—should be your partners. Your job as the top executive is to be certain that your development partners have what they need. This starts with your budget for development. Early in my career, one of my mentors told me that, as the development professional, you should be certain that you have one of the best computers, a CRM that is highly functional, administrative support, a travel and entertainment budget, and professional development. I agree with all of this. You have got to be certain that your development team has what they need to be effective communicators to your donors.

What's in your development budget? I would start by asking your professional development staff what they need. Is their CRM working for them? Be certain that they have the right people, with the right skills, doing data entry. Do they have dedicated staff? People trying to do two tasks, like development and marketing, will be pulled in different directions. Someone being a receptionist and also doing data entry will likely mess things up in the database, or provide poor customer service because they will constantly be interrupted or pulled off-task.

While development budgets vary extensively from one organization to another, here are a few expenses that are often overlooked in the development budget:

- Software training and updating (CRM/database, online marketing tools such as Emma, MailChimp or Constant Contact)
- Professional development for staff and board
- A skilled data-entry person
- Travel budget
- Entertainment expenses (for meals and beverages in donor meetings)
- Donor recognition Structures or online publications like annual reports, impact reports and one-page Donor Offers (especially for capital and other large campaigns)
- Minor donor appreciation items (awards, framed pictures, books, etc.)
- Access to copiers and other office equipment
- Postage
- Marketing and communication expenses to assure high-quality materials, engagement with social media, and so on—including your web page and online giving platform

Meeting weekly with your top development professional is also a way to invest in development as the top executive. It will assure that you are on the same page and that a Culture of Philanthropy is top of mind. You should have a strong development plan that's updated periodically. See the section on creating a development plan in the next chapter on development professionals. As a way to focus on the activity that has the best ROI, you should have weekly strategy meetings with the group of you who have Major Donor Portfolios. See Chapter 17 to learn more about how managers can support those with Major Donor Portfolios.

One distraction to an effective Major Donor Program is the conflict between management responsibilities versus development responsibilities. If you have a Development Director, he or she likely got into that position because they were a good fundraiser. They had success in building relationships, perhaps coordinating events, or maybe they moved up from fundraising administration or volunteer coordination into this role. But once they took on this Development Director job, they acquired a large responsibility managing staff. These staff might be in charge of data entry, grant writing, special events or donor research.

This parallels a classic mistake that frequently occurs in sales. Someone gets good in sales, so they become the sales manager. Their customer portfolio or their territory starts to bomb as soon as they start managing, as it takes too much time away from sales. Management feels like an important job, and an exciting promotion, and doing sales seems passé. If you have someone good at donor relations, promote them to a position of Major Donor Officer. If you need a manager, get a manager. It will be well worth it to focus appropriately.

One organization that I worked with had, over time, hired a series of Development Directors, only to find that each of them would spend much of their time managing staff, finding little time for working with top donors. One after another would be fired for failing to care for the best donors.

Eventually, the Executive Director decided that he would take over the management of the development team. He also maintained his own portfolio of Major Donors. He hired a Major Gifts Officer, who had no other responsibilities than her portfolio. This worked out brilliantly, and to this day, they're having the greatest fundraising success in the history of the agency. He shifted his own organizational responsibilities to more than 50 percent on development. Not every organization can do this, and you will need to be creative to establish the team that serves your plan.

Likewise, the CEO should be receptive to receiving support from the CDO in her or his Major Donor Portfolio goals. They should partner around goals and individual strategies in weekly meetings. There should be a strong yet comfortable accountability Structure in place. Again, more details on this in Chapter 17.

Foundations! Corporations! And Events! Oh My!

There are three different potential fundraising streams that I feel the need to warn you about. I don't want to take these opportunities away from you, just have you be cautious. Each of them seems compelling, but they each have flaws that you should be aware of.

We've talked a little about the role of foundation grants and corporate giving. As the Total Giving chart in Chapter 7 indicates, individual giving accounts for 79 percent of all giving in the United States. Foundations are at a mere 17 percent, and corporate gifts account for only 5 percent of all philanthropic giving. I recognize that there are many of you who depend upon large grants or corporate gifts, and they take a lot of time to prepare for and write. I want to recommend an approach to these income streams.

Large Foundation Grants

If you are in a field that gets state or federal grants, you need to maintain those. They are often a heavy lift of writing and editing. You need someone to do this. If at all possible, have this work done by someone who is not also managing Major Donors. These two tasks require unique skill sets—writing and relationship building are very different animals. Writing takes focused uninterrupted time, and often donor relations require being able to respond quickly to donor questions and incoming phone calls. It has also been my experience that a development professional who has a range of responsibilities, has difficulty focusing on the strategic and methodical work of Major Donor planning and implementation. If you have an existing relationship with one or more foundations, you should have someone maintain those relationships, similar to a Major Donor relationship, but have a grant writer do the work on reports.

Corporate Relations

If you have already had success with corporate sponsors, be sure that someone maintains those relationships. Have a staff or consulting grant writer partner with program staff to report back to the funder, illustrating how the gift made an impact.

Any grant or corporate initiative should be evaluated for its ROI. Consider how much time and human resources are utilized for proposals. What is the likelihood of getting the grant or corporate gift? Do the math to determine how much you spend to get the grant versus the amount of effort that goes into it. Smaller grants often have a worse ROI.

Don't spend a ton of time seeking new grants or corporate gifts. There are two reasons for this. The first is that seeking new grants is prospecting. You likely have individuals who give to your organization that you are not giving any of your attention. Taking care of your existing donors is a significantly better use of your time and resources. Donor engagement and stewardship has a much better ROI.

Secondly, in corporations or foundations, it is likely that you will not have the opportunity to build a relationship. If you have a local business or family foundation where you know the owner or family, then by all means, go for it. But without the relationship of the decision-makers, you are unlikely to be able to build a long-term partnership. Additionally, both foundation and corporate giving strategies change. There is seldom a sense of loyalty to a particular cause as leaders change and giving can shift.

One of the great shortcomings of disproportionately large gifts of any type from a single donor, a foundation or a corporation, is that they do not contribute to you having a diversified portfolio, and this undermines the security of your mission. A single funder can pull an agency off mission and distract you from building a community of supporters surrounding your organization. While it may seem easier to deal with just one person, do not make the mistake of putting all of your eggs in one philanthropic basket. A Culture of Philanthropy does not exist if you have all of your funding from one wealthy individual, a few state and federal grants, or a giant foundation or corporation.

Events

Events should also be evaluated by their ROI. If you are going to have events, their purpose should be clear. Focus them on your mission. Think of the steps of fundraising and be certain that you know which of them you want to be touching on. My suggestion is that you focus on donor engagement and stewardship and be clear if you are hosting a fundraiser or a stewardship event.

Once you get clear of your purpose and strategy, map out the expenses. Be certain to include the labor cost and the intended impact. Volunteer hours need to be included, even if the individuals contribute their time with no expectation of compensation. According to the Foundation Center and Guidestar (Candid) the value of a volunteer hour in the United States is $27.20 (philanthropynewsdigest.org, "Value of Volunteer Time Rose Nearly 7 Percent in 2019," 2021). Why is this important? Because the ROI on volunteers helping you with donor relations and connections is so much more valuable than coordinating logistics for a gala. Events, especially the gala model, typically have a terrible ROI, and they take staff away from donor relations.

How to Inspire Your Board to Build a Culture of Philanthropy

The best thing you can do to inspire your board to build a Culture of Philanthropy is to lead them through a full organizational implementation process as outlined in Part 4 of this book. Second to that, use these approaches:

- **Speak Abundance and Possibility**. Notice your language and attitude about fundraising. Is it coming from a place of scarcity or from abundance? If it's abundance, spread the joy! If not, see what you can do to get a fresh perspective.
- **Start board meetings with a Mission Moment**. It should be a bright spot or time where you saw evidence for the difference that your agency makes. Prepare and practice the story illustrating your relevance. (Seriously, take the time to practice it!) Tell the story using direct quotes, not

generalizing. In other words, share something like this from a program serving adults with developmental disabilities.

Instead of generalizing, saying, "We heard from Robert's mother, and she's really pleased in his progress," try saying, "When I pulled up the van in front of Robert's house, his mother enthusiastically came over to my window and said to me (and she had tears in her eyes), 'Robert used to be so lethargic. Now, every day that he gets to go to your program, he wakes up excited, and when he comes home, he has a story to tell of something he learned. Yesterday, he told me that he loved showing other participants in his program how to do an exercise because he had learned it so well. I can't believe how much he's grown.'"

When you share your Mission Moment with your board, do it wholeheartedly. Encourage them to share your story with their friends and come back and report on it to their board peers. By sharing successes, you give hope and possibility to your board members. In addition, you affirm the wisdom of their decision to be a board member and give you their time and money.

Have your frontline staff help you gather these firsthand stories. This will empower them as well, as they will quickly get in touch with why they do this work. When you ask for their stories, it shows that you respect and understand what they do, and that their stories make a difference with board members and people who are invested in your work.

- **Find a board member to create an active development committee—if it doesn't exist already.** This leader should be inspired and excited about the vision of your organization and understand that fund development can help manifest that into reality. They should either currently understand or be willing to learn about a Culture of Philanthropy. If you want to get really inspired, read about Nancy (Chapter 14), who started a Culture of Philanthropy Committee on her board.

- **Provide training for your board on building a Culture of Philanthropy.** The training could be an in-person or online session, or they could simply read this book together and do the various exercises.
- **Have time devoted to development at every board meeting.** And be sure that it is near the beginning of the meeting, not at the end. Focus less on reporting and more on engaging the board in learning and practicing.
- **If there is reluctance around development at the board level, start with stewardship.** Work with your development staff to set board members up for success. Teach board members the distinctions of stewardship as a tool for funders to see that what they gave, their investment, was well spent. Find creative ways to show people what a difference they made! If you want to learn more about this, read about it in the next chapter.
- **Focus on the talents of your board members.** Match them with the development efforts that work for them. Sit down with board members and find out what they like to do. Do they have a particular skill? Would they be comfortable meeting with donors, getting to know them? Would they want to be part of an ask? What would be fun and inspiring for them? Help them find their development niche. Don't try to force people to do things that don't work for them. Download our chart on distinct roles for board members from our Book Hub at www.ChooseAbundanceBook.com, which will give them a number of choices to consider.
- **Infuse your strategic plan, or your Strategic Planning Process, with a Culture of Philanthropy.** Set goals including board roles in donor engagement and stewardship. (See Chapter 14 for more on the board, or Chapter 16 on Strategic Planning Through the Lens of a Culture of Philanthropy.)
- **Be the visionary of your organization. Make an inspired case for why your organization is worth investing in.**

Organizational Silos—Killers of a Culture of Philanthropy

As an Executive Director, you should be cautious of the dreaded silo. As some agencies grow, they begin to departmentalize into organizational silos. I've seen a number of places where this causes competition of resources and the complete opposite of a Culture of Philanthropy. Eventually, it can become rare that staff interact outside of their silo, and jealousy and resentment can occur. Perhaps one silo brings in a lot of resources because of the nature of their work. Things like ticket sales, earned income or donations may be abundant. Another department might be key to the mission but may depend on the resources generated in another part of the agency.

Imagine being in the cash cow part of the organization—"Why can't we spend the money to enhance our program and make it even better?" Or imagine being the needier department—"We have so few donors! I'm not going to let that other department know about this new one. They'll recruit them and take all our money!" Obviously, these scenarios are full of scarcity thinking. As the Executive Director, your job is to break down those silos, and build strong cross-agency communication Structures.

There are a number of ways that you, as the Executive Director, can help break down silos. Here are a few.

- Have development staff be part of the leadership or "Chiefs" of your agency.
- Provide Culture of Philanthropy training to all staff so they understand that they have a role in development.
- Meet with development every week to form a partnership so that you can help connect people in different departments with development.
- Work with development to create Donor Offers (see next chapter) that will result in different departments understanding the value of development and, inversely, allow development to get to know the programs deeply so they can help channel donors' philanthropy appropriately.

If you're the Executive Director, your Culture of Philanthropy role is to:

- Lead the charge of building a Culture of Philanthropy.
- Make a visionary call to action for your surrounding community to fund your agency.
- Assure that development is at the table of the top organizational conversations.
- Break down silos.
- Empower all staff and board members in finding their niche in a Culture of Philanthropy.

Getting into Action

The following is a pathway to take what you've learned in this chapter and put it into practice. Use this exercise to map out how you can begin to imagine and build an organization-wide Culture of Philanthropy.

Exercise

As the Executive Director, my goals for how a Culture of Philanthropy will impact our organization are (utilizing each of the 5 Points of Possibility):

1. **Culture of Philanthropy Is Integral to Our Mission**

   ____

   ____

   ____

2. **Everyone Shares Some Responsibility for a Culture of Philanthropy**

   ____

   ____

   ____

3. **We Build and Maintain Deep Donor Relationships and Partnerships**

   ____

   ____

   ____

4. **Community Engagement Is What We Do**

   ____

   ____

   ____

5. **We Recognize Every Contribution of Service, Items or Money as an Expression of Philanthropy**

   ____

   ____

   ____

Hearts & Minds

I will address the following areas:

1. ____
2. ____
3. ____
4. ____

Structure

I will address the following areas:

1. ____
2. ____
3. ____
4. ____

Behavior

I will address the following areas:

1. ______________________________

2. ______________________________

3. ______________________________

4. ______________________________

My partnership with development will include:

____

My work with all staff will include:

____

My work with the board will include:

____

I imagine these could be my obstacles:

____

These are my potential blind spots:

____

Chapter 13

Development Staff

Being a Superhero: Actions You Can Take Even if You Aren't in Charge

Abundance is a fact of nature. It is a fundamental law of nature, that there is enough and it is finite. Its finiteness is no threat; it creates a more accurate relationship that commands respect, reverence, and managing those resources with the knowledge that they are precious and in ways that do the most good for the most people.

—LYNNE TWIST

Your Job Title Should Actually Be Chief *Enrollment* Director

If you are a development professional, either in a one-person shop or part of a team, you have an opportunity to lead up and sideways, even if you aren't in charge. You may be in a situation where you are fully empowered to lead this effort, or, more commonly, you may feel frustrated with the resources that are available to make development and a Culture of Philanthropy a success. Either way, this is a moment in your professional career to enact culture change, and culture change takes persistence, wisdom, patience and fortitude. But you are up to it! Let's address some of the obstacles, one by one.

First Things First: Set Priorities and Make Time

Grab a pen and pad of paper, or an equivalent electronic device. Stop and think about your job for a minute. Make a list of all the things that are on your plate.

- Are you in charge of direct mail?
- Do you write grants?
- Do data entry?
- Put on events?

- Do marketing and promotion for events?
- Work with Major Donors?
- Work with the board?
- Do you get pulled into other organizational activities and tasks?
- Are you responsible for certain board functions like getting food for meetings, sending out minutes?
- Are you part of larger agency initiatives like strategic planning, or a capital campaign?
- All of the above?

Write it all down.

I'm well aware that you may be a development department of one, or a department of many. Regardless, it's good to know the parameters of your job, and within that role, what your priorities are.

Now look at that list, and highlight or put a star next to the things that you are responsible for that are consistent with one or more of these:

- Deepen donor relations (get two stars!)
    - Make personal connections and get to know Major Donors and their passions and preferred type of engagement through meaningful conversations.
    - Engage and steward donor relationships so donors don't feel like an ATM (only being contacted for an ask).
    - Ask funders to give to things that you feel confident are meaningful to them.
- Build community engagement.
- Connect with individuals in the community to partner on your mission.
- Inspire people to give to your agency.
- Engage staff and board in development.
    - Get to know these individuals and find out what their skills, interests and passions are.

   - Teach them about a Culture of Philanthropy.
   - Enroll them to be part of your extended team, and have them help the cause with whatever resources they feel they have in abundance.

- Demonstrate that every gift of money, service or objects is valued at your agency:
   - Show value for volunteer and donor engagement by acknowledging its worth verbally and in printed communications. Have a Structure in place to highlight all different types of gifts.
   - Have donor recognition and stewardship include all size gifts and gifts that are not monetary.

Now that you've done this, look at the things that have stars. Are there activities that have little to do with building a Culture of Philanthropy? Should those be your priorities? Should you push back on having these activities be part of your workload?

There is no doubt in my mind that the most effective activity is to focus on building and strengthening connections to the top 10 to 20 percent of your donors. As you begin to consider the entirety of your workload, it will take substantial fortitude to prioritize those things that advance your Culture of Philanthropy.

Major Donor Relations and a Major Donor Program

If your organization does not have a Major Donor Program, and if you do not currently have a Major Donor Portfolio with specific plans for each of the top donors, you are missing a tremendous opportunity. I resisted the temptation to repeat the chapter on how to build a Major Donor Portfolio in multiple places throughout this book. So, please, go to Chapter 17 to learn what it entails. You won't be sorry you did.

If you do have a Major Donor Program, but you feel that it could be greatly enhanced if framed within the context of a Culture of Philanthropy, please do the same—read up on how you can enhance your existing program (see Chapter 19).

Support from Leadership

One thing that can significantly help you build strength in development is having your CEO empower you being at the "Chief's" table, or the equivalent within your agency. If that hasn't yet happened, you need to request that development be part of the leadership team. In my experience, this commonly is a problem in social service agencies that have relied on fee for service or large state and federal grants as their main sources of income. They started doing true individual fundraising much later in their evolution, and it is yet to be a formidable source of income. If the intention of the CEO is to have a Culture of Philanthropy *and* fundraising success, development must be in the inner circle of leadership.

This also occurs with smaller not-for-profit agencies that are just starting to have professional development staff. The program staff and operations and finance have seats at the table, but development does not.

If this is the case in your agency, it matters that your leadership team knows that you are actively out in the world advocating for programs. I know that seems obvious, but until development is known to produce financial results for the various departments, and that those departments experience the value of your work, it is unlikely that you will get your department's marketing needs prioritized, or that program staff will consider your efforts to be relevant to them. This work takes time. My advice is to be patient and build bridges within your agency.

Leaping Over Silos with a Single Bound

It's possible that silos are among your greatest obstacles. Everyone is too overwhelmed with their own job to stop and pay attention to the needs of development, there is competition for vital resources among departments, and finance doesn't track contributions in a way that works for donors. The demands on marketing are so high that development is often not on the top of the priority list, and program staff and frontline administration staff don't seem to know how to treat donors. And, in some cases, with larger organizations, you are working with multiple databases! In most cases, your department is short-staffed. You'll see that we touched on all three domains of the Wheel of Change: Structure, Behavior and Hearts & Minds.

How do you make a difference here? You start by being curious (even if you've been there a while). Now that you're at the leadership table, get the blessing from the various program department heads to visit and observe their programs in action. If that isn't appropriate for confidentiality reasons, you can meet with the program staff. Your intention is to be moved and inspired by the different programs and gather stories. Ask questions, intent upon finding out what impact the program has on your community members.

As you get to know the program staff, first ask them, *Why do you do your job? What difference does it make?* Really listen and try to understand the heart of what is so meaningful about their work. Next, ask them, *If you had a magic wand, what would you need to bring the program to the next place?* Do they need items, volunteers, special equipment or special talent? They may say *money*. If they say it, ask, *What for?* Take copious notes. Do this for every program area. If you are asked if you are intent on providing these things, do not make promises—other than you'll do your best—and see what you can do!

Be sure to meet with various non-program staff, as well. How could you better collaborate with finance? How could your department and finance synch up better? What are their needs? Consider marketing and the front desk. What are they in need of? Share with them what you've been learning about the impact of the agency, as they may not see it as clearly as the on-the-ground program staff. Toot the horns of the various departments and their commitment to the agency. Share the success stories, the bright spots.

You'll notice that these conversations are not about you and your department's needs. They are about learning, sharing and understanding what it takes to run the agency. While development may come up in these conversations, they shouldn't be about your needs, but about how to serve the greater staff team.

As you accumulate a list of needs and suggestions, look at what you've got. Are there some things that are needed that could be shared across the silos? Are there individuals you know who might be able to provide items or skills to one of the departments?

Finally, meet with the Executive Director/CEO and share what you learned. Express your sense of impact that the organization is making and ask to have regular time at all staff and board meetings to share Mission Moments by the program staff, so that everyone gets in touch with how moving and effective your work can be. If you get the nod to make this happen, put the Structure in place to make it a reality (part of the Wheel of Change). That might mean that it is a regular agenda item in your weekly team meetings, that Mission Moments are shared at the start of all board meetings, or that there is a communication Structure to spread the inspiring stories throughout the community.

Also talk about the needs that have been expressed to you, and any ideas you have about funding specific items. Share if you know people who might want to fund particular things in different departments. Suggest that you and the CEO take a walk for the purpose of learning what needs to be funded so that you can create Donor Offers.

Donor Offers

What if you and the CEO did a tour similar to your previous curiosity chats? Imagine going together to each department and making a more formal wish list. The program staff would rearticulate their needs and desires. And the CEO would determine, *yes, this is something that would be great if we could get funded*. Or, *no, I'm not willing to buy a new piano, but if you find someone giving away a good piano, we would certainly take it!* And, in some cases, *no, I'm not committed to prioritizing that at this time.*

And what if you worked with the program leaders who helped you turn those needs into Individual Donor Offers; mini one-page descriptions of the need, why it would be impactful, and what it costs? This concept of Individual Donor Offers is a tool invented by the Veritus Group (https://veritusgroup.com). If you are unfamiliar with them, I strongly recommend checking out their blog, white papers and other resources. I've learned a tremendous amount from their work and expertise. Individual Donor Offers are different from making a proposal after a donor comes to visit. By having different programs, staffing needs or physical items written up in a one-pager *before* a donor comes to see you, you are able to have clear costs outlined of items that they are inspired by, in the moment.

And look here if you want to see examples of Donor Offers: www.ChooseAbundanceBook.com.

Following is an example of one organization that jumped on the opportunity of Donor Offers. Remember our friends at the Harry & Rose Samson Jewish Community Center of Greater Milwaukee? Well, when it comes to Donor Offers, Lenny, the camp director, is at it again.

Guidepost

Lenny the Camp Director Embraces Donor Offers

Lenny has a great story about how a donor embraced one of his top Donor Offers. The Chief Development Officer, Elyse, and the Chief Executive Officer of Lenny's organization did just what I described above. They went to camp one day with Lenny and walked around discussing the various needs of camp. They wrote up a number of Donor Offers for various camp priorities. One day, a donor came out to camp at the end of the season.

Lenny had in mind that this donor, who is an artist, would be interested in funding something in arts and crafts. He already had a number of Donor Offers prepared ahead of time, and he was certain that he had one for enhancing the arts program that was in stretch gift range for this donor—$6,000—according to predictions based on her historical giving.

As they walked around the campus, they went by the pool, and the donor noticed how lovely it was to see such diverse ethnicities at this camp that typically served a higher percentage of privileged white families from their community. Lenny exclaimed that he, too, was thrilled to have these children get to have the experience of a rural outdoor camp. Their parent organization had partnered with city planners to assure that city children had many of the same experiences that the suburban children had.

The donor also mentioned that it was her suspicion that many of these children didn't have access to a public pool, and certainly not one that was as lovely as the one they were looking at. Lenny commented on the importance of children learning to swim, and noted that *black children drown at a rate seven times higher than white children.* The donor was horrified by this news and asked Lenny what he was doing about that.

He informed the donor that there was a highly effective water-safety training program that was also fun for kids that he was hoping to start the next summer. She asked why he was waiting to do that, and he said that he needed to get it funded. She asked how much that would cost, and he said $20,000. He knew this with certainty because he had prepared a Swimming Safety Donor Offer. She said she would like to fund the program in its entirety.

Without this prepared Donor Offer, Lenny never would have suggested a program or equipment or materials that costs so much money. They had believed that six thousand dollars would have been a stretch gift for the donor. But because he had written something up including the cost of the program, and he was clear about why it was urgent, he was fully prepared to tell her exactly what it was. He learned that it spoke to her

> values. In fact, on the wall of their agency's pool was a traditional Jewish expression which emphasized the importance of water safety for children: *"With regard to children, a parent is obligated to teach them how to swim. The reason? Their lives may depend up on it." Babylonian Talmud.* He didn't need to prepare a proposal for her. On the spot, she said yes to the gift, and it became a reality.

Why are Donor Offers so aligned with a Culture of Philanthropy? First, they cause the Executive Director and Development Director to have to listen closely to the frontline program staff people. This alone is an important learning moment for all three parties: program, development staff and executive leaders, all putting their heads together to think through an organizational fundraising challenge. The program people see that they have a team. It helps to break down those silos. The program people, when inspired to think of their biggest dreams, start to see that maybe development could provide a good partnership. If development does a great job listening, it will go a long way. That program staff person might be inspired to share Mission Moments with development, which then inspires the donors, which leads to better funding! This team approach is critically important in the success of an organization-wide Culture of Philanthropy.

The way to have development and a Culture of Philanthropy become an integral part of the entire agency, and for you to get help from the various departments and board, is for you to become an enrollment master. Remember the story about the rappel where I learned that every conversation is an enrollment conversation? And I discovered that I had a choice in whether I would get enrolled in the fear of the person belaying down a cliff, or I would enroll them in some greater opportunity? You need to figure out how you can brilliantly enroll people in the possibility (the possibility of more Mission Moments happening) and see if it is a possibility that they are aligned with. Then, roll out a plan to cross silos, leaping them with a single bound, and create partnerships throughout your organization to build a Culture of Philanthropy.

Getting into Action

Go meet with various program staff and find out what items or resources they need to do their jobs well. Get approval from the CEO to seek funding for those items. Create a sample Donor Offer to share with the various program areas. Choose one that you believe is particularly clear, moving and inspiring.

Again, go to www.ChooseAbundanceBook.com if you want to see a couple of examples of Donor Offers by the team at the Harry & Rose Samson Family Jewish Community Center.

Showing Impact: Communications That Support a Culture of Philanthropy

Impact Take One: Marketing and Mission Moments

Your work connecting with the various departments should include marketing. If your organization is large enough to have a marketing department, they're likely pulled in many directions. How do you get marketing support when they have so much on their plates? Sit down and talk with them about their needs and yours.

When you collect great Mission Moment stories from the program staff, you will essentially be gathering narratives that illustrate the impact of your agency. Remember that, in your role, you are about stewardship. And stewardship is about illustrating to donors that their investment in your organization was worthwhile. It made a difference. It made an impact. Your marketing team wants to show impact, as well.

As you get to know the various programs, ask staff to share and record short Mission Moment videos (under three minutes) of themselves telling their story. If appropriate, they can also take video of their participants' experiences, if individuals are willing to be recorded. Use these short videos with individual donors or a group of Major Donors. Also, bring these to marketing so that they can incorporate them in their work.

If you work for an agency that has strict confidentiality rules, like a social service program, the staff person might become a spokesperson for the people who they serve. Jennifer McCrea, in her book, *The Generosity Network* (McCrea and Walker, Deepak Chopra Books, 2013), refers to this program staff person as being an *avatar*; the trusted individual who goes out and does the field work and translates the impact through stories that illustrate the front lines. You may be familiar with the use of an avatar in video games. It's an illustration of a representative person who is doing the work for you. In this case, an avatar isn't a cartoon, but a live staff person who has the ear of your agency's supporters and gives them access to an inside narrative of what it is like on the front line. It allows someone, via video or photo or script, to relay what it is like in the life of the individual receiving your services.

This is especially useful for remote international NGO (non-governmental organization) work, and for work in our own country that requires strict confidentiality and anonymity. The intention is to have the avatar be the extension of the donors' hands and hearts, out in the field.

Impact Take Two: A Graphic Impact Report

A second way to demonstrate impact is to produce an impact report. There are numerous ways to do this, whether you frame your stats in engaging graphics or send an email newsletter that's simple, yet filled with powerful quantitative data and accomplishments. An impact report is a way to put front-and-center what your organization—in partnership with your funders—are getting done.

Go here to see fun and playful examples of Impact Charts: www.ChooseAbundanceBook.com.

As you think about these different ways to demonstrate impact, remember this: When you show a donor that their investment in your organization made an impact, you show them that they made a wise investment; it proves that they put their money into something that had an outstanding return on investment. If they give to various organizations, and one of them demonstrates impact, but the others are silent, where would they be apt to reinvest?

I have to share this example. My husband and I have given instruments to a few different organizations. We love music and love to contribute to kids learning how to play music. The first time we bought a couple of guitars and amps for Lighthouse for Teens in Holyoke, MA, we dropped them off, and then we drove home. By the time we reached our driveway (about four miles away), we'd received a video of some teenagers picking up the guitars. We could see through their enthusiasm and their pretend playing of the instruments that they were lit up. They could not wait to learn what to do with these cool-looking guitars!

As I mentioned, we've given to other organizations as well. Now, let's pretend that we similarly dropped off instruments, but this time, we never heard from those organizations at all. We didn't get a thank you—or, if we did, it was a month or two later, and it seemed like an afterthought. If you were me, if you were that donor, where would you imagine you made the bigger impact? Think about it—two organizations. Which was the better investment?

Again, when we thank donors and demonstrate the difference that their gift makes, we confirm that they made a wise investment in our organization. Notice that taking a quick video wasn't a lot of work. It took, more than anything, being authentically appreciative and thoughtful (Hearts & Minds) and taking an action correlated to those thoughts (Behaviors).

The single most important thing you can do as a development person is to continuously tell people the difference their money is making. If you don't do this, you are throwing away money, wasting the effort that was involved in acquiring that donor to begin with, and contributing to the national statistic of poor donor retention.

Be a Culture of Philanthropy

As the development staff person, you need to take a lead role by *being* the Culture of Philanthropy. Lynne Twist gave me a signed copy of her book, and it said, "To Laurie, May the message of this book bless, affirm and nourish your life and work."

Lynne's work became a powerful gift that had my career path, development, rise high above simple fundraising to something that was profoundly meaningful. It is my invitation to you to embrace development and frame it in a Culture of Philanthropy, a transformative model that has the ability to manifest the world that we want.

Start with your own Hearts & Minds. Just as I advised the Executive Directors, speak abundance and possibility. Notice your language and attitude about fundraising. Is it coming from a place of scarcity or from abundance? If it's abundance, spread the joy! If not, see what you can do to get a fresh perspective.

If you feel intimidated leading from your seat, get some coaching. Especially if you are the Development Director or the Chief Development Officer, you should prepare yourself to lead. If it isn't something you've been trained for so far, this might be a good time to ask for some input from someone you admire and trust. Look at the exercises for Executive Directors (Chapter 12) related to getting your mindset aligned with a Culture of Philanthropy.

Put Structures in place to support donor engagement. Make your database work to track contributions, pledges, donor passions and communications. Take a stand that it will be impeccable and be unwilling to have people do data entry who are unskilled. If you inherited a database mess, clean it up. How quickly are thank-you letters sent? Again, take a stand that all letters are out the door in forty-eight hours. Do you track donor retention? You should, as this is a Key Performance Indicator. Pull quarterly reports and be sure to check in with those you haven't heard from. And, lastly, establish or enhance your Major Donor Portfolio as outlined in Chapter 17.

Communications That Support a Culture of Philanthropy

The three buckets of the Wheel of Change—Hearts & Minds, Behavior, and Structure—will support your communications strategy to build a Culture of Philanthropy. Let's look at each one from the communications perspective.

Hearts & Minds

As you plan your communications, put yourself in the shoes of your donors. What would you want to know? What would give you confidence in the agency? What would show that your investment in this agency had been worthwhile?

Your message should not just be about your agency, but about how the reader could be a part of it. The voice of the writer should be friendly, as if talking to a peer. It should come from a place of assuming that you're in agreement, have similar values and are committed to the same thing. You want to show that you know them, that you're on the same page.

This is where marketing can come in. If you have a larger agency, with different departments offering different services, you want to be clear what attracted the donor to your organization and try to segment mailings by donor passions. For example, you don't want to be the environmental organization that ignores that the donor came to them in response to your mailing about saving elephants, and solicit them on a campaign for solar panels.

See the section on Mission Moments earlier in this chapter. How can you tell the story of the impact of your agency? This is another example of the importance of connecting and learning from your program staff, as covered earlier in this chapter. This is where you allow yourself to be moved to tears. This will help inform your work of grabbing hold of the Hearts & Minds of your donors.

Structure

- Create a plan that is multilayered. It should include some mass communications and more individualized communications, all designed to engage your funders.
- There should be specific strategies for the different strata of donors. Your communications should be timed to stay top of mind with your funders and so that you show up reliably. They shouldn't be so frequent that most people would tune you out. Let's start with mass communications. Is there a regular time that you send out a newsletter?

- The content of your e-newsletter should be exciting and moving. Even though it might be broadcast widely, it should feel personal. A newsletter should grab the attention of your supporters. E-blasts (with just one message) can work even better, and because they take less time to write, you can more easily segment your messages for different populations. Create a format that is consistent yet pleasantly surprising. Have the Structure serve your goal of community stakeholder engagement. While I recommend having a storytelling feature, if it makes sense to change it up for some reason, don't let the format cramp your creative style. Use an engaging photo—one or two people are better than photos with a group. The bottom line is that you don't want each newsletter to look like every other not-for-profit communication they're receiving in their inboxes or every prior newsletter that you've sent them before. Use consistent brand and identity to tie your letters together without being boring.
- Do you invite people to see your programs (either in-person or virtually)? Is there a way to tour your agency? If so, plan a forty-five-minute tour that's brilliant, moving and exciting—with no ask attached. Plan stops along the way, each with a staff person making a key point. This is a great way to get staff to take an active role in development. The Executive Director could be available for ten minutes to share their vision. This should all be tightly planned, and the Executive Director's message should get illustrated along the way. If a tour doesn't work, given the work you do, what could be the alternative? A group video meeting where different staff each share a few minutes of their experience? Be creative!

Behavior

- Who is helping these communications happen?
- Are the various staff members supplying Mission Moments?
- Does marketing connect people to get the best resources possible?

- Do communications go out in a timely way that support donor relations?
- Are donors sometimes interviewed for newsletters?

Asking from Possibility

We've discussed how to get to know your donors, how to partner with them and how to have them feel more connected to your work through cultivation and donor stewardship. How do you know when it's time to ask? And how do you ask within a framework of a Culture of Philanthropy?

When it comes down to asking, it's not unusual that people get nervous about it. Mostly, they get nervous because they don't know how people will react. If you're about to ask someone for money and you don't know how they'll react, especially with major gifts, you're probably asking prematurely.

As you build a connection with each of your donors, you start to have a sense of who they are. You learn what is important to them and what their values are. You get to know what they have in abundance. You know what it was about your agency that inspired their giving. You know if they're interested in direct service, in infrastructure, or if they care about and are happy to fund staffing, capital or specific programs.

Once you've established this relationship and you know these things, it's likely time that you ask them to give financially.

How do you ask from possibility? The bottom line is this: you discuss what is possible. When you get in touch with the difference that their gift could make, you identify that it is consistent with their philanthropic desires and generate a conversation to move them to partner with you. Together, you make this enhanced vision of what is possible, real.

When you see your donor as a source of tremendous possibility, and you know you've connected them to something that they are committed to, it becomes easy. It requires no strategizing, manipulating or strong-arming. It becomes authentic and very powerful. Reread Chapter 8, where Lenny's experience reframing his perspective on donors versus investors is discussed. It's a great tool to shift your view of who you are talking with.

If You're the Development Professional, Your Culture of Philanthropy Role Is Not...

Be clear as you think about this Culture of Philanthropy—what things are assigned to you that *are not* part of a Culture of Philanthropy?

As a leader in building a Culture of Philanthropy, your job is not:

- Putting on events that are designed to entertain versus enroll funders in your mission.
- To ask everyone for the same thing (let's get fifty donors to give $1,000!). Remember that people have unique financial capacities, life circumstances and desires. For one person, $1,000 may be way above their ability, and the request would feel like a burden. For someone else, $1,000 may be an appropriate amount. For a third person, it could be an uninspired gift if they could give so much more. Whenever possible, lean toward a more personalized approach.
- To ask a donor who you know is not ready to be asked.
- To be the note taker or caterer for board meetings.
- To *pressure* all staff or board members to make an annual gift (*inviting* them to give is another thing, entirely).
- To constantly seek the elusive savior donor (someone not currently giving who might make a mega-gift).
- To focus on all new funders rather than caring for your existing donors.
- To ignore donors until you need money from them.

If your CEO is committed to fundraising success, he or she should understand that these bullet points are not what you should be doing. I encourage you to have a conversation with your direct supervisor about the need to focus on activities that are consistent with building a Culture of Philanthropy.

Getting into Action

The following is a pathway to take what you've learned in this chapter and put it into practice.

Remember the 5 Points of Possibility (Chapter 8) and think about the things you could take on as a development staff person at your agency. If you are willing to step into the role of positive change-maker for your agency, do the following exercise. This exercise can help if you decide to take on leading an organization-wide Culture of Philanthropy strategy, or if you want to just start to infuse the organization with your own Behaviors, Structures and personalized mindset (Hearts & Minds).

Exercise

As the development professional, my goals for how a Culture of Philanthropy will impact our organization are (utilizing each of the 5 Points of Possibility):

1. **Culture of Philanthropy Is Integral to Our Mission**

   ____

   ____

   ____

2. **Everyone Shares Some Responsibility for a Culture of Philanthropy**

   ____

   ____

   ____

3. **We Build and Maintain Deep Donor Relationships and Partnerships**

   ____

   ____

   ____

4. Community Engagement Is What We Do

____

____

____

5. We Recognize Every Contribution of Service, Items or Money as an Expression of Philanthropy

____

____

____

Hearts & Minds

I will address the following areas:

1. ____
2. ____
3. ____
4. ____

Structure

I will address the following areas:

1. ____
2. ____
3. ____
4. ____

Behavior

I will address the following areas:

1. ____
2. ____
3. ____
4. ____

My partnership with the Executive Director/CEO will include:

____

My work with all staff will include:

____

My work with the board will include:

____

I imagine these could be my obstacles:

____

These are my potential blind spots:

____

Chapter 14
Board Members and Other Volunteers

The difference between extraordinary people and ordinary people is as simple as the difference between the two words. Extraordinary people are committed to doing the extra things that ordinary people won't.

—CHRISTINE KINNEY

Roles for Board Members to Build a Culture of Philanthropy

What are the roles a board can play to build a Culture of Philanthropy? The board of directors, as the governing leaders, has both an obligation and an opportunity to show up as strong stewards of the mission through the development effort. When someone gives their hard-earned financial resources to your cause, they are entrusting you to deliver the services that they're investing in with their gift.

Remember that culture is a construct. While it may seem to have just mystically appeared, it's likely that you could review the organizational culture over time and see how you got to this place. But more important than tracking this past is being intentional about what values are most important in driving the agency forward. As a governing leader, you have a role to walk the talk—and demonstrate your commitment to those values with your Behaviors.

If you care about the mission, you seek funding for it. You model donor cultivation and engagement. This applies to all board members, but especially if you are the Board Chair. Your involvement with donor engagement, for example, will impact the other board members and the staff.

Remember the first law of *The Three Laws of Performance*: How people perform correlates to the way that a situation occurs to them. If the board members see the Board Chair leading by example, they are apt to step up. If the staff see the board taking initiative, they are apt to feel that they have partners in the board. Both examples will inspire leadership.

How will you positively impact the culture of your organization? If you walk the talk, you have the capacity to make a tremendous difference. You have a say in what sort of culture will exist. Think about it from the Hearts & Minds, the Structure and the Behavior perspectives.

One of the easiest ways for a board to start building a Culture of Philanthropy is to start with stewardship. It also *makes sense* to start with stewardship. Here is why:

- When board members practice and become skilled at talking about the difference the agency makes, it will reinforce their own commitment to the organization.
- As we've discussed, many people are uncomfortable with asking. Starting with stewardship will have them get comfortable with talking with funders and hear their genuine joy in giving. This will demonstrate to board members what a gift it is to give.
- Stewardship is often overlooked. It is the single most important action that can be done to assure donor retention. Part of asking them to do this should include teaching them the value of stewardship as a means to building donor loyalty.

Support of donor stewardship from the board of directors reinforces to funders that their gift has made a difference. When a donor understands the impact they have made, they'll come back again and again to support your cause. If that message isn't reinforced, they'll go to another agency that does a better job at communicating. While it's the staff's job to send thank-you notes, hearing from a board member acknowledging the contribution, and the difference it makes, is very powerful.

There are many small things that board members can do to be good stewards and support development. Here is how a Board Chair, Development Chair, development professional or Executive Director can engage board members in building a strong Culture of Philanthropy.

Exercise

Enroll Your Board Members in Building a Culture of Philanthropy

How do you get your board members involved in a Culture of Philanthropy? Be a matchmaker! Make a list of your board members. Think about them. What do they do for fun? What rocks their world? The idea is that you want to find fun things for them to do, not annoying or burdensome tasks! If you don't know these things about them, invite them to have a cup of coffee or a beer. Set an intention for the meeting: to get to know them better and learn how they might want to be more involved in the organization.

Once you sit down for a beer or cup of coffee, ask what their favorite thing to do is when they aren't working. Ask what their favorite volunteer experiences have been and why those were such fulfilling roles. What do they like doing with your organization currently? Listen closely about what they like to do. You might ask *why* questions. *Why* is that meaningful to them?

Don't throw out your ideas of how they might want to be more involved. Just listen! You will likely find things that they enjoy doing that are unrelated to development, but if you listen well, you will likely find ways that they can provide something that they have in abundance to your organization.

Let's first pretend that they mention things that are directly related to development, and then we'll address those things in abundance that *seemingly* have nothing to do with development.

1. **If they are adamantly passionate about the vision of your organization,** give them opportunities to speak up. If they are particularly adept with expressing their love for your work, tell them that. Invite them to tour your facility, where they can share their enthusiasm when you have guests and potential donors. They can attend donor meetings where there is no ask. They can attend meetings and be part of the ask (see number 3 below). Invite them to take the role of secondary participant at donor meetings where someone else does the ask (if that isn't their strong suit). *If they are good at public speaking,* invite them to speak at an event or to be a media spokesperson. Interview them for a newsletter and ask them to share their passion on social media. *If they are good writers,* ask them to write a piece for your newsletter or website.
2. **If they are great connectors,** request that they sit down and review donor lists, particularly of people who development doesn't know well. Ask them if they would be willing to help make a connection to the people they already know. The connection could mean that the board member participates in the meeting or simply provides an introduction over email, and then someone else takes it from there.

   They could also potentially introduce you to people who aren't current donors, but who would likely be interested in getting involved in the organization. Ask a board member who knows a ton of people to sit down and talk about their community connections. Don't do this with the whole board, as it isn't everyone's strong suit.

3. **If they like the idea of asking people to give to your agency,** work with them when you are planning a donor meeting. Would they come to the meeting and ask on behalf of the board? One warning about this: it's actually best if the person who knows them the most is involved with the ask, which is the reasoning behind number 4, below.
4. **If they love donor relations,** ask them to take on one or more people as part of a Major Donor Portfolio. Unless you have a seasoned development professional on your board, start by giving the board member one individual to start with, and if that goes well, build a small portfolio. A staff person from your development department should work with the board member to make a plan for this donor for twelve to eighteen months. Think through the critical contact points, and verify with the board member whether they are willing to take some of these on. The staff person should be in charge of keeping track of the calendar and reminding the board member of next touch points. Asks should be coordinated with the development person as well.

So now, let's consider that they list a number of fun things that don't *seem* to be connected to development:

5. **If they love entertaining,** perhaps they would help you put on a small garden party for a few

donors or community stakeholders. They could help you think creatively about how to demonstrate the work you do if confidentiality issues make it difficult to hear directly from clients. Or they could focus on how to have the garden party be mission-focused. What is it that they like to do when they're entertaining? Are they a self-described master griller? Would they come and work their magic?

6. **If they're artists**, perhaps they help you come up with an innovative way of stewarding donors. Perhaps designing blank cards with artwork from your program participants or gift bags full of all things related to your organization would be a nice touch.
7. **If they're passionate about making their own microbrew,** perhaps they would contribute some of it for a gathering of clients' families or alumni of your organization's programs. My guess is that they'd be honored!
8. **If they're gardeners,** perhaps they'd consider sharing their knowledge of gardening with a summer children's program, or inviting people to their home garden for a stewardship gathering for some of your donors.
9. **If they're woodworkers or handy people,** maybe they'd help you with a project at your facility that needs doing or teach people in your program how to do what they do!

While some of the steps above are very much about development, and others don't seem to be, in a Culture of Philanthropy, all gifts are honored and appreciated. When you are a matchmaker and you connect someone to a passion that makes their heart sing, and your organization sincerely needs and values that gift, then people will feel great. They'll feel useful. And they will get involved.

This can have a snowball effect. It will likely result in more sharing of resources—more connections, more of their time, and more of their financial contributions as well. This sort of matchmaking pays off as people will *feel known and valued.*

It's my experience that, oftentimes, board members are perceived as a disappointment because they don't step up when vaguely asked from the front of the board room to help with development. This doesn't go over the board members' heads. They know you're disappointed. And that doesn't feel good. Choosing instead to find something that will make board members feel that they are authentically useful will build a long-term connection and loyalty.

A Culture of Philanthropy Committee

Here is a story of the first organization I worked with that had a Culture of Philanthropy.

Guidepost

The Culture of Philanthropy Committee

It will be no surprise to you at this point that the board of directors of the Harry & Rose Samson Family Jewish Community Center in Milwaukee has been on the leading edge with regard to creating a Culture of Philanthropy. As mentioned in Mark Shapiro's story, one of the first actions taken by the board after their training was to establish a Culture of Philanthropy Committee. A board member, Nancy, said she would take on leading the charge. The bylaws of the board of directors stated that to form a new committee required a vote and sketching out the roles and responsibilities of that committee. Since they didn't yet have clarity on what this entity would look like, she established a Task Force to define how the Committee would operate.

In this temporary form, the Task Force explored what the Committee could mean for their agency. They knew that they wanted the board members to take an active role in development. They knew that they wanted to address the culture of the board in regards to participating in development and overall attitudes about fundraising and development. They ultimately wanted to lead the culture of the organization so that people embraced development and the possibility that it held for their organization.

Over time, this Task Force became clear as to how they could go forward as a full Committee, collaborating with the CEO and Chief Development Officer to build funding abundance.

I adapted the following bullet points from what Nancy had to say when I interviewed her on the process of creating a Culture of Philanthropy Committee of the board of directors.

What They Did That Worked

- **They started with a Task Force.** This way, it had a beginning, a middle and an end. It was finite. Its purpose was ultimately to form a Culture of Philanthropy Committee on the board of directors.
- **They mapped out the goals of the Committee and the expected outcomes.** They established a mission statement for the Committee.
- **They instituted a Culture of Philanthropy agenda item at every board meeting.** Sometimes, it was a report on what the Task Force was doing, and other times, it was about stewardship or what they were learning as a team while participating in my course. It was intentional that they had a

variety of different contributions to the board meeting so as to illustrate the multiple ways that people could participate in a Culture of Philanthropy.

- **They took on providing a Culture of Philanthropy orientation for new board members.** They put in place a slide deck and narrative to assure that it became a consistent part of their onboarding process.
- **They reinforced both the mentality and the mindset.** Nancy began her Culture of Philanthropy Task Force meetings with a d'var Torah, an interpretation of a passage or portion of Torah, like this: "The one who causes others to give is greater than the one who actually gives." Or, "If you could help someone give, you're giving them a gift to be able to give." And Nancy loves that it connects Judaism to a Culture of Philanthropy. Judaism teaches the belief that donors benefit from *tzedakah* (giving) as much or more than the recipients. This practice ties the values of the organization to building a Culture of Philanthropy.
- **They took their time establishing the Committee**—and it worked—as buy-in was done in stages and methodically, over time. It took an entire year to build the Committee, but once it was fully initiated, the Task Force ended.
- **Through the entire time, initially as a Task Force and then as a Committee, they were first aware of—and then intentionally altered—their mindset and language to be abundant and bold.** When it came time to fill the seats on the Culture of Philanthropy Committee, in Nancy's words, "We shot for the moon." They wanted some of the big philanthropic players in their community to be part of their committee.

Lessons Learned

Mark and his team are candid about mistakes made and lessons learned.

- As Mark Shapiro mentioned back in Chapter 8, this process began many years ago with a consultant providing a training for how board members can ask for money. This was a misstep. It led the board members to think that a Culture of Philanthropy was simply about asking. The board was not ready to be asking. They needed to understand the role of culture and a broader framework for a Culture of Philanthropy. They needed to understand relationship building. This pivot took extra time, as they needed to address the missteps of the past. It took numerous reassuring conversations that they were not instituting *a culture of asking*.

- They found that having non-board members on their committee to expand community buy-in made a tremendous difference as it showed everyone that there were numerous people beyond the board who were willing to help development.
- Nancy, the board member, suggests getting people used to the idea that it takes a while to do this. It may take fits and starts. It doesn't happen in a straight line. Taking the time up front to get buy-in will build a strong foundation for a Culture of Philanthropy.
- To see an example of a Job Description for the Harry & Rose Samson Family Jewish Community Center Culture of Philanthropy Committee, go to our Book Hub at www.ChooseAbundanceBook.com.

Nancy, from the Board of Directors, Shares

The day that I interviewed Nancy for this book (during the 2020 COVID pandemic), she said this: "Today, we have a Culture of Philanthropy Sustain the Mission meeting at four o'clock. Because I was going through my Task Force binder for you and going through my old messages in my own reports, I found out that I wrote to the community that we should look like 'an

> inclusive mission-centric, social service agency with depth and impact—and less like a collaborative of revenue earning business.' That was written on October 24, 2018. How perfect it was to see that, with COVID or without, we're actually doing what is on our plan."

What if Your Executive Director Doesn't Want to Ask for Money?

I've run into this scenario a number of times now, where the Executive Director is either the founder or was hired because of their passion for the agency's cause or their expertise in the field, but they have no propensity for fundraising. In fact, they may not like it and feel that it's beneath the work of programs. This can be a big deterrent to building a Culture of Philanthropy. So, of course, in the best-case scenario, hire someone who has a proven record of donor engagement and success in fundraising.

If you began your board leadership after the Executive Director was hired, and, as a board member, you're hoping to get them enlisted in fundraising activities, start a conversation about what could be possible for the agency if there was a Culture of Philanthropy. I'd list a number of advantages, including the obvious (enough financial resources to fulfill the mission), but also more volunteers, a community that is receptive to your work, and being better known in the community.

Also, the 5 Points of Possibility could inspire a reluctant Executive Director to be willing to learn more about the topic. Of course, you could encourage them to read this book!

Getting into Action

The following is a pathway to take what you've learned in this chapter and put it into practice. Read through the 5 Points of Possibility (Chapter 8) and think about the things you could take on as a board member of your agency. If you are willing to step into the role of positive change-maker for your agency, do the following exercise. It can help whether you decide to take on leading a full implementing team or just want start to infuse the organization with your own leadership.

Exercise

As a board member or volunteer, my goals for how a Culture of Philanthropy will impact our organization are (utilizing each of the 5 Points of Possibility):

1. **Culture of Philanthropy Is Integral to Our Mission**

   ____

   ____

   ____

2. **Everyone Shares Some Responsibility for a Culture of Philanthropy**

   ____

   ____

   ____

3. **We Build and Maintain Deep Donor Relationships and Partnerships**

   ____

   ____

   ____

4. **Community Engagement Is What We Do**

   ____

   ____

   ____

5. We Recognize Every Contribution of Service, Items or Money as an Expression of Philanthropy

____

____

____

Hearts & Minds

I will address the following areas:

1. ____
2. ____
3. ____
4. ____

Structure

I will address the following areas:

1. ____
2. ____
3. ____
4. ____

Behavior

I will address the following areas:

1. ____
2. ____
3. ____
4. ____

My partnership with the Executive Director/CEO will include:

____

My partnership with development will include:

____

My work with all staff will include:

____

My work with the board will include:

____

I imagine these could be my obstacles:

____

These are my potential blind spots:

____

Chapter 15
Nondevelopment Staff

Too often we underestimate the power of a touch, a smile, a kind word, a listening ear, an honest compliment, or the smallest act of caring, all of which have the potential to turn a life around.

—LEO BUSCAGLIA

While the responsibilities of fund development often go to the Executive Director and development staff, there is potential for other staff to identify ways that they can positively impact a Culture of Philanthropy. As you'll see in this chapter, and similar to the Guidepost: Fundraising That Feels Like Magic story from Chapter 10, from the frontline program staff to the van drivers, to finance, to reception, to IT, everyone has a role they can play. And if everyone is finding their niche, the organization has a significantly better chance at success!

The Program Staff

As a program staff person, you may have the thought that you shouldn't be responsible for anything related to development. It seems challenging enough to do one's job!

Let me introduce you to another person at the Harry & Rose Samson Family Jewish Community Center. In a recent training of board and staff in their larger community agency, I worked closely with the Chief Development Officer, Elyse, to co-lead multiple training sessions over three weeks. In the first session, we introduced scarcity versus abundance thinking and gave them an assignment to be Scarcity Detectives. I told them that if they identified their own scarcity thinking, they would win a prize.

A woman named Ronna is the Director of Youth Programs at their JCC. She had a real insight when doing the Scarcity Detective exercise. She noticed that she had an attitude about having to be part of a fundraising training. *It wasn't her job!!* Then she noticed that her thoughts were a brilliant example of scarcity thinking. She was fascinated to have this insight!

While you may feel overwhelmed at times by the sheer volume of work you have to do as a not-for-profit professional, I hope you'll notice that Ronna didn't really have to add anything substantial to her plate. A simple change in perspective created an opening where she could see opportunities for collaboration and connection with families that she already works with.

There are three main things that you as a program staff member can do to help build a Culture of Philanthropy, none of which are a heavy lift.

- Capture those Mission Moments that demonstrate the most moving and inspiring parts of your job and share them with others. As you learn about Mission Moments in other parts of your organization, share them freely, as well, helping to break down organizational silos.
- Connect about your organization's work with people who you are already in touch with—vendors, community members who impact your organization, and even funders or politicians.
- Know what you would make an investment in if you were a donor. If you had $100 to give away, what would you give to? This will have you reflect on what is most meaningful to you and what speaks to your highest values.

Sometimes, in the course of doing one's work, a blindness can start to occur where you become oblivious to the difference you make, instead focusing on the shortcomings, failures and frustrations. Whatever work you do in your organization, the experience of making a difference must be communicated widely. The best way to do this is to listen. What is it like for the individuals who benefit from your programs? How can you seek, capture and spread stories in the user's words?

Keep your eyes open for everyone that your agency touches. Open up communication between different program areas, administration, development and marketing. Advocate for leadership meetings so that you hear of the successes and struggles of the other departments. Brainstorm together to establish positive changes. Share the successes you hear from other departments among your team. Share resources and ideas generously. You can be a critical connector for the whole organization.

Marketing

Over and over, I've heard from participants in my classes that the marketing staff play a critical role in organization-wide Culture of Philanthropy implementation. I couldn't agree more. As the keepers of communications, you have your finger on the pulse of the various constituency groups. Are you accessing powerful Mission Moments? Are you tailoring communications to reach your funders and stakeholders? Here are a few things that can be done by marketing staff to enhance a Culture of Philanthropy:

- Have development be on your radar. It is often the case that programs are the primary focus of marketing. As you put yourself in the shoes of the public to do your marketing work, remember the philanthropic aspect of the public. Remember Point of Possibility 5: We Recognize Every Contribution of Service, Items or Money as an Expression of Philanthropy. This is not just about money. Where have there been inspiring stories of volunteerism, people speaking publicly about the difference your organization has made (and they made a gift of sharing brilliantly), as well as monetary gifts of all sizes? Legacy giving is also inspiring to share about. In all cases, be certain to seek permission from the individual.
- Work with development to produce methods of donor engagement, cultivation and stewardship. Think of opportunities to move and inspire funders and potential donors with both visuals and copy.
- Consider how Mission Moments could be a part of your communications strategy. How could direct-mail pieces be sent to different special interest constituency groups? Work

with development to clarify who should get what communication. Who should not be on a mass mailing list?

- Think of how you can help break down silos. What ways can you be receptive to the various departments and help feed information of successes to development so that funders are inspired to give more?

Front Office

If you are a receptionist or front desk person, you inevitably have opportunities to meet clients, members, families, board members, staff, funders and vendors of your agency. If you think of your job as making everyone who walks in the door feel welcome and appreciated, you will go a long way toward building a Culture of Philanthropy.

The story of the museum in Chapter 10 showed the importance of the front reception staff paying attention to who was walking in the door. While that story focused on the front desk recognizing the name of a Major Donor family, what if your job was to have *everyone* who walks in the door feel a sense of belonging and connection? Don't be that person who makes someone feel invisible. Instead, give them a unique and wonderful experience of your organization and programs. Think of how you might embody the values of the organization and relay the mission as people walk into your building or dial into your office. Identify people who might step up as a volunteer or perhaps as a donor, and connect these individuals to development or a volunteer coordinator. See your role as a bit of a matchmaker for people's interests.

Getting into Action

The following is a pathway to take what you've learned in this chapter and put it into practice.

Read through the 5 Points of Possibility (Chapter 8) and think about the things you could take on as the frontward-facing staff of your agency. If you are willing to step into the role of positive change-maker for your agency, do the following exercise. This exercise can help you whether you decide to throw your hat over the fence and enroll your organization's leaders to take on building a Culture of Philanthropy, or if you want to simply infuse the organization with your own leadership.

Exercise

As staff person, my goals for how a Culture of Philanthropy will impact our organization are (utilizing each of the 5 Points of Possibility):

1. **Culture of Philanthropy Is Integral to Our Mission**

   ____

   ____

   ____

2. **Everyone Shares Some Responsibility for a Culture of Philanthropy**

   ____

   ____

   ____

3. **We Build and Maintain Deep Donor Relationships and Partnerships**

   ____

   ____

   ____

4. **Community Engagement Is What We Do**

   ____

   ____

   ____

5. **We Recognize Every Contribution of Service, Items or Money as an Expression of Philanthropy**

   ____

   ____

   ____

Hearts & Minds

I will address the following areas:

1. ______________________________
2. ______________________________
3. ______________________________
4. ______________________________

Structure

I will address the following areas:

1. ______________________________
2. ______________________________
3. ______________________________
4. ______________________________

Behavior

I will address the following areas:

1. ______________________________
2. ______________________________
3. ______________________________
4. ______________________________

My partnership with the Executive Director/CEO will include:

____

My partnership with development will include:

____

My work with all staff will include:

____

My work with the board will include:

____

I imagine these could be my obstacles:

____

These are my potential blind spots:

____

Part V

A Culture of Philanthropy Approach to Common Development Projects

Chapter 16
Strategic Planning to Build a Culture of Philanthropy

Culture eats strategy for breakfast.

—PETER DRUCKER

Sometimes, when I get a call for strategic-planning services, I find leaders seeking help in setting up Structures within their organization. They have a vision that they want to implement. Often, it's an incremental step forward. They're fearful about the process. They don't want the goals to be too audacious, and they want the process to be quick. They want it over with. They want a plan, whether a full strategic plan or an abbreviated one, and it needs to happen quickly.

Their hope is that they can do it internally. They don't want to bother anyone. Their donors and stakeholders don't need to be at the table. It just makes the process longer. And they know how intolerant external players can become. "We don't want them too much in our business."

It might be tempting to just create this sort of plan and be done. But I promise you, if you want to create an extraordinary organization, it requires thinking differently and looking more deeply. If you are going to have a visionary strategic plan that directs your agency for the next five to ten years, it will take deep thinking, key stakeholders, and a strategy to fund it.

When I sit down with a potential strategic planning client, I start to ask questions:

- How did your last strategic plan go?
- Was it inspiring?
- Does your board embrace it?
- Does it sit on a shelf (and get ignored), or is it part of your work at every board meeting?
- Was your greatest vision of the last strategic plan funded?

- Were the board and staff committed and actively involved in having the goals realized? Why or why not?
- Were your supporters aware of your vision and its evolution over time?
- How many funders do you have in your database?
- How well do you know them?
- How many people in your agency are involved with and connected to your donors?
- Do you track things that you learn about your donors' interests and desires?
- Do you have a CRM system?
- What does stewardship look like?
- Who helps with it?

These questions help me learn about the culture:

- How much buy-in is there from different staff and board members?
- Is there an expectation that funding for visionary programs will magically appear?
- Is all the fundraising effort on the shoulders of the Development Director, or is it a shared endeavor?
- Who knows the donors?
- How much engagement is there with them—or is attention given to supporters only when it's time to ask for money?
- Does the agency invest in development, or is it assumed that it will get done without a commitment of financial resources?
- Is development talked about in a good way, or is it treated like a necessary evil?

If it isn't obvious, we're digging into development and asking about stakeholders because to build a visionary organization requires buy-in from people. It requires funding. To get that money, it takes a village, as they say.

Moving from Pain to Possibility

After understanding the basics, I begin the process of talking about what's most unique about strategic planning. It should be *strategic*. But here's the thing. If you don't address the culture, you won't be successful.

Think about it. If, through reading this book, you've started to notice the scarcity mindset that exists in our country and most likely in your organization, you will see that it will block fundraising success and a Culture of Philanthropy. If you ignore it, it's most likely that the best-laid strategic plans will fail! You won't fulfill your strategic plan. You'll fulfill your Default Future.

It's a waste of your precious resources to:

- Build a plan with no one to implement it.
- Try to build relationships with donors if the organizational leaders don't think it's valuable.
- Invest in a sophisticated relationship database (so you can get it right with donors), but not invest sufficiently in the staff to assure that the job is done properly and without frequent staff turnover.
- Hire a Development Director if you think fundraising is a necessary evil.
- Do a direct-mailing campaign if you don't have people willing to build relationships with the funders that bubble up through this effort.

So, where do we go with this prospective client who really wants a strategic plan but doesn't want to address the culture pushing up against their vision? (Pause for a moment and feel our pain.)

This is where I'm apt to say, "Sometimes, we've gotta put the *duh* in fun*duh*raising"—a great new perspective from Eric Phelps, Rainmaker Consultant and Chief Comedian! I have to carefully explain that not paying attention to culture is like cutting off your nose to spite your face! It's like wanting to eat unlimited desserts and fried food and lose weight at the same time. It ain't gonna work out!

A reminder:

The bottom line for leaders is, if they do not become conscious of the culture in which they are imbedded, those cultures will manage them.

—Edgar Schein, *Organizational Culture and Leadership*

The Strategic Planning Process

The Strategic Planning Process is a tremendous opportunity to create an invented, generative and bold future you desire—including a Culture of Philanthropy. When an organization pauses and begins to explore its plan for the next several years, it's an opportunity to dream big and consider what it will take to fulfill their wildest dreams. If the dream is powerful enough, and if the leaders are brave enough, they will use this opportunity to address anything in the culture or the day-to-day mindset of the staff and the board that might be in the way of this inspiring vision. To state the obvious, an inspiring vision without the internal and external buy-in, which ultimately leads to the dollars to pay for it, is going to fail. Given the right coaching and outside perspective (so that they can better disclose the culture), the organization can start to build something powerful.

Taking a stand to have a strategic plan grounded in a Culture of Philanthropy is a significant first step for altering the culture of your agency. Each department will have goals consistent with advancing community engagement, great customer service and building enduring and meaningful relationships with your clients, board members, staff and donors.

The Strategic Planning Process can either be a boring, insular phenomena or a brilliant community engagement endeavor (friendly reminder: this is also Point of Possibility 4: Community Engagement Is What We Do).

If it's one of your worst nightmares to involve outsiders in your Strategic Planning Process, then this might not be your favorite part of the book. A Culture of Philanthropy isn't for those who just want to *go it alone*. I'm going to make a case for community engagement as a deliberate tactic to construct a powerful Culture of Philanthropy throughout your organization. In fact, and this might be hard to consider, if you are a go-it-alone leader, your version of an insular strategic plan *will be in the way* of you achieving an organizational Culture of Philanthropy. A Strategic Planning Process can forge important relationships on every front. Let's walk through a typical process.

Phase 1: Planning

Initially, you want a small team to just think through the process. This usually consists of one or two staff, including the Executive Director and one or two board members. They are each there to be lead communicators for their team of people. With this small team, you should start to think through who should be a part of the process. Think on multiple levels. Consider the following and make a list of important stakeholders:

- Who are experts in the field?
- Who would really push us forward?
- Who has skills that we are lacking?
- Who would we want to be part of our organization in the future (that we would want to start or continue to build a relationship with)?
- Who would we like to enroll in our work?
- Who is visionary?
- Who is well connected in our area? (I've intentionally used the word *area*, a rather ambiguous word, to inspire you to think creatively about your community.)
- Who is either fundraising savvy or supportive of a Culture of Philanthropy?

No one will be all of these things, but you can certainly find people that have some of these traits. Once you have a good list, start to think about the various roles. Should they be invited to:

- Be a part of the entire process (six to eight months for three to five hours each month)?

- Be on a small working committee digging deeper into issue areas? This group meets a total of three times for a couple hours each meeting.
- Participate in a focus group or a one-on-one interview?
- Advise you in the background if you have some questions or want some input?

Once you have your team, design a process to intentionally involve the people on your list, utilizing their skills. Let them know your organization's strengths, its challenges and your dreams.

To see our outlined Strategic Planning Process, go to our Book Hub downloads at www.ChooseAbundanceBook.com. What is unique about this process is that, right from the start, you frame it by imagining your organization as the middle of a hub of a wheel. Use Axelrod's Treasure Map Exercise from Chapter 9 to do a thorough scan of the stakeholders surrounding your agency who could help you advance your mission.

Phase 2: Mission and Vision

In Phase 2, you review and perhaps update your existing Mission and Vision. There are a few reasons this is important:

- Getting clear about the Mission and Vision is critically important for the rest of this process.
- The world is changing. Is your Mission and Vision still relevant? By examining this, you get to consider if the need is still there and if you are the best people to be addressing it. Be honest with yourselves. It may take setting aside your own self- interests. I've known of more than one organization that needed to decide to end itself or wind down its services because of its diminishing relevance. It takes tremendous bravery to admit that your job is done and let the program go.
- For the individuals who are part of this Strategic Planning Process, especially those who do not do your work every day, you are bringing them into the folds of your organization. You are articulating the full possibility that your organization holds and letting them in on it. They will likely "own" your

agency to a greater extent. They may want to become more involved as a result of this process. They may want to give more time or other resources to your work. They may connect you to people they know who they think should learn about you.

- For the individuals who are part of this process who do the work every day, it's an opportunity to step back and get in touch with why they do it. Especially for individuals who have been on staff for a long time or who have served on your board for a number of years, it is easy to get caught up in the day-to-day and overlook the impact on people's lives.

In a powerful Strategic Planning Process, one that is building a Culture of Philanthropy, this first meeting is an opportunity to have everyone involved in the process be moved to tears by your work. You'll clarify and powerfully articulate why you do this work. What do you do, and why? What impact are you having? How are things different now that you exist? Are you moved and inspired by the vision of your agency, or are you resigned and frustrated? How do you envision the world or your community different as a result of your vision?

Exercise

Circle up to access your Mission and Vision. In the beginning of the first meeting, have people sit in a circle. Before the meeting, pull aside someone who you trust to be an open and articulate person and ask if they would help you out. Explain that you are going to ask a question to the whole group, and that you would like them to help set the stage by sharing first.

The question you are going to ask is this: What is it about this organization that moves and inspires you to give your time and resources? Their share should last two minutes at the very most. (Be certain that you trust that they will truly keep it to this timeline, or this will fail miserably!) Let them know that they are being asked so that others will follow suit and share authentically about why your work is so meaningful.

Once the group convenes, after welcoming guests, have them go around the circle, sharing what it is about the organization that moves and inspires them to give their time and resources. Be sure to say that they should limit their share to two minutes. Start with your colleague you asked to share first. This exercise will get everyone in the mindset of deep appreciation for the work done by your agency.

Writing your Mission and Vision is a time to have your donors and volunteers be a key part of your organization. What does that mean? Start to think of why it's important to have your community be a part of your work. This will vary a lot from agency to agency. For example, an agency serving individuals with developmental and intellectual disabilities that I've worked with states that their mission includes education of the public. Why not take that to the next level—include the public as stakeholders in the support and care of all individuals living in our community?

It is critical that you have volunteers and investors be part of this conversation. Why? Here are five key benefits:

- Educating investors about why you do what you do.

- Having them increase their stake in your agency by contributing their ideas to your vision.
- Hearing the perspective of funders about what they think is important for their community.
- Exposing everyone in the strategic planning process to the unique points of view held by individuals who invest in your work.
- Enrolling individuals (who are not currently contributing money to your organization or who are afraid of fundraising) in the idea that donors are just humans who are committed (like they are) to making a difference in your cause.

The information gathered from these shares should be captured and used to inspire a small group of individuals to look deeply first at *what* you do with whom. This will inform your draft mission statement. A similar statement should be drafted that gets at *why* you do what you do and how the world will be different as a result of what you do: the *vision* of the agency. Be bold and create the organization of your dreams.

Phase 3: Identifying and Addressing Key Issues

At Phase 3, addressing key issues means being authentic about your challenges with your stakeholders, and this lets people in. They get to be part of the solution. This is a very good thing. Donors and other community members are often thrilled to help. You may have specific donors who would be good to include in this phase, and who truly model transparency and deep donor partnerships by troubleshooting your agency's challenges and issues with them.

You identify your key issues by asking questions of people. You can do this in broad strokes by reviewing past surveys and program evaluations, feedback from staff, and by community input. You may find that you need to dig deeper and get more information to reveal what the key issues actually are.

Phase 4: Data Gathering

Data gathering allows for deeper community engagement. In this phase, volunteers are divided into subgroups to dig into key organizational areas, addressing the issues that came out of Phase 3. It's important to make time to assure that issues bubble up. Otherwise, dormant issues could thwart your success. For example, if there are staffing issues, but everyone sweeps them under the rug, it's possible that you won't get authentic feedback on the viability of a goal from the start. The outcome of suppressed feedback is that your strategic plan, or at least that goal, will fail.

It's important to dig into a number of issues such as staffing, customer service, development, board engagement, facilities, programs and finance. The following are some examples of key issues that might come out of Phase 3 that are aligned with these areas:

- **Staffing**—What are the causes for staff turnover? This is a way to have staff give feedback about what works and what doesn't in the agency. They can share ideas on what would improve programs, what tools and resources would help them do their jobs well, and what they need in order to perform optimally. It is also a chance to take the pulse of the internal culture.
- **Customer Service**—How well do we respond to clients' needs? This is how you would find out how you're serving your clients. Everything from the initial call to your location, to navigating registration or members' services online, to day-to-day services provided, can all be examined by this group. This also includes any donor who might call in or send an email seeking help or clarification on their giving.
- **Development**—How are we doing building a Culture of Philanthropy? This would examine how involved people from different parts of your organization are in helping

development efforts. It could include speaking with funders to see if they feel appreciated, as well as examining how each of the three parts of the Wheel of Change are being addressed. Be sure to remember Structures, such as database management, Major Donor planning and ROI on events. It would also be appropriate to use the Choose Abundance Culture of Philanthropy Assessment, which you will find at our Book Hub, www.ChooseAbundanceBook.com.

- **Board Engagement**—Are our board members feeling good about their involvement? Do they feel appreciated and acknowledged? Are they serving our agency? Do the board Structures support the agency's mission? Their Behavior? Their Hearts & Minds?
- **Facilities**—Do our current facilities serve us? Are we in need of a capital campaign? Will the current facilities be sufficient a few years out? Do the facilities serve our greatest vision?
- **Programs**—Are we being effective? Are we aware of best practices in the field? How do we compare to other like-missioned agencies? Are we being innovative and responsive?
- **Finance**—Is our business model working for us? What do we do if there is a major change such as a catastrophe or a severe economic downturn?

It is well worth it to get an abundance of volunteers to be part of this phase of your Strategic Planning Process. If you do, you'll have a group of smart individuals on each subcommittee focusing on each topic area. These volunteers do not have to (but could) be part of the entire Strategic Planning Process.

In Phase 4, members look at data that currently exists (client surveys, internal financial reports, fundraising reports, and growth or reduction of program participants), and data that you would like to get (qualitative data from interviews of individuals from the neighborhood around your agency, information on client satisfaction, past employee-exit-interview information, one-on-one interviews with thought leaders on your agency's work, and financial reports that show trends within the agency or in the field, donor-retention reports). It's also important from a culture perspective to look at the three parts of the Wheel of Change: think Hearts & Minds, Structures and Behaviors.

Phase 5: Establishing Basic Goals

If you have your mind focused on building a Culture of Philanthropy, setting your goals will be a blast. Think about it. If there were unlimited resources, and if everything you needed already surrounded your organization, what would your most inspired programs look like?

- How many people would you serve?
- What would your materials look like?
- How would you attract the brightest and most inspired staff to get the job done?
- What would your development team need to look like?
- Who on your staff or board would need to be involved in development?
- What would be the Executive Director's role?
- How much money would you need to raise?

Trigger warning: don't get overwhelmed worrying about raising all that money to fulfill your organizational dreams! Don't go down the tunnel of scarcity thinking. Ask yourself these questions: Who do we have to be to build this organization to its highest vision? Who do we need at the table? How can we enroll the right people to make this happen?

While strategic planning is about building a plan (aka, a Structure), establishing a Structure that is consistent with a Culture of Philanthropy has to have Behavior and Hearts & Minds aligned with it. Remember, all three buckets have to be swinging forward in concert. If you've ever been a part of a Strategic Planning Process that didn't get implemented, those other buckets weren't engaged. I like to say, "If not, why not?" My guess is that the attitudes, thoughts and feelings, aka the Hearts & Minds bucket, would reveal things that are in the way.

In fact, developing a powerful Strategic Planning Process without Behavior and actions being aligned produces a strategic plan that sits on the shelf. Having a strong strategic plan and passing out tasks without buy-in (Hearts & Minds) would also be useless. Imagine having a new mandate that the board will take on development tasks when they haven't bought in to that idea. This type of thing happens all the time! To expand on Peter Drucker's famous quote, without your Hearts & Minds aligned with your highest vision, you could be having your culture eat your strategy for breakfast.

When you have the right team of people in your Strategic Planning Process, and if you are really listening to that team, they should have the opportunity to discuss their perceived barriers. Then, together, as a team, you all work on potential solutions to those barriers. I've been in more than one Strategic Planning Process where I watch the program staff slowly sink as board members paint a grand vision without the understanding of what it takes to implement it. Be certain that you take the time to map out what it will take to get there—and that you have what it takes to get there.

This may appear to be the opposite to what I indicated in the beginning of this step, which was *dream boldly and wildly*! The opportunity is to first dream boldly, but there is no doubt that you eventually have to get realistic about how that will happen. That is why it will be important to have development be a part of your configuration. It's why everyone needs to know their role in creating funding abundance. Now, let's explore why Phase 6 is so important.

Phase 6: Critical Success Factors

If you truly desire your boldest vision, your Critical Success Factors have to be well thought out. These are simply the things that will assure your success. Think about items that, if they are in place, will nearly guarantee you will reach your goal.

When you make decisions based on what might work, not from a mindset of fear of change and scarcity, but possibility, then you may find yourself going places you never imagined. This applies to your resource development work. If there is a desire to create new programs or strengthen existing ones, getting your entire Strategic

Planning team enrolled in these possibilities will be inspiring. What is critical for your success (the Critical Success Factor)? It may be a focus on fundraising for this program or a new Culture of Philanthropy Committee created to work with the development staff to increase revenue or increase engagement of all staff and board members in development. It may be a new hire in the development department.

A similar fund-development initiative could get sparked by the group working on board engagement. One person might say it is a great idea to have board members be more involved in development. Going from the idea to the reality might be much more effective if there are multiple people weighing in. Instead of one enthusiastic board member strong-arming their peers to do this, there's an opportunity to create a broader strategy and form a board Culture of Philanthropy Committee to implement it. If your Strategic Planning Process has board members deeply engaged, then you are beginning to build your future Culture of Philanthropy.

When you have a strong, engaged team, you have the possibility of identifying what the attitudes need to be to pull off this grand organizational vision. What would leadership need to do to inspire this sort of greatness?

Phase 7: Prioritization

As mentioned above, if you've followed this process well, you will have identified myriad goals and opportunities. How do you narrow it down if you can't fund everything now? One way is to spread your visionary ideas over time. Make your top priorities happen first.

You might be wondering how to prioritize your goals. I have a useful tool for this at www.ChooseAbundanceBook.com. It is an exercise to think through and set priorities for all your goals.

Phase 8: Implementation

A Strategic Plan is as good as your Implementation Plan. This is a key piece of your organizational culture of accountability. Embrace the importance of this plan by:

- Setting clear measurable goals (SHMART goals and KPIs).

- Assigning someone to be accountable for each of the goals.
- Having a part of every board meeting devoted to checking on progress of your Strategic Plan (Structures and Behaviors), and having the accountable person provide an update.
- Establishing a small committee or even a single person that is accountable for bringing the implementation to everyone's attention.

To assure that this Strategic Plan becomes realized and doesn't just sit on the shelf, there are a number of things you can do. Consider taking these on, which fit within the Wheel of Change buckets.

Structure

- Create buy-in at the different stages of the Strategic Planning Process, particularly when setting goals.
- Set up your subcommittees to intentionally engage the community.
- Create an easy-to-read Implementation Plan that has clear goals, timelines and accountability.
- Have an agenda item at each board meeting to check in on the status of your Strategic Plan goals.

Behavior

- Assign a visionary leader to move and inspire people and keep everyone on task.
- Assign individuals accountable for specific goals.

Hearts & Minds

- As an organizational leader, be open to getting input from community leaders.
- Be courageous, and be transparent with challenges.
- Be willing to explore the degree to which you and your organization might be stuck in a mindset of scarcity.

A Strategic Planning Process is an opportunity to reinvent your organization. By bringing the right people to the table, you can reach for inspiring goals. While you may not reach every one of your intended goals, you have a much better chance of doing so with a Culture of Philanthropy as a visionary, aspirational goal. If you need help facilitating this sort of process, reach out to us at www.rainmkr.com and we'll be happy to assist!

Chapter 17

Steps to Build a Major Donor Program

I alone cannot change the world.
But I can cast a stone across the waters to create many ripples.
—Mother Teresa

A Major Donor Program in a Culture of Philanthropy is one where the Structures, Behaviors and Hearts & Minds all support a strategy to build and deepen relationships with your top donors. This strategy is consistent with Point of Possibility 3: We Build and Maintain Deep Donor Relationships and Partnerships.

Based on the size of your organization and the number of larger donors that you currently have, your parameters of what constitutes a Major Donor is apt to vary. Usually, this is determined by a minimal, annual, financial giving threshold that the top 10 percent of your donors fall into. For some smaller organizations, that amount is as low as $500 and up each year, and in larger organizations, it may be $5,000 and up. Larger universities and hospitals often have much higher-tiered Major Donor thresholds.

In a Major Donor Program, multiple staff and board members take on creating individual plans for a number of Major Donors. A board member may take on a small handful. The CEO may take on a larger elite group who want their primary connection to be the organizational leader. A development professional may have the largest number of funders in their portfolio. If you have no development professionals, it may be that the CEO and a few board members do the lion's share of the Major Donor work, building and maintaining the Major Donor Plans. Each of these players would have their own large or small Major Donor Portfolio. Together, these portfolios make up the vast majority of your Major Donor Program.

There are some people who may fit within your agency's Major Donor giving threshold, but who prefer not to be engaged. They should not be part of anyone's Major Donor Portfolio. They don't want to meet or get to know your work any deeper, and they typically don't answer your calls or emails. They just want to give financially. There will be a separate strategy for these individuals, as I explain below. But first, let's talk about the Major Donor Portfolio.

Major Donor Portfolios

What does it mean to build a Major Donor Portfolio? It means that instead of having Major Donors be part of a broad mass-communication strategy, you build customized donor-relation plans. One per donor. It is proven that customizing the donor experience provides the very best ROI in development. As with any human relationship, the more that people feel known and heard, the more that they trust. The more they trust you, the more they'll trust you with their money and their investment in your cause.

Universities are known for how they create their plans and maintain their individual donor plans in a disciplined way. For-profit businesses are the same. If you were the owner of a company selling high-end items, you would know your best customers very well. You would know their birthdays, if they have families, what their passions are, and what's important to them. You'd know what makes them tick so that you could provide the best possible experience for them. You would have goals of how they'd grow their connection and partnership with you and your business.

As I map out a Major Donor Program and customized Major Donor Portfolios, I make these assumptions:

- **You have a donor database that supports relationship building.** What I mean here is a CRM (Customer Relationship Management) tool. While it's important that you can sort by date, and so on, what I *also* mean is one that includes information about the person in the database (birthdays, anniversaries, names of children, awards, what programs are their greatest passions, who they are most connected to within your organization, etc.). If you don't have this, get one before embarking on this process. If you are a new agency, it is still possible to build strong donor relationships without one, but it is *far* from ideal.

- **You have a cause that you are passionate about and that you have a strong case for support**. See the importance of a strong case for support in the next chapter.
- **This isn't about donor acquisition.** When you build a Major Donor Program, you forego that elusive savior donor. This hope for a wealthy individual to come along and save you from the day-to-day work of fundraising is wrought with scarcity thinking. Further, it is a common time drain for a professional Major Gifts Officer or staff person with a portfolio of Major Donors. There's a time and place for donor acquisition, but this is not it.

This method of establishing a portfolio is critical for both start-up and experienced fundraising programs. Having a current group of funders is helpful, but for agencies just starting to work with individual donors, this will be useful to build a fundraising program from the ground up. In fact, starting out this way, building individual plans, will make for great practices and a Structure that you can build upon into the future. For those organizations with established fundraising programs, working through your data might be more cumbersome up front, but it will be worth it. This will require you change how you do things.

Another commodity that you must have to make this a success—and this is the number one killer of implementing a program like this—is time. You need to commit time to make this happen, and it will not happen overnight. It will likely take several months of building before your program is highly functional. Patience will be critical, as this isn't a light lift. If you're fortunate enough to have a development professional (or more than one) who will be focused on Major Donor relations, you should be going through these steps together. Perhaps there's a board member or development committee member who will join you in this endeavor.

Creating a Major Donor Portfolio

So, you've adjusted your mindset, you've purchased a relational database, you have someone very skilled who is able to do data entry and produce reports for you, and you've perhaps assembled a team of people who will be together implementing Major Donor Portfolios. And now you're ready to get started. Let's go!

To create Major Donor Portfolios in a not-for-profit organization takes focus and discipline. I recommend looking up and getting on the mailing list of the Veritus Group to receive useful tools, resources and wisdom on how to do this. Over the years, I've shared the Veritus Group tools with development professional classes that I taught, and they found them to be very useful. However, I noticed over time that a number of the professionals I worked with struggled with fully establishing a Major Donor Program—and it wasn't due to the materials and resources that I shared with them.

Those barriers had much to do with not having full buy-in from the CEO and not getting support and help from the board. Now, as I teach about establishing a Major Donor Program in the framework of a Culture of Philanthropy, I make sure that the leaders are all around the table, and that there are adequate resources to get the job done.

I've created a Major Donor Portfolio Spreadsheet that you can download from our Book Hub at www.ChooseAbundanceBook.com and use for tracking and managing your portfolio. Here are the steps that you need to take to fully implement a Major Donor Program.

1. Dedicate time. This has to be deliberate. Schedule focused time on this substantial project over the next six to eight months. Make no mistake, it is a real project. Your organizational leaders should understand its value and commit to it fully. Know that if it's one person setting this up, assuming the data is in good shape, they could spend twenty hours a week for four months just conducting discovery interviews and creating the individual plans. Once these are established, it could easily take an equal amount of time to work your plans and maintain them. This, of course, is based on the size of the portfolio. I use a simple sketched-out sheet of paper or a digital file to map out my weeks so that I have time reserved for this Major Donor work. This illustration shows one example.

TIME MANAGEMENT FOR A PART-TIME MAJOR DONOR PORTFOLIO

	SUNDAY	MONDAY	TUESDAY	WEDNESDAY	THURSDAY	FRIDAY	SATURDAY
6:00 am							
		WORKOUT		WORKOUT		WORKOUT	
9:00 am		PLANNING	MANAGEMENT RESPONSIBILITIES	STEWARDSHIP	DATABASE CLEANUP	PLANNING	
		TEAM MEETING					
12:00 pm							
		STRATEGIC THINKING & CREATIVE TIME	MAJOR DONOR PORTFOLIO				
3:00 pm							
			EMAIL CLEANUP	EMAIL CLEANUP	EMAIL CLEANUP	EMAIL CLEANUP	
5:00 pm							

TIME MANAGEMENT TOOL: The idea with this tool is to have you map out and put those things that are most important into your schedule. Be certain that your Major Donor Portfolio and Planning time are both prioritized (they are in white). They should be treated as an appointment. You should also include items that assure that your health and well-being are being considered (like sports, recreation and cleaning up emails). Periodically refresh your calendar template as needed.

17-1 Major Donor Portfolio Management Calendar

(Laurie Herrick, Rainmaker Consulting)

2. Determine the desired portfolio sizes, including that of the Executive Director, development professionals and board members who agree to take it on. Here is a way to figure out how many people you could include within one professional's portfolio. Private colleges have become proficient in managing Major Donors. At one private college, each of the Major Gifts Officers (MGO) has a portfolio of approximately 120–125 individuals. The industry standards for portfolios have shifted in the last few years as donors have become more involved and connected. Unless you have a larger shop with gift processors, researchers, proposal writers and communications, start with one hundred people for a full-time MGO. If you are spending half of your time doing this, then fifty people should be sufficient for your portfolio.

In the case of universities, an MGO gets hired, and they inherit a portfolio. In your case, you're likely going to have to verify that you're focusing on the right individuals through a discovery process, and from that process, you'll build your list of Major Donors. Each person who is part of your Major Donor team should determine how much time, and, therefore, how many people, will be within their portfolios. Going back to the time commitment in number 1 above, each person should look truthfully at their calendars and block off time for this project.

3. Pull key reports. I imagine that you, the readers of this book, come to this conversation with a varied spectrum of giving to your agency. As mentioned above, some of you have a number of large funders stretching from $5,000 to seven-figure gifts. Or, you might have a smaller number of individuals who have given $500 to $5,000 or more. Regardless, the opportunity is the same: by establishing a Major Donor Portfolio, you strengthen the capacity of your agency.

You can increase or decrease the dollar amounts on your spreadsheet, based on the size of the gifts and the number of donors you have. In our sample at the Book Hub, and in the examples that follow, I've used $1,000 as a middle-of-the-road threshold for smaller not-for-profit organizations that have been fundraising for a few years, at minimum. You will want to have enough people in your Major Donor Portfolio Spreadsheet so that each person managing a Major Donor Portfolio can start with approximately three times the number of family units/individuals as they can ultimately manage. This may require that you include data on individuals whose giving is slightly lower than your threshold. Starting with three times the number of family units/individuals than you can manage, allows you to narrow down your portfolio to those who truly *want* to engage with you. But more on that shortly.

Here are the key reports I recommend you build:

> **Report A:** All donors who have given a *total sum* of $1,000 or more in the last four years, in descending order (with those who gave the largest sum on top)

Report B: All donors who have made *a single gift* of $1,000 or more in the last four years, again in descending order

Report C: All donors who made a one-time significantly larger or noteworthy gift over the last five to ten years

Earlier, I touched on corporate and foundation giving. If you have a relationship with people at a corporation or within a foundation, you want to include them in your list of possible portfolio members, assuming they meet your giving threshold. You will vet these individuals to see if they want more of a relationship with you, just as you will with the other individuals in this pool of potential portfolio members.

Take the first report, A, and drop it into your spreadsheet. Review the info from reports B and C and determine who stands out that is not already in report A. Add those individuals to the spreadsheet. This is your starting list of existing donors who have potential to be in your portfolio.

4. Determine which funders are already interested in being engaged with your organization. There are two pieces of criteria for your portfolio. One is that they have given of a particular threshold ($1,000 suggested above, or an adjusted threshold based on your range of donors and giving), and the other is that they desire engagement with your agency. The reports help you to identify the giving threshold.

As a reminder, Point 3 of the 5 Points of Possibility is We Build and Maintain Deep Donor Relationships and Partnerships. You will find that some of your largest funders want to have a deep and meaningful connection with you or the leadership of your agency. Others do not. Let's use a dating/relationship metaphor. There are some people who want to be our best friends and chat and hang out often. There are others who are good with a periodic wave from across the street. None of us like it when someone pushes being our pal when we don't feel it. Just because someone does not want to meet with you, it doesn't mean that they don't like you or that they don't care about your cause. It just means you should not be wasting time trying to have a deeper relationship with them.

A note about current and past board members: a common mistake is that leaders overlook current board members and assume they don't need to be part of this process. Don't do it. Learn from my past mistakes. These volunteers have put in countless hours for your cause—they're among the best informed and most committed. They've likely given financially in a substantial way as well. Be sure to include them in your process, just as you would any other donor. The same goes for past board members.

Next, you will set up Discovery Meetings, which are designed to figure out who wants to engage with you and to discover what drives their passion for your organization. If you can call or email someone right off the bat and get a meeting, you can advance to Step 6, the Discovery Meeting. If you are unclear if the individual is interested in deepening their connection to the agency, then you should go through Step 5.

5. Steps to verify who should be in your portfolio. These are the steps to reach out to the individuals who you don't meet with regularly, to find out if they want to meet with you. This is important. Don't avoid these steps. What distinguishes a successful portfolio from an unsuccessful one is focused attention on the individuals who want to engage with you and your agency. (You will not ignore the individuals who do not want to engage with you. They will be part of a different strategy and not in your portfolio.)

This process includes the Executive Director, the individual who is taking on a portfolio (I'll call them MGOs—Major Gifts Officers, though others besides an MGO will likely take on portfolios.) and any board or staff member who is connected to the Major Donor. Again, the Veritus Group has wonderful tools for this including scripts and sample letters.

a. Starting at the top of your list, identify who knows each donor the best. If there's a board member or staff person who has a relationship with the donor, speak with that person to learn more about the donor. Take notes as you learn what you can about their connection, the donor's interest in your agency and what their passions are. Be sure to put this information into your database. A staff person, either a development professional or CEO, should be the main contact. Ask the contact to introduce you via the following process.

b. Send a personal letter from the person with the closest relationship, making an introduction to the MGO (or chosen staff person), requesting that they meet. This can be done with email or snail mail, based on what you know this individual prefers. They should be told that they should expect a call or email from the MGO within the next few days. If no one knows the individual, this letter should come from the Executive Director/CEO.

c. Within two days, the MGO should make the follow-up communication. Again, this should be a highly personalized communication or voice message asking for the opportunity to meet. Be sure to use the name of the individual who they know within your agency. Let them know that you appreciate their support and that you'd like to meet to get to know them more and see how you could keep them in the loop in terms of the work of your agency. Assure them that you are not soliciting them, you just want to get to know them better.

d. If there isn't a response in four days, the MGO should do a follow-up call or email. Do this three times.

e. After the third attempt, give it five additional days, and then have the original contact pick up the phone and call the individual directly, or however they are most commonly in touch with this donor. They can check in and be sure that the donor is okay and ask if they're open to meeting with the MGO.

f. If you still don't have any response from the donor, the MGO should send a final letter or communication saying, "We tried to reach out and didn't catch you. I'd love to meet sometime if you are interested and available. We'll keep you on our mailing list, and if there is anything you need, please call me."

Through this process, you will find a number of people who don't want to get together. This is good, as you will stop reaching out to them to try to get to know them better. This will allow them to have what they want: to give financially, but not continuously or sporadically get calls requesting to get together. If you followed all the steps above, remaining committed to the desires of the donor, they'll remain loyal. Statistically, two out of three people who you contact this way will not want to be more deeply engaged. This process of elimination saves the staff person tremendous time. There is no reason to periodically pester someone who doesn't want pestering. Again, those who don't want engagement will be part of another strategy.

In some cases, you may have found that the original contact for a particular donor is the only person they want to connect with. That's okay. You can work with the board member or staff person to build a customized plan that they manage. More on that below under Step 10.

That leaves you with a number of people who want to meet. Now what? Time to begin!

6. How to have an effective Discovery Meeting. These meetings may take place face-to-face, or with donors who live farther away, with a phone or video call. Be sure to do your homework first, learning about their past with your agency. Review what information is in the database and reach out to anyone who might have some connection with the donor. Is there anything that they have been unhappy about from the past? Were there mistakes made with this donor? Have they focused their giving with your organization in one program area or another? Gather this internal information and add it to your database and your knowledge for this meeting.

Also, if you have it available, use a donor research tool like Donor Search and run a report on the funder. It isn't at all required that you have a report from an external source, but if you have it, it will be helpful. Once you have gathered any available information, you've done your homework and are ready for a Discovery Meeting.

With someone who's known to the agency (like a board member or more active donor), or in the case of a first-time encounter with a donor, as the MGO, you want to get to know them and listen to how they would best be served by the agency. You don't need to have a pitch for the agency, but have a heartfelt story of how your work has made an impact on an individual's life.

It matters that you be genuinely interested in them. Do not take these steps in order to get money. People can see right through it. If you find yourself having to rally because you are disinterested but think you should be interested, take a break and see if you can connect to a sincere and authentic curiosity.

Your primary tasks during this meeting are gathering information and having the donor come away from the meeting with an extraordinary experience of your organization. Much of what will make it extraordinary will be based on how well you listen. People love to be heard. Listen closely to learn:

- About their values, their passions, their frustrations, and their wisdom.
- What they have in abundance and what they truly don't have in abundance. For example, they may not say it directly, but it could be clear from things they say that they feel scarce with their free time but generous with their money. Or, even though they give to you, they may feel scarce about money.
- Something unrelated to your agency that they're passionate about. Make a mental note of and record it in your database, so that you can later share something relevant to this topic, illustrating that you listened and get who they are.

Here is how you can accomplish your goals in your Discovery Meeting:

a. **Be clear about your intention of the meeting.** This will impact your mindset and how you address the donor. The intention should be clear in your head that you want to get to know them and their desires. Enter the meeting with a mindset of curiosity.

b. **Start by thanking them.** Have them know how important their support is. If they've given to a particular program, let them know how it makes a difference. This is where a heartfelt story of the impact of their giving comes in. Come to the meeting prepared with this. Chapter 13 has resources on how to tell a powerful story of impact.

c. **What are their values and what makes them tick?** Jennifer McCrae in her book, *The Generosity Network* (McCrae and Walker, Deepak Chopra Books, 2013), talks about how to connect with people in a meaningful way. She suggests that you, the development professional, Executive Director or board member, think about your life and how you got to this time and place, working with this organization. Think about the various turning points or changes in your life's trajectory. You see, when we make a big change in our life, it is usually because we recognized that our values were not aligned with what we were doing. When we hear that someone makes a change, it often indicates what is important to them. Having a conversation on this level is actually quite intimate. When you share this way, you reveal what motivates and moves you.

   Using bullet points, make notes of your life's path that brought you to your current involvement with your organization. Next tell the story out loud. Time it. How long does it take? Is it impassioned? Take out the parts that are less powerful, until it takes under three to four minutes to tell.

   In your introductory meeting, tell them that you'd like to get to know them and that you'd like to start by sharing your story and how you got here. Share your three-to-four-minute story, and then ask them how they ended up here, at this point in their lives, focusing their philanthropy on your agency. Listen closely and take good mental notes. (You don't want to literally take notes, as you want to be listening and *focusing on them*). The more heartfelt your story is, the more it will inspire their story and deepen your connection.

Be clear. While this exercise may move and inspire others, it is equally important that you are deeply in touch with and can channel your "why." This is an important pre-meeting grounding mechanism. When you are aware of your personal choices that led you to this place in life, and why they represent your deepest values, you will be much more effective with everything you do. You will be grounded in and motivated by the work that you do. It will help you genuinely articulate your passion for your mission.

This conversation also has an equalizing effect; you are meeting with someone who, just like you, is an individual who traveled through life to get to this moment. And here you are, sitting together, expressing your commitment to making the world a better place. You each have your unique paths and your own way of expressing that commitment.

d. **What was their most inspired and meaningful giving? What made it so meaningful?** I've been surprised again and again to learn what people reveal when I ask this question. People will interpret *meaningful* in various ways, but I suggest that if they share dollar amounts and specific gift amounts, you push further into *why* it is meaningful to them, emotionally.

e. **Do they have questions about your agency?** Take time to listen to their questions and answer to the best of your ability. If you don't know the answers, promise to get back to them (and follow up). This is a good time to pull out a pad of paper and let them know that you've made note of their question.

It may come up here, or at another time in the meeting, that there is something that they are unhappy about from the past. If this is the case, your job is to be an extraordinary listener. Ask clarifying questions, and ask if there is anything that you could do to help resolve the issue. Do your best to not get attached or defensive. If you are going into this meeting knowing that there is some preexisting baggage with the donor, be sure to see Chapter 20 for some coaching from Zemo Trevathan on how to get grounded with a centered mindset to address challenging situations.

f. **How do they like to be communicated with? How do they like to be recognized for their giving?** This is an opportunity to hear directly from the donor about what they like and what they don't like. Be certain that you incorporate anything that you learn into your database and your Major Donor Portfolio Spreadsheet, with details. If you do this well, you will have earned a tremendous amount of trust from the donor. By contrast, if you lack needed Structures, such as a robust database to track this information, you will likely ultimately harm the donor's relationship with your organization. (Remember, if it is in your head, and not part of a useful Structure, once you leave the organization, the next person responsible for working with the donor will be at a tremendous disadvantage. If you care about your organization and its cause, put the needed Structure in place, now.)

g. **Is there some way that they would like to be more involved?** This is a critical question to ask. If you can find the way to engage your top donors on a deeper level, and in a way that feels comfortable to them, you have the potential to substantially enhance their loyalty and commitment to your agency. Remember my story in the beginning of the book about Peter, my volunteer friend who became the million-dollar donor for RESULTS? He was already committed to the organization, but he became a different kind of leader, an even greater stakeholder in the organization through being more deeply engaged.

If you want to learn more about how to engage volunteers, review Chapter 14 and the exercise on finding out what each of your board members has in abundance. Using that tool, you will find examples of questions you can use to discover more about what makes your donor's heart sing!

7. Set your priorities. Make sure that you first have a prioritization process for your funders. Then, start to build your plans. Each individual or family unit should take up a row in your spreadsheet (again, a Major Donor Portfolio Spreadsheet can be downloaded at www.ChooseAbundanceBook.com). You prioritize them by working on a formula based on the sum of scores, including:

- The number of meaningful conversations you've had with the donor.
- Their capacity based on their largest giving to any organization from Donor Search or other sources.
- How much they've given to your organization (cumulative giving).
- Their desire to connect, their inclination to give (based on frequency) and their stated passion from your Discovery Meeting.

When you add up those scores, you will get a sum, the Tiering Calculation, which will allow you to prioritize your donors by A, B, C and so on.

8. Goals and plans for individual donors. Once you know the answers to the questions in number 7 above and you have a score for each person (plus you have notes in your database from your Discovery Meeting), you can start to estimate what might be an appropriate goal for each individual or family. What has been their largest gift to your agency so far? If they expressed a high level of enthusiasm in your Discovery Meeting (or any subsequent meeting) about a particular program, would it make sense to aim to ask them for a stretch gift down the road to enhance it? What would be a long-term goal (2–3 years down the road) from this individual based on the largest gift they've made to other agencies?

If in the Discovery Meeting, they shared with you that they made a much larger gift to another organization than they have ever given to you, what do you think it would take to get them to think of your work in the same light? Of course, they may have shared that their most significant gift happened because of an inheritance that they gave away, or that they are not apt to give as much to your organization. This information should be reflected in your goals. Once you determine a goal for the year, as well as a stretch goal, be sure to add both types of goals in subsequent columns in your Major Donor Portfolio Spreadsheet.

Once you've established goals, you can work backward (starting with the achieved goal) and include interim goals and calendarized touch points. While twelve months spread out (each with three columns) makes the spreadsheet particularly wide and difficult to print, this is a great way to track activities by month. The three columns are labeled with the month and **General (e.g., January General)**, the second column has the month and **Specific**, and the third has the month and **Actual**.

Use the **General** column to identify any mass communications that will be going out from your agency, with a special focus (noted in the **Specific** column) on targeted program areas that are your donor's sweet spot. The **Specific** column is also where you should put individual touches that are highly personalized. This includes handwritten notes, meetings, phone calls or emails that indicate the donor is important, and any stewardship touches that show what a difference their giving has made.

For example, in the case of Lenny's story with the investor and the swimming safety program, Lenny might want to mark in his calendar to show that program in action the following year. In an ideal world, plan to invite the donor to see the program in-person. If that is impossible, then plan to have someone video an event or take a photo and send it off with a personalized note.

Your plan should also include sending something (a note, an article, a book) that seems to say, "I know you." It might be related to that passion that they shared about (one that isn't relevant to your mission). As the "owner" of this donor in your portfolio, you'll likely be the person making the touch. But there will be times when it matters to have someone else show their appreciation. Be specific regarding how this will work.

Lastly, be clear about when it will make sense to reach out again and make an invitation to give. Your calendar should schedule the prep involved so that you are ready for a powerful and impactful meeting. Your plan for an individual will be complete when you've filled it in for an entire year to eighteen months and set an aspirational longer-term goal.

9. Working your plan. Get support in strategy and implementation. Lastly, meet weekly with your supervisor and others with Major Donor Portfolios to support each other in implementation. Below is a section on Portfolio Management Meetings complete with an agenda. Talk about successes, challenges and goal setting, and brainstorm brilliant ideas so that each and every person in your portfolio has an extraordinary experience of your organization. At this point, you just roll out the plan that you've designed. You can periodically customize any mass communications (that you typically send to everyone) for your top donors. Simply take the e-newsletter you personally received and forward it to your donor with a note on the top pointing out an article that you think they would be particularly interested in.

Use the **Actual** column to note what actually happened. If it is as simple as a newsletter going to the donor, then note it. If you personalized it, note it. If a meeting failed to happen, note it and indicate why it didn't occur. Your database should be used for any narrative and details.

10. Review your plan. Pay attention to the plan and periodically update it. Do you want to add something? Did you hear that a donor just had a significant life event that requires an extra communication? Does it become appropriate to take someone out of your portfolio? Be sure all of these details end up in the plan, as well as your database.

Incorporating Major Donors Who Don't Want Deeper Engagement

It's still very important to take care of those individuals, corporate givers and foundations who don't want to be deeply engaged, yet give at or above the Major Donor threshold. I recommend using the same chart, but without the detailed, individualized parts of it. Use the calendar columns of the chart as described above and have the next tier of Major Donors receive the mass communications and perhaps some individualized touches.

You might be able to personalize some stewardship. For example, you might know the donor's birthday or send out a card congratulating them on a success that you saw in the news. You can also calendarize asks if you know that they like to be asked at a particular time. Take what tidbits you have and incorporate them into your plan. It may be appropriate to have some individuals eventually moved up to your Major Donor Portfolio if they are both within your specific threshold of giving and they shift to being more deeply involved with your agency. Otherwise, resort to mass communications. Segmenting this group of Major Donors this way will keep them top of mind, assure that they get some communications, and, at the same time, allow you to focus on the Major Donors who want deeper engagement.

You can also use this spreadsheet for other groups of donors who don't fit in your Major Donor category. In this case, you can segment them together, not listing a single name, per row as we did for all of the Major Donors—but a group per row, for example:

- Ranges (examples: $500–$1,000, $250–$499, under $250)—This allows you to consciously move people up in their giving from one category to another.
- Corporations and foundations could be batched together if you have a number of them.

These three ways of segmenting are useful for targeting communications:

- Constituency groups (parents, alumni, members, past board members, etc.)

- Types of donors (monthly donors, direct-mail donors, Giving Tuesday new donors)
- Program interests (based on the different unique program areas of your agency)

Portfolio Management Meetings

For everyone who has a Major Donor Portfolio, it's important to establish a weekly management and accountability structure. These meetings are a chance for your team to connect and share wins, progress and challenges. Here's a sample agenda.

Agenda

1. How many letters went out this week requesting Discovery Meetings?
2. How many Discovery Meetings do you have scheduled?
   a. Are your calls seeking Discovery Meetings effective? Are you getting meetings? If not, what do you think is going on?
   b. Who do you have meetings set up with?
3. What Discovery Meetings did you have with current donors?
   a. How did they go?
   b. What did you learn?
4. What is your plan for each of those you met with (review the Major Donor Portfolio Spreadsheet)?
   a. What is your goal?
   b. What is your strategy? Use the group to think this through.
5. What, if anything, is in the way of doing this work?
   a. Were you stuck at any particular part of this process? If so, examine what might be off.
6. What are promises for next week's meeting?

Setting up the portfolios and having Discovery Meetings will take several months. Once you have the plans in place, your task is to work the plans, and then periodically update them. You may need to add people to your portfolio if someone gets moved out of your portfolio, or if someone moves up in ranks and becomes a new Major Donor. Continue to have weekly meetings and use the support of your team to constantly enhance your plans and provide an extraordinary donor experience. If you find you want to implement this with some assistance, reach out to us at www.rainmkr.com. We'd love to be of service!

Chapter 18
Making a Case

There are only two ways to influence human behavior: you can manipulate it or you can inspire it.

—Simon Sinek

A case for support is a valuable tool to help get you clear about why it's so important for people to give to your organization. It will inform your print and online audio and video communications. It isn't often a document that you share with someone, though I've seen some organizations borrow heavily from it. A typical *case for support* is used for a capital campaign. The idea is that you write a document that makes your case for support, and then someone in marketing works their magic and creates beautiful materials. In the end, you want something that can be used to inspire online and print literature for a capital campaign, a direct-mail campaign, an e-newsletter or a brochure.

A case for support is also great for any type of fundraising work that you do. I'd like to propose you consider both using this exercise of creating a case for support for large campaigns (like a capital campaign) and also to provide an array of Donor Offers (as described in Chapter 13) for your Major Donors *when you aren't* in a capital campaign.

In this chapter, I focus on the steps for establishing a case for support that is consistent with building a Culture of Philanthropy. Then I'll show you how to use it for the average Major Donor who might be interested in giving to your agency.

Step 1

Get in touch with why it's so important to do your work and for your organization to exist. One way to do this is through the exercise I shared in Chapter 16, where everyone circles up and shares why it's meaningful to be involved with your organization. Notes from that sort of meeting will make it apparent to you why your organization is in existence and why *it needs to be in existence.* Spend some time writing an emotionally compelling and moving narrative about why it's critical for your organization to thrive. It's the first element of your case for support.

Guidepost

Here is an example of why an alternative educational program for teens is so critical in my community.

In traditional schools, a number of kids fall through the cracks. At Lighthouse for Teens in Holyoke, Massachusetts, we've adopted an extraordinary model from higher education—where students receive guidance from staff counselors to create their own educational plan. We found that it works for teens who are being homeschooled and need some extra structure, teens with learning disabilities, supersmart teens who are bored in public schools, teens from low- and high-income families, teens from a variety of different ethnic backgrounds, and teens who feel bullied in public schools for being uniquely themselves or for being gay or transgender. At Lighthouse, we have a diverse community with one common goal: creating a powerful learning environment and experience for the students who go there.

The results are outstanding. Students who hated school are beginning to love learning. Those who were "troublemakers" are getting serious about their futures. Students who lacked confidence because they didn't fit in are embracing what makes them unique. In the last few years, Holyoke Public Schools has placed some of their students at highest risk of not graduating at Lighthouse. The vast majority of these students receive their diplomas through attending Lighthouse.

Step 2

What are you up against? What is in the way of you achieving your goal? Make bullets that illustrate what is in the way. Specifically, why are you raising money for a particular thing? Craft a few paragraphs that illustrate why you need partners in funding your project. If you need a new building that can handle increases in the number of people participating in your program, it might read like this: At Lighthouse, we are limited by our physical space. We currently have the space for fifty students, and we consistently have a waitlist. This waitlist is of young people who are falling through the cracks. We believe we could have up to 120 students and maintain the intimacy and focus of the program.

Step 3

What is the solution? What could be done that would make a difference? Don't only say *what* the solution is, but *how you're going to do it.* What is your plan? Our example solution is this—we are embarking on a capital campaign to purchase the Steiger Building in downtown Holyoke, Massachusetts. This former department store from the late 1800s is an extraordinary space that would allow up to sixty more students to participate in programs. Additionally, this new space would give Lighthouse room to expand its program in the following ways:

- A first-floor, student-run café that serves the public, provides lunch for Lighthouse and other renters in the building, and includes a demonstration kitchen for health-center-connected nutrition classes for community members.
- Maker space in the basement that serves Lighthouse during the day, and then is open to the public in afternoons/evenings/weekends.
- Classrooms and offices.

- A music studio/performance/dance space on the fourth floor that serves Lighthouse during the day, and then is open to the public in afternoons/evenings/weekends.
- A rooftop urban garden that similarly serves Lighthouse during the day, and then is open to the public or other programs, or both, in afternoons/evenings/weekends.

Step 4

What does it cost? Map out the basic costs. Be sure, if you are embarking on a larger project such as a capital campaign, to include campaign costs.

Step 5

Make it urgent. Why is it important to act now? This is where you make the case that the reader needs to take action now. For example, in the last several years, our community schools have had increasing dropout rates and have started to partner with schools in a program called Opportunity Academy, where the public schools recommend certain students (who are at high risk of dropping out) to attend Lighthouse. Whether students come to us through Opportunity Academy or through word of mouth, we have had repeated success, and the number of students (and families) seeking an alternative educational option is overwhelming.

It's a game changer for youth, and their families recognize this. When a teenager shifts from being at the whim of their education to owning their success, their life trajectory changes. This is a pivotal time in young people's lives, and we owe it to them to make this option available.

Step 6

Make your request. This is where you directly ask for the gift. For the case for support, you may not have a specific dollar amount written, but it is where the donor goes to find out where they might be helpful.

Chapter 19

How a Capital Campaign Can Help You Build a Culture of Philanthropy

I look at my own body
With eyes no longer blind
And I see that my own hands can make
The world that's in my mind.

—Langston Hughes

Similar to a Strategic Planning Process, a capital campaign can be a way to engage your community, build deeper donor relations and have staff and board see their role in building a Culture of Philanthropy. As you read this chapter, look at ways that you can:

- Clarify and better articulate your mission and highest vision.
- Share your Mission and Vision with more stakeholders.
- Encourage people to step up and be bold.
- Reach out to individuals who are less engaged.
- Build the skills of your board members and staff.
- Save money on consultants while gaining deeper donor partnerships.

Guidepost

Dana Marie Lupton Co-Founded Moving in the Spirit in Atlanta Thirty Years Ago with Leah Mann and Genene Stewart

Eric Phelps

Moving in the Spirit uses the discipline of modern dance to teach young people the social, emotional and cognitive skills they need to thrive. They have won numerous awards, including a national Youth Award Program presented by the President's Committee on the Arts & Humanities. It is not an overstatement to say that they have transformed thousands of lives and have a high level of impact; in Georgia school districts with a 71 percent graduation rate, 100 percent of Moving in the Spirit's seniors have graduated high school and gone on to college, vocational school or military careers.

And yet, while they have a strong base of monthly supporters, Moving in the Spirit has sometimes struggled to garner the financial support they need to succeed and to "dream big." In 2016, they were facing considerable financial challenges and were also undergoing personnel changes that were amplifying these difficulties.

In the midst of this, and building on a vision developed in 2013, Moving in the Spirit decided to undertake their most ambitious project to date: build a brand-new facility in the heart of Atlanta that could serve as center for not only Moving in the Spirit, but also for the broader arts community. Born of a Strategic Planning Process in 2013, there was now a new opportunity that could be taken advantage of: The Metro Atlanta Regional Transit Authority [MARTA] had a vacant lot adjacent to the Inman Park/Edgewood Station that was available for building. This was a perfect location, as students who travel by MARTA could easily and safely go to and from classes and programs. The only challenge: a price tag of more than $8.4 million.

Dana did what most organizational leaders would do at that point. She engaged with a consultant to do a feasibility study regarding the project. As one might expect, they said that the organization was not going to be able to raise the support for this campaign within the year required to secure the funds. This was reinforced by an interview with a foundation considered to be a "gatekeeper" of Atlanta's arts capital campaigns.

Dana called Rainmaker Principal Eric Phelps with a request for some counsel. How could she raise $8.4 million when there were challenges paying the current bills? As you can now see from the distinctions we've made, there was a clear need to move from scarcity to abundance thinking, and to mobilize the broad network of supporters in a concerted campaign to go far beyond previous fundraising success. The recommendations included:

- **Be bold and unreasonable.** There is an amazing opportunity, and it is timely. People may well respond to this sense of urgency.
- **Go back to basics.** Tell your origin story, speak of your vision, engage the students, and talk about your impact on the community as it has been and would be in the future.
- **Rally core supporters and advocates.** Dana had forgotten one of her own mantras, "Don't have any 'Devil's Advocates' on your board. Let the Devil do his own work." She needed to get people behind her—both personally and professionally—to help garner the resources needed.

Dana gathered a group of ten diverse champions, who committed to risk their reputation to make this dream become a reality. They agreed to bring to the table friends, family, colleagues and a personal sacrificial pledge. In short order, she had significant seed money and a new sense of momentum. Then, the champions, along with the students, approached other foundations, met with Major Donors past and present and gained more support. A young couple who was interested in investing in the dream brought additional support, and soon, Moving in the Spirit was nearly at $8 million dollars. The enthusiasm for the project was becoming infectious as people recognized the possibility of transforming a neighborhood, as well as the Atlanta arts community and the people involved with the programs. The final $500,000 gift needed for the capital campaign came from the foundation that had initially said they would not support it. In fact, upon seeing the community support, they felt compelled to be part of the project.

Moving in the Spirit implemented the major tenets of a Culture of Philanthropy, even though they may not have labeled their work in that way. They enrolled people in the possibility of a space that engaged their imagination. They built upon their considerable work and shared the stories that illustrated how they had transformed young people's lives.

Traditional Feasibility Studies—Are You Wasting Precious Resources?

It isn't an unusual occurrence. A not-for-profit organization decides it needs to undertake a major building project, and the board approves a capital campaign—on the condition that they first conduct a feasibility study. That's when a Request for Proposal (RFP) is created, and you reach out to multiple consultants. In this section, I'm going to discourage you from wasting precious resources. It's time to have the conversation about traditional feasibility studies versus having conversations with your funders to more deeply engage them.

In a traditional feasibility study, a consultant is hired by the organization to meet with its top donors. The consultant interviews them and gets a sense of what they think about the organization. Do they still feel good about the mission? Do they have faith in the leadership? Do they feel well cared for by the organization? What do they think about this proposed campaign? Would they support it? To what extent? Ultimately, the job of the consultant is to find out how much money the donor would likely give to the campaign.

This is like dating in junior high school. Imagine the scenario. I like a boy, but I'm too chicken to tell him that I like him. So I go to my best friend and ask her to ask him. She casually walks over to him and says, "Hey, my friend Laurie really likes you. Do you like her?" It's hardly a mature approach to getting to know someone! And while it may have achieved results in junior high, it's not likely to be a fruitful approach for an organization seeking capital.

On a more serious level, that's the lesson that many organizations need to learn: using an outside voice on our behalf has the potential to not help, but rather detract from our chances of building a relationship or making our case. Our dependence on the wrong outsider can make us look less confident, or possibly too lazy to get to know someone ourselves!

Reflecting back to the 5 Points of Possibility, this is an opportunity to dig into Point 3, We Build and Maintain Deep Donor Relationships and Partnerships. This is a time to be honest about how well your agency has done connecting with your funders. Have you only gone to them to ask for something? Or have you provided great customer service, showing your appreciation and love? If you don't have mature relationships with your donors and you're afraid to assess how you've done in stewarding their gifts, let me save you a bundle of money—you aren't ready for a capital campaign. Instead, you should begin by building the relationships and partnerships.

To make that point even clearer: A capital campaign is for an established development program. It isn't a starter project for a new development program. However, a capital campaign can enhance your intermediate to mature development program if you change the conventional approach.

Guidepost

I had firsthand experience of this that made a big impact on my approach. I had been working with an agency on a number of projects related to board engagement in fundraising. They had struggled getting board members to step up, and the development professional was very much on her own. The Executive Director didn't particularly like fundraising, and he found it hard to find time to meet with top donors. In my world, working with that organization was like herding cats, it was very difficult to get them to focus, and while they wanted the end result, they didn't really want to make the effort to build a Major Donor Program.

Then they told me that they needed to do a capital campaign. I told them how we could take on an alternative approach to the feasibility study and save them a lot of money and use it to build those donor relations that they were struggling with. They were intent on hiring a large firm, one that was known widely as *the* capital campaign consulting company. I was introduced to the consultants, and we were to partner. They would do the feasibility study, and then I would help them with the campaign.

The consulting firm conducted their interviews (for a lot of money). When the final report came out, it was scathing. Their top funders (many from years past) felt that they didn't know the current leaders, that they had not been included or consulted on any projects that the agency was doing, and they didn't feel connected to the organization. The consultants strongly advised against doing a capital campaign at that time.

I was shocked. And I wasn't. I had never heard of a flat-out "no" response from a consultant like this: *as a result of our stakeholder interviews, we don't recommend that you do a campaign.* I could see delaying the campaign, but these consultants had found something worse than disengaged donors. They had a number of people who were angry and felt badly about the agency. To a degree, I wasn't surprised, as they had largely ignored individuals who had previously, with prior leaders, invested their hearts and souls.

Shortly after this, the board excused the Executive Director, and there was a large turnover. Our work stopped, and big changes were made. That was probably six or seven years ago. I recently met the new director. Wow! What a change. During the pandemic of 2020, they had a significant outpouring of support from a much stronger base of supporters. Over the years, they had gone out and met with funders and built much deeper relationships with people. When the pandemic hit, these funders knew they could trust this leader and this team. I was so happy to hear that they had turned this around.

I do wonder what would have happened if they had not used the consulting firm and instead reached out directly to the donors and started to build those relationships themselves. There might have been a need to clean some things up. They might have kept some funders who were put off by the consultant. Ultimately, I believe they had to go the distance and strengthen those relationships, one way or another.

Donors would much rather get to know you better than get to know an outside consultant. It is possible that a traditional feasibility study could reinforce to the donor what they already know—that they don't know you! What if, instead of conducting a traditional feasibility study, you used your campaign to improve your donor relations and build a Culture of Philanthropy?

What if, instead of hiring an outsider to interview your donors, you meet with them yourselves, deepening your relationships and engaging them to become partners and stronger stakeholders in your mission? As you do this yourselves, you are building trust, you are asking them directly how you can be a better steward of their gifts, and, most importantly, you are building a stronger organization.

A donor Discovery Meeting, as I described in Chapter 17, will lead to these deeper and stronger connections to your top stakeholders. In this case, when you are interested in getting a sense of what people would give to a capital campaign, modify the meeting to include information on your upcoming capital needs. We call this a *Feasibility Interview.* By doing this, you will get to know your funders better and you will get their early buy-in, which will have them feel included and enrolled in the future of your agency. They will become *more* invested in your work. At the same time, your organization will become stronger as your leaders embrace and begin to see their critical role in strengthening donor relations.

Feasibility Interview

To conduct a successful Feasibility Interview:

1. Identify who will be part of conducting the interviews. Include members of your capital campaign committee, board members, staff, Executive Director and any development staff. This is your capital campaign team. You can start this process by speaking with the team. Get to know them and match up their interests and desires with the skills needed for the campaign. Out of this you should identify the best ways each person can support the campaign. Then, those who are comfortable getting to know your stakeholders should conduct Feasibility Interviews.

2. Similar to how you built your Major Donor Portfolio (see Chapter 17), produce a report of your largest givers. In a campaign, you start with your inner circle and work outward. You typically ask your board first. In the Feasibility Interviews, you do a similar thing, but you are not asking yet.
3. For the purpose of getting yourselves trained in this, get together, pair up and conduct practice Feasibility Interviews.
4. For the practice round, and for the real interviews, pull and review a report of the individual you will be interviewing. Look at their giving history and any contact notes. Make your own notes on what you might say. What do you know about that person? What would you like to know? What are the more specific customized questions you would like to ask that person? Through this process, you build on what you have already achieved with your supporters. If you have done quite a bit with that particular person, think of how to take it to the next level. If you have done very little, how can you build a more authentic and meaningful connection? Are there questions from the Discovery Meeting that would be important to include in this Feasibility Interview?
5. You will have to reach out to people to ask for a meeting. When you make that call or send that email, explain that you are seeking advice on a new confidential project that your organization is embarking on. (You want to be sure that the campaign is kept confidential until you reach a public phase of the campaign.) Tell them how much you value their input. Practice this just as you will practice the face-to-face (or virtual) meeting. Be prepared to leave an enrolling and compelling message on voice mail. If needed, you can roleplay these messages with a partner.
6. As you practice, the pretend donor should take notes about what worked and what didn't. The person conducting the interview should be aware of listening. Don't worry about your next question. Listen deeply to the "donor's" answer.

Ask qualifying questions, but don't pull the topic too much off point.

7. After you warm up to the donor in your practice round, move on to share with them about the campaign. Let them know that as a community leader and stakeholder in your organization, you are seeking their input. Share about the vision of the project, including the scope and estimated timeline. What will be different as a result of the fruition of the campaign? (Review the Guidepost on Moving in the Spirit, earlier in this chapter, or the Lighthouse Case for Support in the prior chapter to inspire you.) Ask the donor what they think about the campaign. Do they like the idea of it? Do they have input to make the campaign successful? Do they have any thoughts about who should be involved in it? Would they like to be involved in the campaign? Customize your questions based on what you know.

8. Once you have tried a practice round or two with your peers, jot down what you learned about the person you interviewed. What did you discover newly about them? How did they answer the questions? Were there any surprises? Now identify what will happen with that information. Is there a Structure in place to capture data? Is there a place to note next steps and a timeline so they don't get dropped? If not, establish these systems.

9. Now, go to your main list and start with your inner circle, board and larger donors. Work closely with your agency's development staff, and if there is a year-long plan for the donor, then the main contact for that person should be consulted. In fact, they may be the best one to initiate and carry out the Feasibility Interview.

10. Be systematic and work through your top funders and see what they say. Get to know them and plan to stay in touch with them. Put it in your calendar or other tickler system. This

is the beginning of an enhanced partnership inspired by your agency's vision for the future.

Here are some standard questions you can adapt to fit your agency. Choose from these topics and complete a number of them that feels appropriate and not too rushed. The last question is an important one. Be certain to get to it before the meeting is over.

- Tell me how you first got involved with our organization.
- What drew you to us? Or, what do you think is most important about what we do? (You want to get at why they care.)
- How do you feel about the mission currently? (Have a copy of the mission with you.)
- Do you feel we are doing a good job fulfilling our mission? Do you have any ideas for improvements?
- How do you think the agency is doing?
- We are thinking about embarking on a larger capital project to _____. (Be sure to articulate the reason why. Share materials in draft form.) What do you think of it?
- Do you see ways that we might improve our case for this campaign?
- What do you think our community's appetite is for this sort of a campaign?
- Do you think that you would support this campaign?
- If not, what is missing from it?
- I know that we don't have our plan fully conceived, but if it goes the way we've been discussing it, at what amount would you consider funding it?
- Would you like to be more involved with this campaign? (Reserve this question, of course, for people who you think might be interested in serving on your capital campaign committee or participating in a focus group.)
- Can I follow up with you as this develops?

After conducting Feasibility Interviews, you will have accomplished a great deal. You will have created deeper, more long-lasting connections, gained a clear sense of what each donor might give to your campaign, and essentially conducted your own internal feasibility study.

If you are considering undertaking a capital campaign, scratch the traditional feasibility study. Instead, articulate your goals. Do you want to get to know your funders better? Do you want your board trained? Do you want to build a stronger infrastructure? Do you want to create a Culture of Philanthropy that will long outlive a series of interviews? Internally run Feasibility Interviews will help you advance all of these goals.

Part VI

High-Functioning Leadership to Achieve Breakthrough Results

Chapter 20

Accountability & Powerful Requests: Leading the Change

Daring greatly means the courage to be vulnerable.
It means to show up and be seen. To ask for what you need.
To talk about how you are feeling. To have the hard conversations.

—Brené Brown

Within your team, you must have somebody who has both the capacity and the authority to hold people accountable. I'm going to repeat that: you *must* have someone with the capacity (ability and time) and authority (either by their position or their endorsement from the highest positioned leader) in place to assure that your Culture of Philanthropy strategy moves ahead. Without those two things, this plan will most likely *not* succeed.

The leader of the Culture of Philanthropy team doesn't have to be the Executive Director or the Board Chair, but they have to be somebody who has the leader's blessing and is fully empowered to roll out this long-term vision. They should work closely with the top executive or board member in establishing Structures to assure that the Behaviors and Hearts & Minds are aligned with the desired culture change. This work takes significant effort and will require altering the status quo.

It's possible that you can be thwarted in your process by not having buy-in from the Board Chair or from the CEO. If you don't have their buy-in and you are trying to do something not aligned with their vision, you are not poised for success. Think about the point I made above. You are disrupting the status quo. How much does the leadership align with the change? If they don't, then you are pushing up against their mindset and vision.

Over the years, I've seen the process of building a Culture of Philanthropy stopped in its tracks repeatedly. Many things—internal and external—can stop you. We've discussed a plethora of them up to this point, and, yes, some of them include members of your own organization. Think about that early in your planning process, *but don't let the potential for stalling stop you from starting and persevering!*

Because building a Culture of Philanthropy takes years, it requires setting benchmarks and check-ins on a regular basis. While the same person doesn't need to lead this team for multiple years, there should be people in this group who are willing to step up and either co-lead or take the baton when the leader isn't up for being the lead driver any longer.

A Board Accountability Structure: The Path to a Strong Culture of Philanthropy

To have a high-functioning board of directors, it's important to have a clear Accountability Structure. Some boards have a culture of rubber-stamping; their membership on the board is easy, and it's a very light lift. Or two or three individuals do most of the work and others just show up and approve things.

The problem is that, in order to have an extraordinary Culture of Philanthropy, the board needs to step up and be extraordinary as well. Some boards have mastered being extraordinary. If that describes your organization, *congratulations and nice work!*

Unfortunately, I've seen this scenario way more frequently than not: the board has a mindset of scarcity, and they're fearful that they won't get enough board members, so when inviting people to be on the board, they downplay board responsibilities. They say things like, "Don't worry. It won't take that much time," and "I promise, no fundraising!" They invite people to take a place on the board, and then cross their fingers and hope they'll volunteer to help out and, ultimately, follow through with the various things that they say they'll do.

The most functional boards I have known are very clear about what it will take to be on the board. They lay out the responsibilities before inviting someone to be on the board. When you make agreements up front, everyone knows what they're responsible for and what they aren't responsible for. This works brilliantly for volunteers and staff alike.

What's fascinating is that some organizations, like the well-known national not-for-profit agencies that have larger events in small towns across the United States, do this very effectively. If you volunteer, to coordinate a walk-a-thon for an organization that has two hundred walk-a-thons every year, every role within that event has a job description and an Accountability Structure. Someone who volunteers knows exactly what's expected of them. People who don't do what they say they'll do are fired (even though they are volunteering). The difference between these success stories and most not-for-profits that I know is that, in our sector, most organizations lack an Accountability Structure. But you can change that.

How do you make this change? You have to have an open conversation about it. You have to acknowledge that there hasn't been an Accountability Structure, and if members want a more proactive board, you're going to need to set that up.

For many at the table, it may not be what they signed up for. You will have to have an authentic conversation about it. It may be difficult, and it may require breaking cultural norms within your agency. Are you committed to transforming the board and having it become more active in development and other aspects of governing the agency? Is there some urgent cause that requires that the board step up? Is the writing on the wall because you took a look at your Default Future? Did this conversation begin because you are committed to a Culture of Philanthropy?

If there is a desire to transform the board, I encourage you to be strong, have the difficult conversations and enroll people into your vision. Building a Culture of Philanthropy is not always an easy task—but trust that if you have the courage to do the (sometimes uncomfortable) work to keep or bring the right people onboard with you—it will be rewarding.

Communication Tools for Producing a High-Functioning Organization and a Culture of Philanthropy

Building a Culture of Philanthropy requires authentic conversations, clear requests, vulnerability and perseverance. I've mentioned a couple of times that there are always different subcultures going on beneath the surface in every organization. The tools in this section are designed to help you build an organization-wide foundation of strong communication. Once you have that foundation in place, the mindset (Hearts & Minds) and the Behaviors required for authentic communication will follow, and you will create an opening for addressing the barriers to a Culture of Philanthropy. In other words, high-functioning communication can accelerate your path to a Culture of Philanthropy.

For example, I just discussed how to shift to a more functional Accountability. Structure with your board. This type of transformational work requires delicate communication skills. It won't build trust or partnerships if leaders *demand* that people behave differently.

The rest of this chapter has High-Performing Leadership tools from Zemo Trevathan (The Aligned Team) that my clients have found very useful when pursuing deep and meaningful culture change. Zemo is a master consultant focused on culture change with his clients. You will see that he has designed tools to help build extraordinary organizations. I strongly advise doing the exercises with your team *before* they become necessary, as it will make everyone familiar with how to use the tools, should the need arise.

Insights from the Field

Requests: The Ultimate Power Tool of Effective Leaders

Zemo Trevathan

Most of us are readily familiar with the cultural default that somehow leading means doing. Most of us, at this point, are also aware what a misunderstanding this is of the nature of leadership. Leadership, whether informal or formal, elicits willing participation and action from others—from your team.

The most powerful way for me to fulfill my ownership/accountability of any important goal, and certainly a Culture of Philanthropy, is to have a strong network of people mutually committed to that goal on whom I can call for help. And the tool for gaining that help in a high-performance culture is *the request.*

Here's a basic definition of the request that clarifies it more usefully than the standard, default definition of requests in our world.

> A request is an invitation to another person to help us get a specific need met in a specific manner. The appropriate response to this invitation is either yes or no.

If we're not open to the other person declining the request, then it's not really a request. It's a demand disguised as a request. And demands don't build high-performance cultures. Demands tend to come from a scarcity mindset. I tell someone else that they have to do something because I believe there are no other options. When we come from a place of abundance, it's easier to approach requests for help with this openness to the possibility of other options.

Now, obviously, there are certain rules, guidelines or even job requirements that are not optional, and we don't want to continuously revisit such core requirements. But even these requirements are best handled, initially, as requests. The powerful thing about a request is that a request requires the other person to choose between yes or no. And once they say yes, they've made an agreement.

For requirements, it's best to ask for people's compliance and alignment from the very beginning as a condition for being in the job or on the team in the first place.

Instead of saying, "You're on my team now. There are some things you must do and some rules you must follow," you could try saying, "I'm about to invite you to take a position as one of our team members. But before we make that agreement, I need to ask for your complete alignment to and compliance with a few team ground rules. If they don't work for you, I will understand. I want to be clear, I can only invite you to the team if these ground rules work, as commitment to these ways of working is a prerequisite to being on my team. Are you willing to commit to and align with these principles?"

In this example, the answer no is perfectly acceptable to the requester, though there would be consequences (as in not getting hired).

Even later, let's say someone has violated one of those parameters. I can still phrase my intervention with them as a request. "Can I get your complete recommitment to honor this ground rule in the future?"

Part of the reason requests work is that we want the team member to have full internal, energetic alignment with the behavior or principle. We want them to do it because they've committed, not because they're being made to do it. We can relate this to the centered versus reactive mindsets discussed below. We want people who are choosing to honor the behavior code or agreements, not doing so because they feel they have to.

Exercise

Make a list of recent interactions in which you have either accepted an assignment or role or given one to someone else. For each example on the list:

- Evaluate whether or not the invitation was made as an effective request (was a yes or no response acceptable?).
- Assess the level of alignment within the assigned person for the task/invitation.

For any of the items on the list in which the assigned person had a low level of buy-in/alignment, how would you restate the invitation so that it would be a more effective request?

As you begin to roll out your Culture of Philanthropy Implementation Plan, you will need to enroll people in taking on different responsibilities to assure that it happens. You will need to make clear, straightforward requests. As mentioned above, with board members in particular, our field is notoriously vague when making requests. There is something difficult about staff making requests of volunteers, and especially making requests of volunteers who are technically bosses. It isn't surprising that Accountability Structures can be nonexistent.

Insights from the Field

Hard Conversations: Simple Steps of Being Direct (Kind + Honest at the Same Time)

Zemo Trevathan

Step Zero: Get in a Centered Mindset

Empowering Mindsets: Centered vs. Reactive—In addition to the abundance mindset (vs. the scarcity mindset), there's another mindset that is key to success for individuals. It is especially useful in creating a high-performance, sustainable culture. This critical skill in intentional culture building is the *centered mindset.*

In the simple diagram below, you can see that we are in a centered mindset when we're in touch with our core self, embodied and present. When something has triggered us or thrown us off-center, we're in a reactive state.

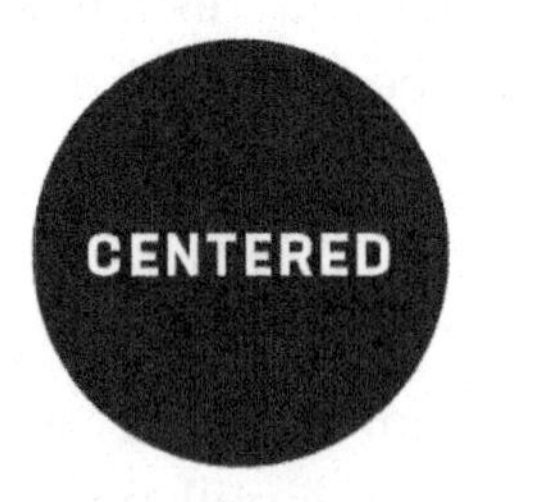

20-1 A Centered vs. Reactive State
(Zemo Trevathan, The Aligned Team)

The key distinction between being in a centered state or mindset, as opposed to being in a reactive (off-center) mindset is very simple. We are in a centered mindset whenever we're "at choice." When we are in reactive state, we have gone into a form of "default" mode, in which we are not truly "choosing," but habitual, previously learned behavior patterns are taking over.

Many times, being in a reactive mindset is easily identifiable, as when someone says something we don't like, and we immediately react with an angry comment. Other times, it is subtler, either because the triggered behavior is quiet or internal, or because it may sound measured and thoughtful, while it is still in actuality, an automatic, unconscious response.

For example, it took years of having other people reflect back to me before I finally became truly aware that when I get angry, I often mask it, from myself and the other person, by going into an automatic reaction of trying to seem calm when, just underneath, I am seething and trying very hard to change or control the other person.

The purpose of this centering tool is never to evaluate whether someone else is in a centered state or a reactive mindset; this is meant only as a self-awareness tool. And similarly, the purpose is not to "correctly" identify whether I'm in a centered mindset. It isn't about being right or wrong. In fact, it's just the opposite. Often, if we're looking through a lens of right versus wrong, that's actually a sign we are in a reactive mindset. When we're in a centered mindset, things don't usually occur as either/or, black/white. In a centered state, we can usually see a range of possibilities or options.

The purpose of the tool is really just to inject a moment of observation and intention. Pausing and asking ourselves, *Am I in a centered or a reactive state at this moment?* tends to have the effect of helping us ease out of a reactive state, if we're in one. By definition, pausing and reflecting is the opposite of reacting. In fact, the pause itself might be the key tool here.

Without going deep into the physiology of these two different mindsets, let me just say a few words that most of us can relate to. When a stimulus happens to or near us that startles us or upsets us, there's usually an instantaneous physical response. Heart rate speeds up, adrenaline is released. That's the physiological part of the reactive state. We can't stop it or control it, as it's an automatic part of our nervous system. If we were deer or mice, we'd have no choice but to act on that physiological response—fight or flight.

But as humans, and especially as "philanthropically oriented" humans, we have another option. We have the option to notice the physiological reaction and make choices about what to do with it. This means simply that whatever is happening around us or to us, whatever stimulus is being presented, does not cause our subsequent mindsets and actions. We pause, consider, and choose a mindset and actions based on our values and intentions, not based on our default reactions.

I want to stress that choosing a centered mindset does not mean suppressing the emotion. The emotional reaction will happen, and it isn't useful or healthy to deny or suppress our natural emotional reactions. The intention here is to notice and allow the emotional reaction. Accept it, even. And then make a choice about what to do or say consciously after the emotional reaction passes, not triggered or caused by it.

Exercise

Make a list of situations, interactions or types of people that elicit negative/unpleasant emotional reactions inside you. For each of them, do the following:

- Name the emotional reaction(s) that tend to happen.
- Identify Behaviors or communications that you sometimes react with as default—unconscious results of the reaction.
- Identify, if you can, what beliefs or mindsets go along with the emotional and behavioral reactions. (There's a good chance you will notice a lot of scarcity thinking among them!)
- Imagine a more empowering, centered mindset that you could choose to operate from around this situation. For example, instead of thinking *I can't believe Gail has no time to meet with our Culture of Philanthropy Task Force—she must not be committed,* I could operate with the mindset that says, *Wow, it's too bad that Gail can't make time for our meeting. I'll let that be a reminder to myself that I easily lapse into a scarcity mindset when it comes to my time, too, especially when I'm up against deadlines.*

This is similar to what we did back in Chapter 7 when we chose abundance thinking over scarcity thinking when reviewing the basic steps of fundraising. This time, we are using it when we are in the moment, reacting negatively to something. You can apply this same technique when you fall into scarcity thinking.

Conversations with others always go better if you take ownership of your own mindset first. Sadly, our culture sets us up to think about the conversation with the other person as being the place where we can work through our issue and maybe feel better. The simple truth is the conversation with the other person is going to go better if you work through some of the issues and find a way to feel better *before* you have the conversation.

Get centered. Assume the other person has positive intent. Go into the conversation believing that you'll get your needs met (if not in this conversation, then with this person in some other way). Apply abundance thinking. Call a coach or a Committed Listener first and get their support in expressing the hardest feelings and in finding a constructive mindset for the conversation. Then, go have that conversation.

That's why we call it Step Zero. Do it before beginning the direct conversation.

Step One: Set Mutual Outcomes as the Purpose of the Conversation

The biggest downfall of most difficult conversations (after starting them in a reactive mindset instead of a centered one) is that both parties are usually trying their best to "win," to convince the other that "I am right, and you need to change your mind." This mode of communication, where I speak as if my own perspective is "reality," has been termed as the Model 1 (Argyris, C., Putnam, R., & McLain Smith, D *Action Science: Concepts, Methods, and Skills for Research and Intervention*, Jossey-Bass, 1985).

It is habitual in our default culture and has been estimated to be in use up to 95 percent of the time. It is how we talk. It is also not very effective at changing anyone else's mind or behavior.

The mode of communication that has been shown to have the highest likelihood of influencing the other person's behavior or beliefs is called the Mutual Learning Frame. In this mode of communication, I take care to let you know that I'm just as interested in learning from the conversation as I am in convincing you. I may have some strong opinions, but I'm going to phrase them in such a way that both you and I can remember that they're not truths, but my opinions, and that my goal in the conversation is for both of us to potentially learn from the exchange and for both of us to be served by the conversation.

Here are some examples of how we might phrase things in a mutual learning frame:

- "I've got some feedback I'd love to share with you about your participation in the meeting yesterday, but I'd like to do it as a dialogue in which we both share our thoughts and both learn something from it. Are you up for that?"
- "I know we've been advocating different paths for the project we are working on together. How about sitting down together and talking about how our ideas are similar and different? In particular, I'd like the two of us to see if we can come to a place where we both understand and support each other's intent, even if our ideas for implementation are different."
- "I know we've been disagreeing with each other about _____. I'd love to learn more about why you think about it the way you do, and I'd love for you to learn more about where I'm

> coming from on this. Would you join me in a conversation about just that, learning about each other's ideas?"

There are a thousand ways to phrase the invitation, but the bottom line is the other person is more likely to be receptive to what you have to share if they're clear that your intention is for both of you to benefit from the conversation.

Steps Two and Three: Separate the Objective Facts from the Subjective Viewpoints

This is the actual mechanism of making "kind and honest at the same time" work. Again, our culture has tragically unhelpful default habits in this area. We are trained to speak as if everything we're saying, whether it is mutually verifiable data or privately held opinion, is simple, true and real. The antidote is very simple to practice.

Share the objective facts as objective facts. Take any interpretations about those facts, or anything the other person might disagree with or label differently and leave it out of this step. Remember the exercise from Chapter 5 where we listed a fact (that we failed to get a grant that we had gotten previously) and the various interpretations that we could make up about that fact? This is similar. We start by stripping away the interpretations and just looking at the fact, the basic observation.

Step Two (the Facts step) will often start with "I saw _____" or "I heard _____." The goal is to share observations that anyone can share:

> Say this: "Yesterday, in the meeting, when I heard you addressing me—."
>
> Not this: "Yesterday, when you were yelling at me—."

> Say this: "I noticed you talking to _____ earlier today—."
>
> Not this: "Why were you going behind my back and talking about our project with so-and-so earlier?"

Then, in Step Three (the Viewpoints step), we can share the feelings we had about those facts, or the perceptions we formed about them, but the key here is to own our viewpoints as ours, not state them as if they are objectively true for anyone:

> "Yesterday, in the meeting, when I heard you addressing me, it seemed to me that your voice was elevated, and I felt quite deflated, like I was being talked down to."
>
> "I noticed you talking to _____ earlier today, and I felt concerned that you might have been speaking about our project before I feel ready for them to be brought into it."

Brené Brown talks about this idea in some of her videos. She says that when she and her husband are particularly reactivated with each other, they use a method of starting their sentence with "the story that I made up is...." It has the speaker own their fabrication of the facts. This is all deeply connected to the idea of how things occur that was discussed in Chapter 5. We noted the difference between what happened (the fact), and how it occurs *to us* (our made-up interpretation).

Step Four: Ask for Their Facts and Viewpoints...and Listen

Once you've presented what you've observed and what you think or feel about it, you're halfway there.

Again, the default in our culture is often to think that is the whole conversation. "There, I said it. Now I'm done with that conversation!" But, of course, a conversation is not a conversation without both sides. So, the next step is to ask for, and listen to, their perspective, like this:

> "Now I'd love to hear your perspective. Have I missed something? Are there other things you've observed? And what would you like me to hear about your viewpoint?"

It is helpful to phrase the invitation to have them separate out the facts versus viewpoints. They may or may not present it that way, especially if they have not been trained in a direct conversation model. But the great thing is that whether or not they do, you can practice *hearing* it that way, and you can even reflect it back to them in separate pieces:

> "It sounds to me like you saw and heard a couple different messages in that meeting yesterday than I heard."
>
> "And, if I hear you right, the impact it had on you was that I was trying to assert my power over the group, instead of facilitate a group decision? Is that what you felt?"

As we discussed earlier, the important part of listening for understanding is that you don't let your experience of agreeing or disagreeing interfere with simply hearing and taking in what they're saying. The agreeing and disagreeing will come out in later iterations. When the other person is speaking, your job is to hear what they are saying and understand it.

Step Five: Making Agreements and Actions

Step Five won't actually happen in order right after Steps Two, Three and Four very often. Usually, it will take a few iterations of those steps. We take turns comparing facts, stating and hearing viewpoints, and seeking a place of mutual understanding and agreement. Once both parties feel fully heard, with a commonality of perspective, then we can proceed to agree to next steps.

Once again, the default of our "normal" culture shows up as a very bad habit. Most of the time, conversations in our culture take the form of opinions stated right up front as facts, with a request/demand stated right up front without letting the other person speak:

> "You yelled at me in the meeting yesterday again. If you can't refrain from raising your voice, please just skip the meetings." Judge, jury and executioner, all in one.

In the direct conversation model, we wait to suggest a resolution or action until after we've explored the issue and given both parties a chance to share and learn. Sometimes, the understanding is all that is needed.

If there is further action now implied, the key is to make the agreement for action SHMART goals (as discussed previously): Specific, Hearts & Minds Oriented, Measurable, Achievable, Relevant, Time-Bound:

> "So, by tomorrow, will you circle back to ___ and make sure they know that the information you shared with them was confidential and not to be acted on

or communicated to anyone else, and report back to me when you've had that conversation? Great."

Exercise

Make a list of anyone in your organization (or life!) with whom you've been avoiding or withholding communication. Pick one of those people and answer these questions:

- What mindset am I in right now as I avoid that communication (centered vs. reactive)?
- What would a more constructive/centered mindset for having that conversation sound like in my own head?
- As I imagine having that conversation, how might I phrase an invitation to the conversation that creates the possibility of mutually beneficial outcomes?
- How might I state the observable facts of the situation?
- How might I state my perspective/feelings about it in a nonthreatening way?
- How might I invite them to share their observations and viewpoints?
- By when will I have this conversation?
- Would having someone coach me through it first—to help me get in a centered mindset—help? If so, who will I ask to do that, and by when?

Repeat the exercise for as many of the people on your list as you find helpful. If you are reading this book as part of a group, it helps to practice with others in your group, with the direct conversation model open in front of you so you can support each other to practice the steps.

Step Six: Clean Up and Recommit

Two specific situations in which it is important to communicate directly and kindly, especially when we have leadership responsibilities, are when we have in some way missed the mark in something we are committed to, or when we have had a negative impact on someone else.

Right off the bat, let's take a moment to notice and acknowledge that most of us have been misinformed and shamed about these kinds of situations. Most of us grew up being "forced" into apologies because we had "been bad" in some way. "Now, say you're sorry!" we were told, over and over, at the end of a pointed finger.

The intent of using apologies as a team and leadership tool is not to apologize for "being bad" or "doing a bad thing." It's not about judgment or moralizing, and our old training here tends to be more of a limiting perception than a helpful mindset. So, let's set it aside.

The intent is to acknowledge to another person that I am aware I've had a negative impact, or I haven't fulfilled something I am accountable for. This isn't to say I am "bad." It is simply to acknowledge I have a commitment, and I missed fulfilling it. And, most importantly, that I continue to be committed to fulfilling it going forward. There are three critical components to communicate when carrying out a clean-up:

- I take full accountability for what I did/didn't do, said/didn't say and for the impact it had on the group/other person.
- I apologize for that impact.
- I make a commitment for what will be different going forward.

Here are some examples of how one might take responsibility:

> "Gang, it has been pointed out to me that I've been late several times now to our team meetings. I understand that this interrupts the flow and effectiveness of the meeting start, and that it shows disrespect for the rest of you and diminishes how important our time is together."
>
> "I apologize. I do value our time together and mean no disrespect to any of you and take that seriously."
>
> "I have already had a conversation with my spouse about it, and we've changed our morning routine so that I can come a half hour earlier in the mornings, whether we have a meeting or not, and I'm committed to being on time from now on."

Think for a second about the things that make you cringe when someone tries to apologize to you. There are several classic elements of apology attempts that don't work:

- When it's forced or otherwise seems insincere.

- When it's explained away or justified so that there's really no responsibility being taken.
- When the behavior doesn't change and the negative impact continues.

All three of those characteristics are useful for instructing us on how to make cleanups effective and meaningful. Make sure you're sincere, that you're fully taking accountability and not explaining it away, and that your commitment to change is real and executable.

In my three decades of consulting with leaders and teams, sincere cleanups on the part of leaders toward their teams have been some of the most impactful and transformative actions I have ever witnessed. Whole organizations have changed directions as a result of a sincere cleanup that actually gets followed through on by a leader.

One last pointer: It is often useful to ask questions, and not do this as a one-way communication. For example, sometimes, I think I might have had a negative impact, but I'm not sure. So, I'll ask. "Do I owe you a cleanup for how I spoke to you yesterday?" Or, "Did you have any hard feelings from our meeting yesterday? I want to make sure you felt respected by me, even while we disagreed. Did you?"

Similarly, sometimes I need guidance from the other person to know what form of recommitment might make a difference in the future. If I'm not clear, I'll ask something like, "I'd really like to make sure you don't get left with feelings like that again from our interactions. Is there anything specific I can do or commit to that would feel good to you?"

Exercise

Do a survey in your mind of everyone you know. Who comes to mind that you have had, or may have had, negative impact on (or any impact that is different or less than what you're committed to)?

- Make a list of these people.
- Pick one or two to write out a full cleanup and recommit conversation.
- Pick out at least one or two of these people to go have clean up conversations with—and set a completion date.

As you build your Culture of Philanthropy, these concepts detailed above from Zemo Trevathan will empower you to:

- Stay in a centered mindset (particularly when it's time to acknowledge when something didn't work, or someone didn't keep their word).
- Recognize the difference between the Subjective Viewpoints and Objective Facts. Notice how your team members may have Subjective Viewpoints about money and fundraising—for example, "I don't know anybody with money" or "I think that fundraising means, by definition, arm-twisting," versus these examples of Objective Facts—"We didn't hit our goal" or "I don't know what people want to give until I ask them."
- Make bold agreements and commitments to take action (even when it is hard and feels risky).
- Clean up and recommit (so that you become trusted as being good at your word).

I hope that you will embrace these practices. Similar to any action related to true culture change, the changes we've discussed may seem challenging to take on. I do promise you that stepping into the vulnerability of doing the exercises will be worthwhile. Ultimately, adopting clear, transparent communication practices can transform your relationship with your team and the outcomes you achieve.

Chapter 21

Making It Happen: Creating Time for a Culture of Philanthropy

I challenge you to become a possibilitarian.
No matter how dark things seem to be or actually are,
raise your sights and see possibilities.
Always see them, for they're always there.

—Norman Vincent Peale, *The Power of Positive Thinking*

Time is one of our most valuable commodities. Using your time to work toward your highest ideals is one of the most meaningful things you can do as a high-functioning leader. Creating and prioritizing time to build and maintain your visionary Culture of Philanthropy is a powerful way to cause a breakthrough in fundraising for your agency.

Conversely, the obstacle that has the greatest potential for getting in the way of the rollout of your Culture of Philanthropy Plan is time. Specifically, the scarcity of time. It will likely show up in two ways: constantly putting out fires over more long-term measures and lack of patience (*This Culture of Philanthropy is taking too long. We need results now!*). Prepare for these debilitating mindsets and be proactive.

Let's first address the issue of simply having too much to handle in the present to take on more long-term strategies. To make this greater vision happen, you will need to set aside the time to make it a reality. Put Culture of Philanthropy implementation into your calendar over time. Everyone on your team should do the same. Make it a permanent item on board and staff agendas. Put reminders in your office to help keep Culture of Philanthropy top of mind. There are a number of downloads from our Book Hub at www.ChooseAbundanceBook.com that can be very useful for that purpose. As you develop your Culture of Philanthropy Plan, be sure that you have goals scheduled for fulfillment multiple years into the future. It is important that everyone working on this understands that you are in it for the long haul.

During the tenure of this project, there will likely be turnover. Be sure to have a pipeline of new partners, and train them on your desired culture. Squelch expectations that things are going to change instantly. To keep it alive and vital, celebrate when you've made a step forward. Use Structures such as board and staff meetings to acknowledge your progress in building a Culture of Philanthropy. Build reporting of KPIs (Key Performance Indicators—see Chapter 9, Step 8 on creating your Implementation Plan) into board and staff meetings. Establish and maintain regular communications about your forward movement to assure that it remains top of mind, and that it doesn't get dropped.

Day-to-day, you'll run into people who will fill the air with scarcity thinking. No doubt, this scarcity thinking will include skepticism about your vision of an organization-wide Culture of Philanthropy. Your job as a leader (whether authorized or self-declared) is to be the *possibilitarian* and help people keep the faith that progress is happening and culture change is advancing.

If you are a flying or boating enthusiast, you may be familiar with the term *trim tab*. It's a mechanical device on either a ship or plane, that, when engaged, moves a rudder, which ultimately steers the vehicle. It allows the pilot or captain to make significant change with little effort. Imagine, without it, the effort that would go into moving a rudder physically with wind or water resistance. Buckminster Fuller, the American futurist, coined the term *trim tab* to represent the small action that has the greatest impact. As you lead your Culture of Philanthropy change, identify those things that have monumental potential for breakthrough. Find your trim tabs.

- You may encounter complicated times where outside forces make your work particularly hard. How can your shortcomings be both personal and organizational growth opportunities? In my career in development, I've seen some very difficult times. *Here is what I know: those individuals and organizations who viewed the difficulty as an opportunity to deepen partnerships moved ahead.* While some organizations folded, others got innovative. Remember to be creative and flexible in the evolution of your Culture of Philanthropy Plan as times and circumstances change.

- You may sometimes feel like, *I'm currently trying to take a sip of water from a firehose, and you want me to stop and build the culture?* The more you evolve into a workplace where everyone plays a role in building a Culture of Philanthropy, that has community engagement, and that has deep donor partnerships, the more you will find that you are ultimately building a more resilient agency—one that can more readily bounce back when things get rough.
- One more thought about the firehose metaphor. Stop trying to drink water from it. Walk away from the firehose. Get quiet and thoughtful. Get in touch with your vision, and don't perpetuate the panic. Remember that you don't need to go it alone. Encourage and empower people on your team to step into their own leadership. Do this now, when you aren't in challenging circumstances, as well as if you are blindsided by difficulties. Seek out that which *might be possible.*

My mindset has potential to be my superpower.
I choose to use it that way.

This is a very useful mantra that helps me make it through moments where my scarcity mindset creeps in. It can help you, too.

- Know and name your weakness. Say it out loud. One organization that I work with is quite self-aware. As they put their plan on paper, they said that *lack of time isn't an allowable excuse for failure to effectively generate a Culture of Philanthropy.* It shouldn't surprise you that the organization is The Harry & Rose Samson Family JCC in Milwaukee. They put it in print right below their Culture of Philanthropy statement! They took scarcity of time off the table as an excuse. Period. Does scarcity of time ever come up for them? Of course it does! But when it shows up, they know it's an excuse, and they remember their commitment: to take it off the table as a justification. What is the thing that is most likely to be in your organization's way? Take the time to figure that out, and compensate for it.

- And lastly, remember to keep expanding your circle of people who support your Culture of Philanthropy Plan. The more people you have working on it, the more the work can be spread out. You'll find that the naysayers will begin to get drowned out by the *possibilitarians*!

Chapter 22
You've Got This

What good is an idea if it remains an idea?
Try. Experiment. Iterate. Fail. Try again. Change the world.
—Simon Sinek

In 2014, the seminal report "Underdeveloped: A National Study of the Challenges Facing Nonprofit Fundraising" (Jeanne Bell and Maria Cornelius) was released by Compass Point with support of the Evelyn & Walter Haas Jr. Fund. 2,700 Executive Directors and development professionals were interviewed.

As the report indicated, development shops across North America are struggling. Donor-retention rates are abysmal, boards and staff members are disengaged, and the turnover rate of development staff averages about eighteen months. The missing link, according to the report, is a Culture of Philanthropy. The opportunity to build a Culture of Philanthropy in your organization, while difficult, is entirely possible. It takes effort and focus. The rewards for this effort are equally large.

As you now have seen, this is not a typical fundraising book. While I have read many very useful "how to" books on fundraising, and many on how to implement specific fundraising models and systems, none have focused on *culture change* in fund development. The difference between these two methods is that, while culture change is certainly more difficult, it has the greater capacity to have a lasting impact. And, further, if you build Structures or attempt to take on Behaviors on top of a dysfunctional culture, you are likely not going to succeed.

Building a Culture of Philanthropy is a process that has the potential to forever change the trajectory of your agency. It has the possibility of bringing in the resources your agency needs to fulfill and even expand its mission. Imagine having volunteers stepping up their involvement and making community connections, donors serving as partners, new innovative programs rolling out, and surprise contributions coming in your door.

As I said previously, building a Culture of Philanthropy is a marathon, not a sprint. And for those who are not athletes, taking on a marathon can be a formidable goal. But I encourage all of you, beginners and advanced-level players, to start training. Set an inspiring goal, one that challenges you.

If you are just embarking on your Culture of Philanthropy journey, it's okay. Don't beat yourself up for what you haven't yet done. Take some notes from others in the field, map out your plan, and then just start by taking baby steps. Soon, you'll be walking, you will move on to jogging, and before you know it, you'll have successes to build on. Be sure to celebrate those.

If you are at a mid-level proficiency in establishing a Culture of Philanthropy, you're probably like most organizations I've encountered. Again, you should set an inspiring goal, one that moves you. Do what it takes to roll it out. Do the same if you are already at an advanced level of a Culture of Philanthropy. What could you be doing better? What are you doing to educate people and name the realities of your culture so you can build a stronger, more viable one?

It's likely that you will have fits and starts. You'll make some progress, and then something will go awry. You'll realize you need to go back to your team and perhaps undo some parts of the cultural change you started. As you may remember, I mentioned one organization that started with asking, and then had to go back and clean up and acknowledge that asking was the wrong place to begin the creation of a Culture of Philanthropy.

There are other organizations I've worked with who started down the wrong path initially, then had to pedal backward before moving forward. This is all part of taking risks and learning from your mistakes. When you clean up a misstep, communicate it, and recommit in an authentic way, you are encouraging a culture of learning. This has an equalizing effect where staff and board can become empowered to step into your team and share their ideas of how to advance your desired culture change.

ORGANIZATIONAL PROFICIENCY LEVELS FOR A CULTURE OF PHILANTHROPY

ROLES	BEGINNER LEVEL CULTURE OF PHILANTHROPY	MID-LEVEL CULTURE OF PHILANTHROPY	ADVANCED LEVEL CULTURE OF PHILANTHROPY
DEVELOPMENT STAFF	Development staff are required to do nondevelopment tasks like arrange food for board mtgs, etc. All fundraising is event-driven. There is no understanding of what a Culture of Philanthropy entails.	Development staff are able to focus on development. They have resources to do their job well, including a relational database, admin support and some marketing help.	There is enough dev. staff to be able to focus on Major Donors and broader dev. needs. Advanced resources like donor research tools, regular meetings with ED, etc. There is an understanding of what a Culture of Philanthropy is and a plan to make it happen.
EXECUTIVE DIRECTOR (ED)	ED does not have regular meetings with the Development Director, and Development Director isn't at the table for leadership team meetings. ED feels fund development is a necessary evil.	ED has regular meetings with Development Director and partners with them.	ED has a portfolio of Major Donors, each with a detailed plan. ED and Major Gifts Officer go over each other's strategy weekly. There is a clear plan to build a Culture of Philanthropy with a team of leaders.
BOARD OF DIRECTORS	Most board members are clear they don't "know anyone with money." There is no understanding of what a Culture of Philanthropy is or entails. Some think it means acquiring wealthy donors.	Some board members are involved in connecting the agency with peers. Board meetings include some stewardship activities like card writing and thank-you calls.	The board fully understands a C of P and some board members help with each step of Major Donor engagement.
BOARD DEVELOPMENT COMMITTEE	There is no board development committee, but there is an events committee that comes up with gala-type events (that the single development staff person has to produce).	A development committee exists that helps connect potential donors to the agency.	There is a C of P Committee, which is charged with orienting new board members, providing training for all board members and bringing cultivation and stewardship opportunities to the board.
CUSTOMER SERVICE	Members, parents, students, program participants and possibly even volunteers are not considered contributors.	There is awareness of the potential for any connection to make a difference for the organization. Customer service is average.	There is recognition that each interaction of every staff and board member with members, vendors and community members can be an opportunity for deeper community engagement.
PROGRAM STAFF	Do not see any relevance between their jobs and development.	A small percentage of staff shares their contacts with the development team.	All staff see the importance of capturing and sharing firsthand, inspiring stories with development and making community connections.

22-1 Proficiency Levels of Culture of Philanthropy (Download full chart at www.ChooseAbundanceBook.com)

(Laurie Herrick, Rainmaker Consulting)

As you start to move forward in developing a Culture of Philanthropy, it's important to note that you can't do it all in the beginning. I've developed a chart (an abbreviated version is shown in the chart on the previous page) to help you identify your organization's Culture of Philanthropy proficiency. The full chart can be found and downloaded at www.ChooseAbundanceBook.com. You can print it out and use it to inspire your momentum.

If, in one of the roles, you notice that you're at a very Beginner Level of proficiency in your Culture of Philanthropy, then you can move from a Beginner Level to a Mid-Level Culture of Philanthropy. If you have started your work and already have a Mid-Level Culture of Philanthropy, you can aim for an Advanced Level.

Find your organization's proficiency on this chart. You'll probably have some roles that are stronger than others. Use this as a way to see that there are some areas where you've advanced, and there are clear ways to move forward. Wherever you are, remember that you can up your game and move to the next level of proficiency. You have the ability to *choose abundance*. Make it a practice to see what you can do to build a Culture of Philanthropy.

Across the field, many have sought the path to build this elusive culture, but few have understood and intentionally engineered a Culture of Philanthropy. *You must create a strong team and intentionally build, name and put into practice your desired culture.* If you are someone who takes on building a Culture of Philanthropy, you are a pioneer in the field, and at the head of the class of a growing national movement.

Your organization's mission is a piece of the larger global work of making our world a better place. We cannot do it without you. As someone reading this book, you have an exciting opportunity to accelerate the possibilities that are inherent in your mission. Too many not-for-profit organizations exist in a world of scarcity, which limits their capacity and capability to fulfill their mission. You have the opportunity to build an extraordinary culture that attracts community engagement and philanthropic generosity toward your goals.

This book has been designed to support your organization in being healthier and more vibrant than it currently is by guiding you to create a Culture of Philanthropy. I hope you find this to be a useful resource for making positive change—and you take on this transformative and meaningful work. May it trickle into your personal life, as well, and may you have many moments of stepping outside of our cultural scarcity mindset and into one filled with generosity and tremendous possibility.

Thank you for your dedication to making a world that works for everyone. We need more leaders like you to be pioneers and take this stand for a greater possibility. If you found this compelling, and you have started to build a team to create a Culture of Philanthropy, I invite you to join the conversation and community of people making this meaningful organizational change. I'd love to hear what works and where you are particularly challenged. If there is anything I can do to help your organization, do not hesitate to ask.

I'm with you—choosing abundance.

About Laurie Herrick and Rainmaker Consulting

Laurie Herrick is a fundraising consultant and entrepreneur with over twenty years' experience in the not-for-profit sector. The emphasis of Laurie's work is creating fundraising breakthroughs by empowering leaders to build a healthy Culture of Philanthropy within their organizations. It is through this culture change that Laurie fulfills her personal mission to make positive social change.

Laurie has served in numerous professional and volunteer roles. She's been a Development Director, Executive Director, board member and Board Chair of a variety of not-for-profit organizations. These experiences led to her profound awareness of the challenges they were facing. One of the noteworthy obstacles she identified in her role as a consultant was the way the culture, and specifically a destructive mindset of scarcity, was getting in the way of fundraising success. She built a coaching approach that addressed this mindset and trains organizational leaders to engineer a culture that is more intentional and grows from a mindset of abundance.

Laurie founded Rainmaker Consulting in 2003 (www.rainmkr.com). Since inception, Laurie and the Rainmaker Consulting team have empowered hundreds of organizations in their individual journeys toward building healthy organizational Cultures of Philanthropy—the proven key to successful and sustainable fundraising.

In 2010, Laurie launched a professional development course (called GIFT) for fundraising professionals employed by grantee organizations of the Harold Grinspoon Foundation. It became apparent that the magic formula for breakthrough fundraising success was to not just depend on the development professional to design and make the intended culture change, but for a team of leaders to take it on together.

As a result of this insight, a team-approach course was piloted: GIFT Leadership Institute. Participating organizations were required to bring a committed team of leaders—including Executive Directors, development professionals and board members—to together build a healthy Culture of Philanthropy. The results have been astounding.

Rainmaker Consulting has adopted this team approach in their consulting, training and coaching in fundraising, board development and strategic planning. Rainmaker Consulting offers the following services that incorporate a Culture of Philanthropy:

- **The Choose Abundance Academy**—virtual and in-person courses to add deeper learning to your Culture of Philanthropy journey. You can select Choose Abundance Fundamentals, Choose Abundance Seminar or Integrated Abundance coaching, customized for your organization.
- **Consulting Services**—in fundraising, board development and strategic planning, all with a focus on creating a Culture of Philanthropy.
- **Capital Campaign Coaching and Support**—walking campaign leaders through Feasibility Interviews, goal-setting, donor strategies, campaign planning and implementation.

To learn about Laurie Herrick and Rainmaker Consulting, go to www.rainmkr.com. We welcome your questions and inquiries.

Favorite Resources

Benevon and the work of Terry Axelrod: https://www.benevon.com/about-us/

Blue Avocado: Practical, Provocative, Food-for Thought for Nonprofits: https://blueavocado.org

Bob Sutton: https://bobsutton.typepad.com

Brené Brown: https://brenebrown.com

David Byrne, *How Music Works*: https://davidbyrne.com

Chuck Collins, *Robin Hood Was Right: A Guide to Giving Your Money for Social Change* (W.W. Norton, 2001)

Jim Collins, Good to Great: https://www.jimcollins.com/concepts.html

***Contributions* Magazine**, "how to" source for nonprofit professionals: https://contributionsmagazine.qwknetllc.com

Roger Craver, *Retention Fundraising: The New Art and Science of Keeping Your Donors for Life*. in 2014., Emerson & Church Publishers, 2014.

Robert Gass and the Social Transformation Project: https://www.robertgass.com

Seth Godin's Blog: https://seths.blog and **Seth Godin's books:** https://www.sethgodin.com

Grassroots Institute for Fundraising Training, journal: archives available at: https://www.grassrootsinstitute.org/2020/10/grassroots-fundraising-journal-now-free-open-source/

Alison Green and Jerry Hauser, *Managing to Change the World: The Nonprofit Manager's Guide to Getting Results* (Jossey-Bass, 2012): https://www.managementcenter.org/our-book/

Evelyn & Walther Haas, Jr. Fund: https://www.haasjr.org

Dan & Chip Heath: https://heathbrothers.com

Jennifer McCrea: https://www.jennifermccrea.com

Nonprofit Quarterly: **Innovative Thinking for the Nonprofit Sector:** https://nonprofitquarterly.org

The NonProfit Times: **The Leading Business Publication for Nonprofit Management:** https://www.thenonprofittimes.com

Positive Psychology News: https://positivepsychologynews.com

Reasons to be Cheerful: https://reasonstobecheerful.world

Sea Change Strategies, Alia McKee and Mark Rovner: https://seachangestrategies.com

Jack Stack, The Great Game of Business: https://www.greatgame.com/the-what-great-game-of-business

Zemo Trevathan, The Aligned Team: https://www.thealignedteam.com

Lynne Twist, Author of *The Soul of Money* (W. W. Norton and Company, 2012) and founder the Soul of Money Institute: https://soulofmoney.org

The Veritus Group: https://veritusgroup.com

Yes! **Magazine:** http://www.yesmagazine.org

Steve Zaffron and Dave Logan, *The Three Laws of Performance* (Jossey-Bass, 2011): https://threelawsofperformance.com

Rosamund and Benjamin Zander, *The Art of Possibility: Transforming Professional and Personal Life*: (Penguin Books, 2002): https://www.benjaminzander.org/about/the-art-of-possibility/

Index

Made in the USA
Las Vegas, NV
01 June 2022